Kansas Jayhawks

History-making basketball

by John Hendel

Quality Sports Publications

Reference Note: Some quotes in this book refer to their source as "official records," "game reports," or similarly refer to a nonspecific document. All of these references are to the files of the Sports Information office at the University of Kansas.

Editors ....Kelly C. Anderson and Susan Maze
Production.............................Reta Nicholson and Karen Robinson
College Basketball Hall of Fame photos coordinated by Kelly Porter of Walsworth.

ISBN No. 1-561-66-072-8 General Edition

For additional copies or more information, Contact:
Duane Brown
Quality Sports Publications
Sales and Marketing Offices
10841 Hauser Court
Lenexa, KS 66210
800-464-1116

Acknowledgments

The author would like to acknowledge the help of the many people who aided this project.

A book such as this could not be put together without the help of the University of Kansas Athletic Department and Athletics Director Bob Frederick.

The Kansas Sports Information Department's involvement was also invaluable. Doug Vance, assistant athletic director, handled many calls and dug up many of the telephone numbers used in tracking down KU's basketball history. Associate Sports Information Director Dean Buchan was gracious in allowing the use of his office, files, photographs, and in acceptance of a modicum of abuse. The media guide Buchan and Vance put together for this past season proved a great asset, as it does during the regular season. Thanks also to Ginger Miller and Terri Burtin, who fielded calls and questions with a patience probably not deserved.

The University Archives at the University of Kansas, as administered by John Nugent, Ned Kehde, and Barry Bunch, proved to be a fountain of information, from Phog Allen's personal letters to the Chancellor's notes on Board of Regents meetings. Never once did these men make a wrong turn, or so it seemed, while weaving through racks and racks of boxes directly to the requested information.

The Elizabeth M. Watkins Community Museum, operated by the Douglas County Historical Society and under the direction of Steve Jansen, is a find worthy of its lengthy name. Perhaps no one knows as much about the early days of Kansas basketball as Jansen, and he is readily willing to share his knowledge and even more ready to add to it, should anyone wish to spin tales with him.

Of course, all of the KU players and coaches contacted, either in person or by telephone, were most helpful. I wish every interview were as easy as my talks with them.

The Big Eight Conference, another storehouse of facts and figures, checked several statements for the book. Service Bureau Director Jeff Bollig, formerly with the KU SID office, has a great knowledge of Jayhawks basketball and is beginning to catch up on the rest of the conference schools. Assistant Commissioner Tim "No Relation" Allen also took questions and sometimes had the answer or, at the least, the sense to refer me to Bollig. Mention was made earlier about the Kansas media guide, but the guides published by all of the Big Eight Conference schools were continually thumbed and scanned, with great nuggets of information uncovered. The SID offices at those schools are also thanked for that reason.

I would like to thank editor Kelly Anderson, who led a first-time author through the book with just enough prodding and probably some undeserved flattery.

Finally, I would like to express my appreciation to Walsworth Publishing and representatives Bob Snodgrass and Duane Brown for their faith, help, and assistance.

Contents

Foreword

I will never forget Jerry Waugh's words in the pre-game pep talk before our initial freshman game of the 1958-1959 season: "Doc always used to say, there's only one group of young men who will run out on the court tonight with 'Kansas' on their jerseys, and you have the responsibility of representing all of the pride and tradition of the past." The message was meaningful but the attribution to Phog Allen did not have real significance until 30 years later.

It was a post-game press conference when after a strong performance by his Jayhawks in December of his rookie season, new Coach Roy Williams told the media, "I tell our players that there's only one group of young men who take the floor with 'Kansas' on their jerseys..." I didn't even hear Roy finish the sentence because it suddenly struck me how the past of Kansas basketball was, almost by destiny, intertwined with the present. The influence of James Naismith and Forrest C. Allen had been passed on to Dean Smith and Dick Harp who had in turn passed it on to Coach Williams.

There is no doubt in my mind that 30 years from now there will be a Kansas head coach who was influenced by Coach Williams who will be reciting similar words to his players. The Kansas basketball tradition will endure because it has meant so much to so many people in the past who will ensure its success in the future.

Through its 92 years, Kansas basketball has been a source of great pride, not only to the University but also to the State of Kansas. In fact, it has been one of the State's greatest resources. When "Danny and the Miracles" won the National Championship in 1988 and "Roy's Boys" made the magnificent run to the National title game with Duke, Kansans everywhere were proud of their Jayhawks and the recognition they brought to the Sunflower State.

Clearly, when the entire 100 years of basketball is considered, no other institution has a richer tradition than Kansas. This account of that tradition is a great story about a wonderful place. I hope you enjoy reading this book as much as I did.

Dr. Bob Frederick
Athletics Director

The Jayhawk

The Jayhawk symbol has had many faces in its history. The little blue bird with the prominent beak and sneakers that today promotes the pride of KU basketball, has been around—in one form or another—throughout most of the twentieth century.

The Jayhawk began as blue bird with skinny hairy legs. The 1910 and 1923 birds, above, both appear happy, as does the 1911-1912 model, shown below right. The 1919-1920 Jayhawk, below left, was a departure from the more typical blue mascot.

Opposite page: The 1923-1924 Jayhawk retained a friendly air, above left, but the bird became more militant by 1929-1930, center left. The 1939 Jayhawk, above right, was among the more fearsome of the mascots. The 1940 bird, below left, has softened considerably, and by 1946, below right, the Jayhawk leaned to the cute and friendly look.

KU

KU
1939

KU

KU

The Jayhawk Tradition

"It is safe to hazard the opinion," Robert Taft wrote in *Across the Years on Mount Oread,* "that while there have been more important contributions to the world made by the members of the University faculty, none has touched more lives and brought greater interest to millions the world over than the invention of basketball by James Naismith. There is then, more than an ordinary tie between the game of basketball and the University."

No university has given more to intercollegiate basketball. Kansas' first team was coached by the game's inventor, Dr. James Naismith. And the Jayhawks' most storied coach, Dr. Forrest C. "Phog" Allen, is considered—by Naismith among others—to be the father of basketball coaching.

Since first calling a team together in old Snow Hall, with its 11-foot ceiling and support posts down the center of the floor, Kansas has amassed a 1,459-677

record, four national championships, 39 conference titles—outright or shared— 26 All-America selections from Tommy Johnson through Danny Manning, four college players of the year, and four NCAA Tournament outstanding players. In the process, the program has won a place in the hearts of thousands of fans across the state and country.

That vista should not be limited to Lawrence, but spread across the nation. Only two teams—North Carolina and Kentucky—have won more basketball games than KU. Those schools' most famous coaches—Dean Smith and Adolph Rupp—learned the game while students at Kansas. Fifth-ranked Oregon State was coached for years by Kansas alumnus Ralph Miller. Through the 1990-1991 season, Allen, Miller, Rupp, and Smith, unquestionably four of the all-time greatest collegiate bas-

ketball coaches, hold a combined total of 2,995 victories.

Kansas basketball luminaries John Bunn and A. C. "Dutch" Lonborg joined Phog Allen to create what has become one of the most impressive sporting events in the world—the NCAA basketball tournament. And then there are the players, such as Wilt Chamberlain, Paul Endacott, Jo Jo White, Clyde Lovellette, Charlie Black I and Charlie Black II, Danny Manning, and B. H. Born.

"A lot of those were Kansas guys and basketball was so important in Kansas," said current KU Coach Roy Williams. "Dr. Allen was so important to Kansas, I think little kids grew up seeing the respect he had and the position he had. A lot of kids wanted to emulate him. Some had the skill athletically to do that. The Ralph Millers, the Lonborgs, the Adolph Rupps, the Dean Smiths, all

those guys were players, too, so they started out having a little bit of the name recognition."

"They also had to be very competitive," said Williams. "They had to admire Dr. Allen so much that they had to think that might be a good way to go, but I think it was strictly the interest in Kansas basketball, the position that Dr. Allen held, the esteem that people held him in.

"What was the comment that Naismith made? That you don't coach basketball, you play it. Well, I think that Dr. Allen proved that you could coach basketball and you could enjoy doing it forever. Most of those guys who did it, did it for a long time."

Williams, a native of North Carolina, was not a student of Kansas basketball history until relatively recently. He was the kind of child who "looked into

things," he said. It is a trait he continues to have. He is student and coach of Kansas basketball.

And, after three years as coach, Williams talks about driving down Naismith Drive and turning into Allen Field House with great emphasis on the names Naismith and Allen.

"At first, I don't think I understood the significance," said Williams. "But every time I bring a recruit in and we make that turn and come into Allen Field House, I say something about it because I think it's pretty special. I'm getting cold chills just thinking about it."

"It affected me exactly the same way," said Ken Koenigs, who played at Kansas from 1975-1978. "I had always been a KU basketball fan, maybe that had been bred into me. My father used to take me up to see Jo Jo White play and Rodger Bohnenstiehl and those guys. So when I got there I already had that deep impression."

"That's part of the tradition of Kansas—Phog Allen's years," said Koenigs. "Some of these guys who are playing now have no idea who Phog Allen was

and really don't care. And people don't realize when they look back on the tradition of this or that, they don't really know who Wilt Chamberlain is anymore. But heritage and tradition still mean a lot. That always has been, always will be."

The tradition leads to success and great success in the case of the University of Kansas. But Roy Williams cannot count on the memory of Clyde Lovellette to score points for him, just as Ted Owens could not draw on the talents of Bill Bridges when he needed a rebound. It takes work to keep the tradition going. As Williams said, many recruits nowadays think Julius Erving or Michael Jordan invented basketball rather than some Canadian expatriate looking for a bridge between football and track seasons and landed at a school that needed him to deliver daily convocations and head the physical education department more than it cared about him coaching basketball.

Bob Allen, Phog's son and a KU player from 1939-1941, said James Naismith didn't know what he had invented. Naismith certainly couldn't have envi-

sioned what the game became, with teams regularly scoring 100 points, twisting slam dunks, and physical enough to rival lacrosse, which was a personal favorite sport of Naismith's. And he would have been amazed to see thousands of students fill the west side of the football stadium to watch the Kansas basketball team do the "Cabbage Patch Dance" in celebration of the 1988 NCAA championship.

If there is a drawback to years of success it is that great achievements are no longer measured for what they are.

Fans' expectations, along with those of the coaches and players, can grow to unreasonable heights.

"When I took the job, I was just so amazed to find out more and more and more about Kansas," said Roy Williams. "I'd had a pretty good course in my last two years at North Carolina because Dick Harp [Kansas coach, 1956-1964] had been with us and I loved to sit and talk with Coach Harp. He'd tell the Dr. Allen stories and also about Dick when he played himself and when he came back to coach."

Harp likened those talks, along with the pep talks given by Allen, to Indian warriors passing the lore of generations gone to their children.

The Jayhawk story is not so much about the impressive numbers, but it is about the people who amassed those numbers.

In 1942, on the occasion of Phog Allen's 25th anniversary of coaching, his former players collected money for a scholarship in the coach's name. They also collected letters of congratulations and remembrance from among themselves and from KU faculty. A letter from Frederick Moreau, then the Dean of the Law School, had Allen as its subject. A half century later, his words hold true for the entire program.

"When anything becomes tradition we somehow lose an appreciation of its importance," wrote Moreau. "Winning basketball teams at Kansas are traditional. No one even thinks it possible for our team to land in the second division but we all must realize that it is very difficult to establish a tradition and even much more difficult to maintain it.

"Only a rare motivating force can keep a tradition going."

That "motivating force" is generated about 17 times a year by people in Allen Field House, about 35 times a season by the team and almost every day by the coaches, players, and fans.

While Coach Allen shaped KU basketball, the hiring of James Naismith began the KU basketball tradition. Naismith was not overly impressed with the game he invented. To him, it was just a way to pass the time between football and outdoor spring sports.

Naismith was born in Almonte, Canada, on November 6, 1861. He moved to the United States in 1890. Less than two years later, he invented a game as something to fill idle hours for high-spirited boys forced indoors by inclement New England winter weather.

Late in 1891, Dr. James Naismith was given the charge of a class of 18 men at the Springfield Training School in Springfield, Massachusetts. He was instructed to keep them from being bored.

Naismith tried many simple children's games, but dropped each as the men turned them into violent clashes. Regular outdoor sports, modified only slightly for indoor play, were also found unsuitable.

The instructor fretted over the task, but slowly, Naismith began to formulate a game. After watching indoor football, he ruled out running with the ball and tackling. Remembering a make-shift game played during his time at McGill University in which a ball was tossed into a box on the floor, he decided the goal should be raised since the low goal was too easily defended.

Naismith wandered onto the gym floor and found a soccer ball and decided it was the right size for his new game. He asked for a pair of boxes to be used as goals. The school janitor offered a pair of peach baskets. Naismith nailed the baskets to the running track, 10 feet above the gym floor. He then scribbled 13 rules of play and introduced his creation to his class.

The class was divided into two teams of nine players—Naismith believed his game could be played by any number of people per team. The instructor picked a player from each team and tossed the ball up for the first center jump. Basketball was born.

Naismith knew what he had cre-

ated, but he didn't understand what it would become. He had no desire to profit from his invention. The March 13, 1932, issue of *Time* magazine stated, "Had Dr. Naismith patented some of his paraphernalia he might now have an income that would free him from the chores of teaching Kansas freshmen how to stand up straight." But Naismith remained more interested in benefiting the students who played the game than in retaining control over his invention.

Naismith told Phog Allen that he could not play basketball "because he had played football," but other sources cite Naismith as saying he played the game "twice, once in Springfield and once in Lawrence."

Even if he didn't play basketball, Naismith held a special paternal pride for his game. Early on he saw basketball headed for a completely unintended end.

"So much stress is laid today on the winning of games," Naismith wrote in 1914, "that practically all else is lost sight of, and the element of manliness and sportsmanship are accorded a secondary place."

That, more than anything else, seems to have caused the alienation between Naismith and the game he invented.

Despite Naismith's nonchalant attitude about basketball, it was his presence that brought the sport to the University of Kansas, and it was he who began the Jayhawk basketball tradition as the first head coach.

The Tradition Begins

Basketball was a cross-country rage when Dr. James Naismith, the game's inventor, accepted a job at the University of Kansas. KU did not have an intercollegiate team when Naismith arrived in 1898, although many students hoped his presence would lead to a school team.

Chancellor Francis Snow needed someone to lead daily chapel services—at which attendance was mandatory—and a Director of Physical Education. He asked William Harper, his counterpart at the University of Chicago, for a recommendation. Harper, in turn, asked his soon-to-be legendary football coach, Amos Alonzo Stagg. Stagg immediately suggested a former schoolmate who was currently in Denver, Colorado, and a recent graduate of medical school—James Naismith.

Snow found the match for both his openings in Naismith, who studied as an undergraduate for the ministry while maintaining an interest in physical education. It was the combination of those interests that started a life-long affiliation with the Young Men's Christian Association, YMCA, and led Naismith to Springfield, Massachusetts, where a challenge by Dr. Luther Gulick ended with the invention of basketball in 1891.

With Naismith's arrival at KU, the student body classes fielded teams for a tournament. The best players would be asked to play in the name of the University of Kansas. Basketball grabbed so much attention that even the faculty took part. The 1899 University yearbook stated the actions established basketball on the campus after previous "futile" attempts.

The yearbook staff wrote, "Evidently the faculty realizes the advantages attending basket ball as a game, and has encouraged the sport by organizing a team and participating in match games. That they entered into the matter in no half-hearted way is evidenced by the fact that they played a tie game with the champion Sophomore team."

The yearbook gave the new sport enthusiastic support: "After the men had shown their ability in the class games, a picked team was chosen to represent the University against all comers. The record that this team made is one of which the University may well be proud. On the home ground, not a game was lost, and on strange courts but three."

The yearbook staff seemed to lose track of a game, since the first University of Kansas team went 7-4, including a six-game winning streak.

The record is remarkable because the Jayhawks had no suitable on-campus court on which to practice. Their first home was in the basement of Snow Hall, on a court just 36 feet wide and 84 feet long. Even tougher to battle were the support posts down the middle of the floor and the ceiling that was 11 feet above the floor—one foot above the basket. There was no such thing as arching a shot until Naismith discovered unused space under the floor and had it dropped five feet, giving the court a 16-foot ceiling.

In search of a court, Naismith took his charges to a roller skating rink at 807 Kentucky Street, where the team practiced and played home games until the rink was destroyed by fire. The Jayhawks moved to the YMCA at 937 Massachusetts Street, and called it home until it burned in 1902. The third home for the Kansas team was the new Lawrence YMCA on Massachusetts Street. The Jayhawks played and practiced there—with occasional visits to their on-campus court—until Robinson Gymnasium was completed in 1907.

Without a real home court, Kansas played most of its games in the first nine years on the road. The Jayhawks' first game was played February 3, 1899, in Kansas City, Missouri, against the local YMCA with about 150 people in attendance. Dr. Naismith played the part of the referee, and a Professor Clark served as umpire. Experience controlled the game as the Kansas City team won 16-5, after leading 4-3 at the half.

Kansas did lead, albeit shortly, in that first game. William Sutton scored the first Jayhawk point with a free throw. He also had the first Kansas basket, as the *Lawrence Daily Journal* reported

the following day: "Sutton made one of the most sensational plays one minute into the game. The ball was thrown to him and he rolled it for three yards. He was viciously beset by two Y.M.C.A. men and, bending backwards, he threw the ball fully twelve yards and got a goal."

Kansas was on the board in a spectacular way.

The Jayhawks even drew a celebrity for an opponent in Jesse James, Jr., a Kansas City law student believed to be the son of the famed outlaw.

A week later, the Jayhawks collected their first victory, traveling to Topeka to play a YMCA team, winning 31-6 as "the Capitol City could not pierce the locals' strong defense," according to archive documents at the KU Sports Information Department. Sutton scored 13 points.

Late in that first season, Kansas

Dr. James Naismith asked the school janitor in Springfield for two boxes to use for goals. Fortunately, the janitor had only peach baskets, saving people from boxball.

The first basketball team at the University of Kansas. This team went 7-4, playing only one other college the entire year. The rest of their opponents were city teams, YMCA teams and other amateur teams.

played twice in Independence, Missouri. One of the spectators at the games was Forrest Allen, who was there to see his brother play. That marked Allen's first exposure to Kansas basketball, but Allen, who acquired the nickname "Phog," was destined to have the largest individual impact on the KU basketball program.

Kansas closed the season with its first intercollegiate game, facing William Jewell in Liberty, Missouri. With Samuel Emley earning 10 points "well supported by [Henry] Hess, who sank three field goals," the Jayhawks came away 19-3 winners.

After the first season, Kansas awarded letters honoring Herbert Avery, Samuel Emley, Willis Henderson, Henry Hess, Harold Hoyt, Claude Royal, Rusel Russell, Walter Sutton, William Sutton, and William Yahn.

Russell was the manager of the team and frequently handled the coaching when Naismith did not make trips with the team because of duties on campus.

If Naismith traveled with the team, he generally was called upon to be the referee, since, as the *Arkansas Gazette* recalled in 1937, "Games in which he officiated generally went off smoothly for he knew the game and the players took his word as final."

Although Naismith-officiated games went smoothly, Kansas basketball did not. Without a true home court on which to practice, and with Naismith often remaining at home while the team was on the road, the Jayhawks posted six consecutive losing seasons. KU was 29-41 overall from 1900-1905, but 13-8 when able to play on so-called "home" courts.

Naismith made the trip with the team to Lincoln, Nebraska, although the March 2, 1900, game ended in a reported 48-8 KU defeat.

"No one knows exactly what the score was in Lincoln. Even Manager Russell has forgotten, but it was big," the *Kan-*

4

sas University Weekly reported. "The little Northerners tossed baskets so fast that our men lost count and did not linger to find the score after the game.

"There is not much to be said about this game, says Manager Russell."

As was there not much to be said about the 1900-1901 season that started with six losses, including a forfeit to the Ajax Athletic Club in Newton, Kansas, "in a dispute over knowledge of the rules."

The Jayhawks started 1902 with a 2-2 record when the *Kansas University Weekly*, on January 25, called for support of the team, "The student body must shuffle off its indifference and get on friendly terms with the neglected bunch of Kansas [athletes]. Why not? Do you admire endurance, activity, nerve, a cool head and a quick eye in an athlete? If so attend the next basketball game and see an exhibition of those qualities. Athletics cannot thrive on money alone. It must have encouragement."

It was hard for Kansas students to find their team, however, since it played more road games than contests in Lawrence. KU annually took a long road trip at semester break. In 1902, that trek's first stop was in Des Moines, Iowa, to start a series of six games in six days at various points across the state and, finally, against William Jewell in Liberty, Missouri. The opening and closing games were Kansas victories, but the four in between were the bulk of the losses in a 5-7 season.

The lack-of-court crisis seemed to peak in the 1902-1903 season, ironically, the first that the Kansas Athletic Board financed the team. Kansas opened the schedule at home, but did not play another game in Lawrence and finished the season 7-8.

The 1903 *Jayhawker* decried the problem, saying the team was "seriously handicapped by the lack of a good court on which to practice."

But, the yearbook noted, "During the course of the season [the team] has taken two trips, each one of which was longer than any trip ever before taken by any Basketball team west of the Mississippi. On the first of these trips our team played three of the best teams in the United States. On this trip we got some very valuable information in respect to the way Basketball should be

played. The second long trip was begun Friday, January 30. On this trip our team made a very credible record."

The first trip sent the Jayhawks to Chicago for a New Year's Eve game, to Monmouth, Illinois, the following day and to Font du Lac, Wisconsin, on January 2. The schedule and the travel took its toll in the form of three defeats. The second trek, which started in Liberty, Missouri, and swung through Nebraska and Iowa over 12 days, was more successful, with KU posting a 5-2 mark under the leadership of captain Joseph Alford.

The following season began with five home games, of which the Jayhawks won the first four. But a 28-12 loss to Haskell in which the "Haskell team work was excellent and kept the Mount Oread athletes guessing as what to expect next" set off a seven-game losing streak that explains a 5-8 overall mark.

One of the setbacks was a 27-10 loss

Old Snow Hall was the first University of Kansas "home court." The old gym was inadequate because, among other reasons, visiting teams refused to play there for fear of running into the support beams in the middle of the floor.

The 1906 Kansas basketball team included future coach Phog Allen, back row standing on the right.

to the Kansas City Athletic Club, which featured an "Allen" at guard, probably Forrest by this time. An archive report of the game showed continued moaning over facilities: "The Jayhawkers still displayed a lack of practice and team work as well as poor physical condition, while the Athletics were in fine form."

The 1904 writers of the *Jayhawker* were tired of the grousing and said, quite plainly, "Instead of ceaselessly pleading for a new gymnasium and promising great results *then* the Athletic Department is going to [have to] show itself *worthy* of commodious quarters. That condition is rapidly coming about, and when the Legislature sees that the University merits a gymnasium it will grant an appropriation for one."

The following year, the Jayhawks played all but four of their games from January 28 through February 4 during the usual long journey. They won just two of the seven games. The first game was a stop in Lincoln to face Nebraska Wesleyan. Center William Miller, a sophomore, had eight field goals and five free throws for 21 points and the first 20-point game for a Kansas player.

The 1905-1906 academic year marked the admission of Forrest Allen to the University.

Allen apparently did not judge the entire school by what he had witnessed and participated in against Kansas on the basketball court. He was more taken by the sights of Lawrence when he visited his brother Pete, who was a KU student.

Allen, in 1967, said, "My brother was in school here. He played tackle on the football team and pitched on the baseball team. I came out to see those games... I noticed that Lawrence had wide, paved streets. Columbia [Missouri] had muddy streets. That's not castigating Missouri. They hadn't lifted Missouri out of the mud then... I could see the difference and I wanted to go to a place that was progressive."

By this time Naismith had started his active campaign for a new gymnasium. He did not think only of the basketball team, however, since the doctor's interest in physical education went well beyond the game he invented. He wanted one of the finest gyms in the world for the wrestlers and gymnasts as well as the basketball players.

And the gym was needed, too. Visiting teams refused "to risk their lives among the pillars," according to the school newspaper. There were only three "home" games in 1905-1906 and seven the following season, but Kansas teams showed a general improvement as a seven-game winning streak led to a 12-7 mark in 1906.

Allen, billed by *The Kansas University Weekly* as "the best goal-thrower in the world," was quick to prove his worth on the court, as he scored 23 points against Nebraska. Fans quickly caught on, too, and attendance was "taxing the limit," the school newspaper reported, when Allen played his first home intercollegiate game and helped the Jayhawks to a 39-12 victory over Washburn. Three days later, he scored 26 points in a 60-13 rout of Emporia Normal to close the season.

Phog was destined to move on quickly, however, and before the next season, officials from Baker University asked Naismith if Allen could coach their team.

Naismith called Allen into his office and said, "I've got a joke on you, you bloody beggar. They want you to coach."

"What's so funny about that?" Allen asked.

"Why, Forrest," answered basketball's inventor, "you can't coach basketball, you just play it."

Years later after Allen had proved that statement wrong, Naismith presented his one-time star player with a portrait with the inscription "From the Father of Basketball to the Father of Basketball Coaching."

While the defection of Allen certainly hurt the team, Naismith finally won his battle for a new gymnasium, a victory that would give strong benefits for years.

In 1905, the Kansas Legislature appropriated $100,000 for the task, and the following year ground was broken for Robinson Gymnasium, named for Governor Charles Robinson and his wife Sara, who donated the land at the present site of Wescoe Hall.

Naismith spent two months traveling from gym to gym gathering ideas to make the building at the University of Kansas the state of the art. When he was done with the design, it was more than a little similar to the Springfield YMCA Training School where basketball was born.

While team members could walk past the Robinson Gym construction site every day, they still had old Snow Hall as a home—which is something like living in a tent while your house is built.

On December 20, 1906, *The University Daily Kansan* reported, "The great difficulties in building a team are, the lack of suitable quarters in which to train and the lack of a coach. Dr. James Naismith, the inventor of the game, is so busy with his work as Athletic Director that he rarely finds time to give the men a thorough training. But the time he does spend with them counts."

The 1906-1907 season was Naismith's final one as coach, even if he was coach-in-name-only, and a 3-0 start slipped to a 7-8 finish. The Baker University team coached by Allen posted a clear 39-24 victory against KU, with Naismith refereeing and Allen listed as umpire.

After that season, Naismith was made a full professor and removed himself as basketball "coach," a position he never really treated as a full-time commitment anyway. Among more noteworthy facets in his distinguished career, Naismith holds the distinction of being the only Kansas basketball coach with a losing record. The Jayhawks were 55-60 in his tenure.

By 1908 James Naismith had withdrawn from basketball coaching, and was not very upset about it. The inventor of the game judged basketball as a diversion and found more enjoyment in gymnastics, wrestling, and fencing. Later players said they cannot remember Naismith attending a practice. He would, on occasion, attend a game.

But Naismith was far from a recluse. He remained very active in the Department of Physical Education and answered the call for a variety of local causes.

Paul Endacott, who grew up in Lawrence and played for Kansas in the early 1920s, remembers Naismith as a well-thought-of man around town.

"Naismith was a sort of a father, advisor, and jack of all trades," Endacott said. "He was willing to do things and people would kind of take advantage of him, but he always seemed to like to do them.

"He wasn't known around town for being anything special, outside of being a professor up there. I've tried to remember when I first learned that Naismith was the inventor of basketball. We weren't too conscious of it even when I was in college."

Bob Allen, one of Phog's sons and the captain of the 1941 Jayhawks team, said "Naismith was a really interesting old man" and made so by the many facets of his life.

"[He was] a Christian minister— that's what he studied originally—the ministry," said Allen. "He [had] his M.D. degree, but I don't think he ever [practiced medicine]. I don't know what he did around the university for all those years. I don't think he came to the games or anything like that. He was interested in physical fitness more than competitive athletes.

"He was the only coach there who had a losing record. He didn't care [about that label]. It was just exercising as far as he was concerned. He was just trying to give the boys a game that they could play and enjoy while the football season wasn't on."

On the occasion of the 50-year anniversary of the birth of basketball, Raymond P. Kaighn wrote a magazine article in which he recalled Naismith.

"Few men in history have given to the world so permanent and fruitful a contribution as has Dr. Naismith," wrote Kaighn. "Multitudes of young men and women everywhere have grown strong and healthy through the medium of this game. Perhaps by fortuitous accident basketball is the most American in spirit of all athletic pastimes."

Naismith was more that type of man—one who was happy helping his community rather than accepting accolades for the invention of basketball. Some people claim there was a rivalry between Phog Allen and Naismith, but that rivalry probably existed more on paper than between the men.

Phog Allen, according to Bob Allen, always tried to keep Naismith involved with the basketball team. He made sure the game's inventor sat for team pictures. Phog Allen helped create what Naismith called "the happiest moment of my life," when the International Olympic Committee accepted basketball into the Games. Allen had pushed hard for the sport. He also organized a nationwide drive to collect money to send Naismith to Berlin for the 1936 games.

On November 19, 1939, Naismith suffered a cerebral hemorrhage. Nine days later he had a heart attack and died.

Phog Allen wrote, "Eight nationally known educators, speaking from the same platform, declared that basketball had all the qualities necessary to teach the educable child: poise, rhythm, grace, coordination, development of skills and development of physical vigor. The speakers were not competitive coaches, nor were they athletes. This game, the only international game that is the product of one man's brain, stamps Dr. Naismith as a great educator, a kindly humanitarian and a model Christian. The youth of the world will raise and call Dr. Naismith blessed."

Naismith, humble by nature, might have listed his role in the building of Robinson Gym as one of his finest accomplishments. By giving the basketball team a showcase in which to practice and play, he brought the team back to campus, and playing basketball for Kansas further became a matter of pride.

"The inadequate gymnasium facilities here handicapped the team greatly in the past and the new 'gym' just completed will mean much to the game of basketball at the University," said the 1907 edition of the *Jayhawker*.

Robinson Gymnasium was dedicated at the 1907 commencement, and the following month, the *Kansas City Star* reported, "Boys in abbreviated track suits will not have to crouch behind the pillars and wait for the girls classes to pass by" because of the building's size.

Built of native limestone, Robinson Gym measured 90 feet by 178 feet and had three stories of usable floor space. It was meant for more than just athletics, however, as enrollment and registration used the facility, and it was loaned out for high school tournaments. One of the first events in Robinson Gym was the

The 1908 team was the first coached by Phog Allen, *above, in dark sweater.* Naismith, also in the second row, joined many of the annual team pictures at Allen's insistence.

1907 Prom, although the dance had to be postponed several times before the multi-purpose building was ready.

"Erected at a cost of $100,000 with every detail planned out with great care by Physical Director Dr. James Naismith, the new Gymnasium is a model in every respect," the *Jayhawker* staff wrote in 1908.

There were lockers in the basement for 1,000 men and 500 women, a large swimming pool, a storeroom, and special training quarters for the football squad. On the first floor were the two gymnasiums proper. The west end of the building was devoted to men and the east end for women.

The third floor housed the big auditorium and basketball court, which was "the largest basket-ball floor in the West," according to the yearbook. As many as 3,000 fans could attend basketball games. A large gallery and running track overlooked the floor, a feature Naismith borrowed from Springfield.

"It has made Basket-ball a true University sport, in which the entire student body is interested... The opening of the new Gymnasium truly will mark a new era in University sports," the yearbook concluded.

While the Jayhawks finally had a full-time home, they still had to settle for a part-time coach. Naismith had taken himself out of basketball coaching, and the school was not able to convince Allen to return to KU as the coach until December.

Even then, Allen split time between the Haskell, Baker, and Kansas basketball teams, working with one in the afternoon, another in the evening, and the third at night, finishing the final workout about 10 o'clock. Allen amassed a 74-10 record at the three schools that season.

The Jayhawks opened their new building with a rousing 44-point victory over Ottawa on December 13, 1907—two days after Allen agreed to coach the team. The *Kansas University Weekly* claimed, "In the dedicatory game of Robinson Gymnasium, Kansas defeated Ottawa 66 to 22, and ran up the largest Kansas lead before the opponent scored, tallying 31 points before Ottawa found

Dr. Naismith designed the new Kansas gymnasium, Robinson Hall, based on the YMCA's Springfield Training School in Massachusetts, where he had invented basketball.

four-game losing streak. The final game of the stretch was against a team from Nome, Alaska, that defeated Kansas, 34-28.

But the Jayhawks hit stride. First the Newton YMCA lost to the Jayhawks—for the third time of the season. Kansas then defeated Allen's old team, the Kansas City Athletic Club. KU followed that with a 50-12 victory over Kansas State.

KU archive files report that "Splendid teamwork, coupled with accurate shooting, enabled the smooth-working Kansas University team to pile up a 50 to 12 score against Kansas State.

"The Farmers were cold and could not find the basket as the leech-like K.U. defense kept them bottled up. At the same time McCune, Woodward and Billy Miller hit the bucket with regularity. Every Jayhawker figured in the scoring."

George McCune had 16 points, Earl Woodward 14, Billy Miller 12, and Ralph Bergen and Milton Miller had 4 each for the Jayhawks.

The game had added significance. Allen went over .500 as a coach with the victory. Considering it was the third game of a 12-game winning streak, Kansas made sure its 22-year-old coach would never come close to a losing record.

Four days later, on February 4, 1908, the Jayhawks collected the first conference victory in school history with a 21-20 triumph over Missouri.

Robinson Gym proved to be a comfortable home, as the 1908 *Jayhawker* said, "The splendid new Gymnasium gave the boys a satisfactory court to practice on while as a place for holding match games it had not equal in the West."

The Jayhawks were 8-3, playing before crowds ranging from 200 to 1,000 in their new building and ended with a 6-0 mark in league play. They won the South Division of the Missouri Valley Conference in 1908 and faced North Division titlist Nebraska in Lincoln for the league championship.

Kansas took the first match of the two game playoff 28-26, and "the game was a thriller all the way," files state. "[A]t no time was any perceptible advantage gained by either team until in the closing minutes. The clever Kansans, by

the basket range."

The adrenaline must have been pumping for that game since just six days later Ottawa, this time at home, handed Kansas a 39-33 setback "on a small and miserably lighted court," as recorded in KU archive files.

The Newton YMCA fell twice to Kansas, but the Jayhawks then went on a

smooth team work, made their own breaks. McCune, Billy Miller and Woodward turned in neat performances."

The Jayhawks wrapped up their first conference championship the next night, February 22, as "this game was nearly a carbon copy of the one just preceding it, and the scores were practically the same. Superiority in fundamentals again was shown in the Kansans' play. Every Jayhawker methodically executed his assignments in a manner that would credit any university team.

"There was no individual star—every player turned in excellent games."

The final score was 28-25 and Allen had the first of 24 conference championships he would deliver to the University of Kansas.

During the 1909 season, Allen continued to commute from Kansas City, and it was not until January 19, 1909, that the school announced he had agreed to coach on a full-time basis. The *Kansan* reported that Allen "will now devote two nights each week to showing the Kansans the fine points of the great mid-winter college game."

Even with Allen showing up only part-time, the team captained by Earl Woodward claimed the "state championship" by playing and beating "every large institution in the state except Washburn" between December 10 and December 19. The Jayhawks went 8-0 on that 10-day run through the state.

Kansas won its first 19 games that season, a streak not broken until they met Washington University on the Pikers' home floor in St. Louis. The Jay-hawks also dropped a game at Missouri—their fifth game in five days—but still went 8-2 in winning the division. KU clinched the Southern Division with a 33-28 victory over Washington University.

Again Nebraska was the playoff opponent, with the games played in the Rainbow Skating Rink in Kansas City, Missouri. Tommy Johnson scored 16 points in the opener, and while "neither team played up to the form they showed earlier in the season." Kansas won, 28-22.

The Jayhawks claimed their second league title on March 5, 1909, coming from a five-point deficit with Tommy Johnson, Donald Martindell, and Earl Woodward pulling them back into the game.

The season ended with a 32-29 loss to Nebraska in a game that was "played to raise money for the depleted athletic funds of both schools," according to the official reports.

Kansas' record was 25-3. Earl Woodward, Tommy Johnson, Donald Martindell, George McCune, Robert Heizer, Ralph Bergen, and Verne Long earned athletic letters. After the season, Johnson earned the honor as the first All-America selection from a Kansas basketball team.

"Much credit undoubtedly belongs to Coach Allen for the brilliant record of the season," the 1909 edition of the *Jayhawker* stated, "but he was fortunate in having one of the fastest squads of basket ball men that has ever gotten together at the University."

The Hamilton Years

Phog Allen left the University of Kansas a second time in 1909, unsure that there was a future in coaching so new a game as basketball, but confident that any kind of career in athletics would be greatly enhanced if he knew how to treat injuries. So he enrolled in the Central School of Osteopathy in Kansas City. After becoming an osteopath, he accepted a coaching position at Warrensburg Normal School in Missouri where Allen enjoyed much success coaching football and baseball in addition to basketball.

Other vacancies opened in the Kansas Athletic Department, too. KU needed an Athletic Director, since W. C. Langson resigned to become the business manager of the *Salina Daily Union*, and a track coach in addition to filling the basketball position left by Allen.

There is a "Hamilton, K.C. Central High" listed as the referee for the second game of the playoff with Nebraska in 1909. He was the man who became Kansas' third basketball coach. The high schools in Kansas City, Missouri, were basketball hotbeds, and the move to Lawrence would be a natural progression for an ambitious coach.

Hamilton inherited a team captained by junior Tommy Johnson, who won All-America accolades as a sophomore. Other standouts from the 1909 Missouri Valley Conference champions included Earl Woodward, Vern "Shorty" Long, Robert Heizer, and Donald Martindell.

The Kansas cupboard was far from bare, and Hamilton capitalized by letting the Jayhawks play their accustomed game. KU opened the season with key league games against Nebraska, which finished second to Kansas in each of the first two years of conference competition. But unlike the tight, hard-fought games that marked the playoffs of 1908 and 1909, Kansas romped to 33-17 and 40-16 victories.

"Coach Hamilton's team showed excellent fundamentals and cooperation as well as experience," according to archive files.

The third game was more of the same with a 46-7 rout over Washington University of St. Louis. "The Pikers were in a class by themselves, and that class was just 39 points below Hamilton's huskies," one report read.

Kansas was 8-0 and had hardly been threatened when Missouri visited for a pair of Missouri Valley games, which were described in an official report as "a cross between a basketball game and a wrestling match with a generous sprinkling of football thrown in."

"[Herman] Cohle, Mizzou center, started the fireworks with a field goal, and the battle was on. The feature of this opening half was a sensational tackle of Johnson by [Theodore] Hackney, Tiger guard. Nor were the Kansas representatives especially lamb-like in their tactics."

James Naismith, who had envisioned a game without the roughness of football when he invented basketball, attended the second game of the set. Not long into the battle he was heard to exclaim, "Oh, gracious! They are murdering my game!"

"And so they were," one report answered, "but everyone had an enjoyable time." Especially the Kansas Jayhawks, who came away with 29-15 and 27-14 victories.

Kansas won 12 more games before the rematch with Washington University in St. Louis. One report claimed that Tommy Johnson had a shot in the air at the final whistle, but it was wiped out by the "ill-advised" official. "A more enlightened interpretation of the rules would have permitted the score." Enlightenment not forthcoming, the Jayhawks' 16-15 loss stood.

Kansas quickly returned to form and closed the season with six straight victories, locking up its third conference championship along the way.

"This team has made a most remarkable record, losing only one game on the entire schedule and that by the narrowest possible margin. Technically, the game belonged to Kansas," read the 1910 yearbook. "The play of Long and Johnson at forward was characteristic of the work of the whole team. Their clever dodging and throwing of the most difficult goals early won for them a place in the hearts of the basket ball fans."

Long continued that style of play the following year and led the team with 221 points, including 14 points in the season-opening 40-17 victory over Baker.

Kansas continued winning by "shooting baskets with spectacular accuracy and guarding with leech-like tenacity," according to archive files. The Jayhawks were 7-0, and no team was able to finish within six points of them.

KU welcomed Nebraska for a two-game series on February 10-11—one that was predicted to give a strong indication as to which team would win the Missouri Valley in 1911. And for the first time of the season, Kansas showed a weakness as the Cornhuskers used "the superior playing of [A. H.] Hiltner and [O. A.] Frank" for the 36-27 victory. The Jayhawks "effecting a complete reversal of form" answered in the second game with a 37-12 romp. The first game, however, revealed more about the two teams than the second.

Leaving conference play for a stopover game on the way to Columbia, the Jayhawks were defeated in overtime by the Kansas City Athletic Club as, "Porter Craig, KCAC guard, tossed a basket from the center of the court to give his mates a 41 to 40 victory," archive records read.

Back in the Valley, it was back to business and two-game sweeps at Missouri and at Iowa State. Kansas was 12-2, and clinched the league championship in the first game at Ames, Iowa.

The title could not be disputed, even after the Jayhawks closed the year at Nebraska with 38-26 and 36-24 losses. Kansas went 9-3 in the Missouri Valley, and Nebraska, even with a 3-1 mark against the champion Jayhawks, was 7-5. It was an omen of troubles to come with the Cornhuskers.

Vern Long, Bob Heizer, and Don Dousman each earned positions on the first All-Missouri Valley Conference team, and Hamilton posted an impressive 30-7 record over his first two seasons.

Only one letterman reported when Hamilton opened practice for the 1912 season, but he had a group of 75 players from which to find a team. KU opened the season just as it had in 1911—with a lopsided victory over Baker.

"After a long period of elimination, a team was obtained which proved to be one of the fastest that Kansas has ever put on the court," the *Jayhawker* yearbook reported.

Fast or not, the 45-18 triumph over Baker gave the wrong indications of the 1912 Jayhawks, who were quickly brought to reality by Nebraska.

After four years of finishing second in the Missouri Valley, the Cornhuskers primed themselves for the defending champions.

Nebraska was a "beefy bunch," stated the yearbook. "It seems that they came down with the idea of taking the games rather than winning them. They succeeded in their intention." Kansas was beaten 30-26 and 30-27.

Ironically a change in Missouri Valley Conference rules returned the league to division play and, unlike previous seasons of divisional play, determined

Coach W. O. Hamilton inherited a conference champion team when Phog Allen went to medical school. He finished the 1910 season with only one loss.

The 1909 team was the Missouri Valley Conference champion, a title that became tradition for the Kansas Jayhawks.

that inter-divisional games did not count toward the standings. The losses did not hurt Kansas' title chances.

The Jayhawks rebounded and won their next 10 games, including a 4-0 string against Missouri. Kansas traveled further east for two games with divisional foe Washington University. KU, feeling the weariness of four games in four days, lost both games in St. Louis.

Just two games with Nebraska remained on the schedule. Kansas had wrapped up the MVC Southern Division title with a 6-2 record. The Cornhuskers were 8-0 in the Northern Division, and with 49-21 and 29-28 triumphs over the Jayhawks in the final scheduled games, Nebraska was 14-1 overall.

KU fully expected a playoff—just as the Valley had done in its first two years—between the division champions. But Nebraska balked while debating the site and officials and, after two weeks of squabbling, Cornhuskers Coach E. O. Stiehm cancelled the playoff. Kansas' season was over at 11-7. Conference records list Kansas and Nebraska as co-champions for that season.

"It is needless to say more of the result of the game or Nebraska's or Stiehm's refusal to play off the tie for the championships," the 1912 yearbook staff wrote. "In justice to the coach and the team, it is well to remember that Kansas's chances of a championship must not be determined by the results of the last two games played. The class of 1912 never knew the Kansas Basket Ball team except as Missouri Valley Champions, and they will stand by the Coach and their team in their refusal to 'concede' anybody a championship for 1912."

"Concede" is perhaps not the right word, since Nebraska undoubtedly had the better team that year and beat KU all four times the teams met.

A different look awaited the Jayhawks for 1913 as Coach Hamilton ordered new uniforms for his team. The *University Daily Kansan*, on January 9, 1913, reported what the sartorially correct Jayhawk would be wearing: "The jersey was to have a V-neck with a blue body and carry a red stripe on the chest and neck. The pants are khaki with blue stripes down the sides and around the bottom. The shoes are of white elk skin with heavy red rubber soles. The stockings are red and blue. Altogether this very good looking, as well as novel and probably unmatched in the Missouri Valley."

The smartly attired Jayhawks won their first three games, but they lost two home games to Kansas State before taking two from the Wildcats in Manhattan. Loren Brown, described as a "carrot-thatched Jayhawk forward" in game reports, scored 20 points in each of the games in Manhattan, helping KU to 34-19 and 30-20 victories. Those were the last times the Jayhawks and Wildcats met as non-conference foes because Kansas State joined the Missouri Valley for the 1914 season.

Kansas piled up a 15-4 record by the time it reached the annual showdown with Nebraska, including a record 68-8 rout of Washington University and a 30-24 triumph over the Phog Allen-coached Warrensburg Normal Teachers College.

The Missouri Valley Conference returned to the playoff format for 1913, and Kansas and Nebraska again won their divisions. Conference officials, recalling Nebraska Coach Stiehm's problems with playoff sites and game officials in 1912, determined that each match of the three-game series would be played at different arenas.

Nebraska, which lost just two games in its regular season, got 18 points from Ross Haskell and 10 from Clinton Underwood in collecting a 40-26 victory at Lincoln in the playoff opener. Herbert Stryker "slipped in three timely baskets, one of them ending the scoring near the end of the tilt," according to the game reports of the 18-16 Cornhuskers' victory in Lawrence that clinched the 1913 MVC championship.

Kansas won the scheduled third game 30-24 for a 16-6 season record. For the first time in their conference affiliation, the Jayhawks finished in a position other than first.

"True, Kansas lost a few games, but when it is considered that playing on a strange court and the element of luck itself in basketball is great, they are easily excusable," wrote the staff of the 1913 *Jayhawker*, ignoring the fact that the losses were evenly split between home and road courts.

Team captain Charles Greenlees earned all-conference honors after the season. Ralph "Lefty" Sproull, who led the Valley with a 14.1 point-per-game scoring average, was among the seven other Jayhawks awarded letters that season. Sproull scored a school-record 40 points—a mark that would stand until Clyde Lovellette topped the 40-point mark three times in the 1952 season.

Sproull was something of a celebrity on campus even before basketball season started. James Naismith, in one of his many unpublished researches, measured every incoming male freshman in a variety of ways and compared them with what he considered the "perfect specimen," which, in his medical opinion, was Sproull.

As a junior, Sproull won the vote for team captain and showed his leadership in the first game when he "hit four quick baskets to put his mates out of danger" in a 24-18 victory over Iowa State, according to archive files.

That marked the closest of any of the first five games, which were all Kansas victories. The Jayhawks suffered their first loss of the season in a 29-25 game at

Kansas State, but finished the season with 12 consecutive victories.

KU and Nebraska each won its divisional title in the Missouri Valley. The conference had, again, dropped the playoff format, so the schools, which did not play each other that year, were named co-champions.

Sproull, for the second consecutive season, led the Valley scorers with a 15.5 average. Teammate Edward Van der Vries also had impressive scoring totals with at least seven double-figure games, including a pair of 22-point efforts.

Players served just one season as team captain, and although Sproull was coming back for his senior year, the Jayhawks voted themselves to be led by Ray "Stuffy" Dunmire. The 1914 *Jayhawker* quoted the captain-elect proclaiming his "star of ambition is set for an ever-victorious team, with mighty good chance for reaching it."

Hamilton started practice with returning lettermen Ralph Sproull, Ray

The 1909-1910 season was Tommy Johnson's last at Kansas. He was an All-America selection while at KU.

Dunmire, Arthur Weaver, Ray Folks, and Lawrence Cole and the infusion of new players such as Ephraim Sorensen and Hilmar Appel, the Jayhawks rightly

had high hopes for the 1915 season.

Kansas opened the year with two solid victories at Iowa State and returned home for a game with "Phog Allen's tiny Warrensburg teachers".

"E. J. Sorensen, rookie forward, gave the home fans a treat as he rippled the meshes for nine buckets. Eight Jayhawkers had a hand in the scoring pie as Coach Hamilton used his substitutes for the first time of the season," read the game report of the 46-20 victory.

The routs continued with Sproull, Sorensen, and Weaver combining for 51 points in a 55-21 triumph over William Jewell as the Jayhawks prepared to face long-time nemesis Nebraska.

With Sorensen getting 14 points and Sproull 11, the Jayhawks rolled to a 45-17 victory that "avenged their 35 to 0 football defeat and established themselves as the team to beat in the Missouri Valley," a game report stated. The decision also marked the first regular-season victory by Kansas over Nebraska since 1911.

Sproull scored 24 points to help KU complete a two-game sweep of Kansas State in Manhattan, and Sorensen and Weaver each scored 18 points as Kansas used a 53-28 romp over Washburn to go to 9-0.

Kansas State traveled to Lawrence for the return set, but Kansas, hit by illness, was not ready. A case of mumps kept Ray Folks from the game, and Sproull was slowed by another illness usually found in children—tonsillitis. The Jayhawks failed to find their form and lost 21-18. While it was only the first loss of the season, Kansas found itself in second place in the Missouri Valley behind undefeated Missouri.

KU rallied to beat Kansas State 39-20 in the second Lawrence game and keep tight to Missouri, the next team on the Jayhawks' schedule.

Missouri Coach Eugene Van Gent introduced advance scouting to the Missouri Valley. The Tigers, who had never been a factor in the league race, were suddenly unbeaten halfway through the year. W. O. Hamilton took note.

Missouri's schedule took the Tigers to Kansas State before the two-game series in Lawrence, so Hamilton went to Manhattan to "get a line on a new style of play used by Missouri," he told the

University Daily Kansan.

When he returned, the February 15, 1915, *Kansan* reported that he said, "We are going to play a couple of games with Missouri and I am sure we will win at least two of them."

True to Hamilton's prediction, Sproull scored 20 points in the first game as Kansas knocked Missouri from the unbeaten ranks with a 42-23 decision. Then, because of scheduling quirks, the Jayhawks wrapped up the conference championship with a 44-19 rout of Missouri. Sproull again had 20 points.

In reporting the game, the *University Daily Kansan* took a different angle: "A noisy wedding occurred in Robinson gym last Saturday evening when the Jayhawkers basketball team was married to Miss Missouri Valley Championship.

"A large number of friends of the family were present: E. C. Quigley of St. Mary's conducted the ceremony and the Missouri Tigers gave the bride away."

Hamilton's team rolled through the remaining four games, winning by 11 and 14 points at Missouri and by 32 and 19 over Washington University at St. Louis to finish the season 16-1.

Sproull posted a career record of 49-8, averaged 17.8 points a game, and led the league in scoring for the third consecutive year. He was the second Kansas' basketball player voted to an All-America team. Sproull, Sorensen, Weaver, and Dunmire earned all-conference honors.

But Sproull graduated along with much of the talent from the previous two seasons. Dunmire, Weaver, and Folks all graduated, leaving Hamilton with only captain Lawrence "Slats" Cole to build a team.

The results were predictable. Kansas had to come from behind to beat Iowa State 26-25 in the 1916 opener but dropped the second game of the series 24-21. The Jayhawks used a record 13 players in a 38-10 triumph over Washburn but staggered from there.

The Jayhawks' first road games were at Lincoln where the much-larger Nebraska team expected to take back the Missouri Valley championship.

Kansas played gamely in the first match but, the archive files state, "with the score tied at 33 [Leon] Gibbons, tiny Kansas front line man, sank a long bucket in the final minute of the game. Referee Lowman ruled that Gibbons was out of the playing court when he shot the ball. Gibbie's protest was so vehement that the ruffled official allowed the Cornhuskers a free throw. This gift toss was converted, and therein lay the Huskers' victory margin."

After the demoralizing 34-33 loss, Kansas fell 40-27 to Nebraska, "thereby eliminating the hapless Mount Oread team as a Missouri Valley contender," one game report stated.

That proved to be the case as the Jayhawks dropped two home games to Kansas State to fall to 2-5. Three victories over Washington University and a season-closing triumph over Missouri—24 hours after being routed 41-10 by the Tigers—allowed Kansas to finish fourth

Dr. James Naismith called Ralph "Lefty" Sproull the "perfect specimen" by which all incoming male athletes were compared. *Opposite page:* The teams of KU became accustomed to the number one spot. In the period of 1909-1912, KU was conference champion every year.

KU missed the conference championship of the 1912-1913 season for the first time in its history. The next two teams, pictured above, reestablished the Jayhawk claim to the conference title.

in the Missouri Valley, at 6-12. Hamilton had suffered through his first sub-.500 season.

The team endured what would become a familiar haunt that season as former Kansas player Bill Hargis coached Emporia Normal to a 36-25 victory over the Jayhawks, the first non-conference defeat of Kansas in Hamilton's tenure.

Slats Cole, writing for the 1916 *Jayhawker*, said, "Our biggest problem was to get the big squad of green material worked into an efficient machine. The wonder was that we won the games we did."

Also in the 1916 yearbook, Hamilton wrote: "There is no cause for great anxiety over the prospects in basketball at the University." Because coaches "realizing the situation decided to prepare not only for the present years but also for next year."

Hamilton had an unusual coaching style for the times. Most coaches found a starting five and stayed with it throughout the game except in the most extreme contingencies. Substitutes for any reason were rare. Hamilton regularly used his bench and, in fact, lettered 10 players that season. The optimism Hamilton had when writing for the *Jayhawker* stemmed from the number of experienced players returning for 1917.

Kansas roared out to a 7-0 start, including a sweep of the Kansas State games in Lawrence.

"But it was a lucky brand of ball they were playing and the luck failed to last during the entire season," The 1917 *Jay-hawker* said in retrospect. "In fact, the luck broke down in the middle of the season and the result was disastrous."

The bubble burst in the form of 38-9 and 32-29 defeats in Manhattan. The first game was described, in archive files, as a "bolt of lightning from a clear sky."

Hopes were enhanced with Walter Kauder's "most spectacular shot of the game—a long one from midcourt" tied the score at 23-23 with a minute and a half to go, and Rudolf Uhrlaub's free throw with 30 seconds to play gave Kansas a 24-23 victory over Missouri.

Kansas lost the rematch with the Tigers, but it posted twin 8-point victories over Washington University to keep hold on second place in the Valley standings. After splitting two games with Nebraska, Missouri loomed ahead.

The Tigers won the first game 24-20 and then the Missouri center "rolled in 22 points to lead the [Tigers] in their feast on Jayhawker meat," according to the graphic archive report, of the Tigers' 38-15 victory.

Kansas finished the year 12-8 overall, including a 9-7 Missouri Valley record that left the Jayhawks in fourth place for the second consecutive season.

The 1918 season brought more of the see-saw results, and Kansas finished with a 10-8 record. The Jayhawks played only one non-conference game that year—a season-opening 37-27 triumph over Camp Funston behind team captain Rudolf Uhrlaub's 23 points.

Kansas played its first 10 games at home in 1918 and finished with eight road games. A sweep of Washington in

Lawrence left the team 7-3 when it hit the road.

While Missouri won its first conference championship in 1918, the Jayhawks were able to spoil the Tigers' perfect season after Hamilton shook up his lineup. Missouri pulled within 20-16, "however, Hamilton's new combination managed to curb the [Tiger] rally, 'Scrubby' Laslett making the final basket as the game ended," the game report stated. The 28-23 decision was the one blemish on Missouri's 17-1 season.

Uhrlaub led the Missouri Valley in scoring, and he and Howard "Scrubby" Laslett were voted all-conference while the Jayhawks finished in third place.

While coaching at Kansas, Hamilton supplemented his income with an automobile dealership. The car business boomed, becoming lucrative while coaching went much the other way in terms of money. Even before the 1919 season began, Hamilton thought of resigning to devote all of his time to private business.

As usual, Kansas opened the season with a victory, routing Iowa State 50-17 behind Roy Bennett's 20 points. The Jayhawks dropped the second game at Ames, 29-28, but had two players on the court, John Bunn and A. C. "Dutch" Lonborg, who would eventually be enshrined in the Naismith Hall of Fame.

Bunn, a native of Humboldt, Kansas, was a three-sport star at KU and the school's first 10-letter athlete. After graduation, Bunn coached 42 years, including terms at Stanford, Springfield College in Massachusetts, and Northern Colorado.

Lonborg, a native of Horton, Kansas, won letters in three KU sports and had three all-conference football awards to go with the two he won in basketball. He coached for 23 years at Northwestern, where he was instrumental, along with Phog Allen, in organizing what became the NCAA Tournament. Lonborg also served 14 years, from 1950 to 1964, as the Athletic Director at Kansas.

Even with such a stellar lineup, the 1919 Jayhawks had a tough year, settling in with a 7-9 record—5-9 in the Missouri Valley.

"Kansas played exciting basketball throughout the season," the 1919 yearbook staff wrote, "and the games won

were decisive in determining the championship of the Valley."

Kansas State won its second Missouri Valley Conference title by just one-half game over Missouri, and the yearbook staff assigned the difference to the Tigers' 36-29 loss to KU in Columbia on February 20.

The lure of the private world grabbed Hamilton after the 1919 season. He told the *University Daily Kansan* that "I have been coaching basketball for 23 years." On June 10, 1919, after four championships, a conference title tie, and one second-place finish, Hamilton formally left KU basketball. He remained a fixture in the Lawrence business scene until his death December 30, 1951.

Hamilton had three seasons in which his team lost just one game, and his 125-59 overall record put his winning percentage at .679.

As they had with Hamilton, KU Athletic Department officials looked to their roster of game officials to find a new coach.

While E. C. Quigley officiated many of the Kansas games, the name of "Forrest C. Allen, Warrensburg Normal" popped up on several games. And Phog Allen was asked to return to KU.

Marvin Harms was a KU letterman in the 1919-1920 seasons, after he returned from World War I.

Phog Rolls Back In

Forrest C. Allen received his unique nickname because of his exaggerated call of "Ball" while umpiring a baseball game. Spectators thought he sounded like a foghorn, and sports writer Ward Cauble, as is the wont of the profession, decided to spruce it up with the unusual spelling "Phog."

"What do you expect from someone called 'Peahead?'" Allen asked, referring to Cauble's own nickname.

Allen had another sobriquet. "Doc" was the title his players often found appropriate. "Phog" was reserved for contemporaries.

Allen's previous success at Kansas—Missouri Valley Conference championships in each of his two seasons and a 43-9 record—grew at what is now Central Missouri State University in Warrensburg, Missouri. During his seven years at Warrensburg Normal, Allen won seven league titles and amassed a 102-7 record—0-3 against Kansas.

Bob Allen, Phog's son, told the story that "Drury College [in Springfield, Missouri] got so tired of losing that one year they felt that, apparently there was an epidemic of diarrhea of some kind and they thought that Dad poisoned the water on them. So I think they were glad to get rid of him down there."

When William O. Hamilton left, the University of Kansas again sought an athletic director as well as coaches for basketball, football, and track. Money was tight, so anyone hired was expected to handle the responsibilities of more than one position. Allen enlisted as athletic director and football coach. Karl Schlademan took control of the track and basketball programs.

Allen coached football for one season. And it was a successful year. The football team finished 5-2-1 including a storied 20-20 tie with a powerful Nebraska team.

Schlademan also started his duties successfully, coaching the basketball team to a 37-22 victory over Emporia State in the first game of the 1920 season. Schlademan, however, wanted to devote more time to track. Allen had no qualms about stepping in.

"I was just a dumb cluck," Allen joked to *The Kansas City Star* in 1968. "I wasn't supposed to be a basketball coach in the first place. I took it over because the guy who was supposed to be the coach was too scared of these boys coming back from the war."

The Jayhawks had seven lettermen returning in John Bunn, A. C. "Dutch" Lonborg, Howard "Scrubby" Laslett, Roy Bennett, Howard Miller, and Marvin Harms as well as Ernest Uhrlaub, who had lettered in 1917 before leaving to fight in World War I.

To familiarize himself with his charges, Allen used 14 team members in a game against the Washburn Ichabods.

"Washburn sentinels had a busy evening trying to stop Jayhawker sharpshooters who scorched the netting with 23 buckets. Eleven Allenmen participated in the march of field goals," the game report read.

KU entered Missouri Valley Conference play a week later and defeated Iowa State twice. The winning streak ended, however, when the University of Missouri visited Lawrence.

The Missouri Tigers were the class of the conference in 1920. Out of the four previous seasons, they had won one conference title and were runners-up for the other three. The Tigers lost only one game the entire season, to Kansas State. Even so, the Jayhawks made them work for their victory, forcing them into overtime.

George Rody and Marvin Harms were called off the bench after the Jayhawks fell behind 16-6 early in the second half. With each player getting four field goals, Kansas tied the score at 27-27 and forced an extra period. While Missouri scored all five of the points in the overtime, Allen's team made a good showing.

Kansas split two games with Kansas State and easily handled Grinnell and Drake on the road. Bunn and Laslett broke training rules in Iowa and were suspended from play. In the second half of the Drake game, however, Allen put Laslett on the court. The coach later wrote that Laslett, "like a fiendish ani-

Phog Allen was the driving force behind the Kansas basketball tradition.

mal unleashed" scored or contributed to 16 points in three minutes for a 19-point victory.

The next week, the Jayhawks lost two to Missouri and two to Washington University—the top two teams in the Valley. These losses dropped the Jayhawks to 7-7 on the year.

The Jayhawks closed in a flurry, sweeping two-game sets with new league member Oklahoma and Kansas State. KU ended up 9-7 (11-7 overall) and in third place in the Missouri Valley.

While it marked the first time an Allen-coached basketball team finished lower than the conference championship, the 1920 *Jayhawker* yearbook wrote with pride of the 11-7 showing: "The Jayhawker record was exceptional, considering local basket ball conditions. Kansas teams have had very little coach-

ing in the last few years and the new regime had a bunch of misfit stars from which to round out a machine." Team captain "Dutch" Lonborg, one of the "misfit stars," earned his second all-conference selection.

Many of the experienced players who helped Kansas to a winning record in 1920 left after that season. By the time Allen sent the Jayhawks out to meet Drake in the 1921 opener, only George Rody and Ernest Uhrlaub among the returning lettermen made the starting lineup. The other three starters—sophomores Paul Endacott, "Long" John Wulf, and Armin Woestemeyer—proved to be stalwarts for the next three seasons.

The 1921 season could best be termed a "rebuilding" year. Scores decreased for both Jayhawks and Kansas opponents as Allen's methodical defense and ball

Phog Allen focused on rebuilding in 1921, teaching the team his own style of defense and ball control.

won basket ball championships quite regularly."

Those days were shrouded in the mists of times long gone by. Kansas, which won or shared Missouri Valley Conference titles in seven of the first eight years of the league's existence, had not finished better than third since 1915. Brighter days lay just ahead.

In 1922, Allen instituted a training feature over Christmas vacation in which he arranged with another school to practice on their campus for a week. The Jayhawks went to Minnesota that year to work with the Big Ten Champion Golden Gophers. The teams closed the week of practice with a 32-11 Kansas triumph over the host school.

Allen allowed his team a brief rest after the train ride home, but soon had them back at work. The team respected Allen's practices for the efficiency of the preparation.

"[Allen] was a tactician," Endacott said. "There wasn't any foolishness in our practices. We were using every minute. He knew what he wanted to do and it was always about the same. In those days, everything was defense. It was a cardinal sin to let anybody get behind you. Defense was *IT*."

Just as the trip to Minnesota indicated something extraordinary, Allen often experimented to improve the Kansas team.

Said Endacott, "He was a very unusual, odd person. He was full of fire, very aggressive. He had all kinds of ideas and they worked out. He liked to get into controversies. He liked the publicity. He'd try anything."

"He would make these talks in the dressing room just before we'd go out [to play a game]. Full of fire, I'll tell you. Somebody would say, 'Well, what did he say?' and we'd say, 'Well, what *DID* he say.' We didn't remember just what he did say. It could have been anything, but it got us to play hard."

Kansas won the first five games, posting a 25-15 victory over Nebraska in the final game of the streak by keeping the Cornhuskers scoreless for the first 14 minutes of the game. Missouri handed the Jayhawks their first loss of the season, 35-25. Six days later the Kansas City Athletic Club, with center and future Hall of Fame member Forrest "Red"

control came into effect.

KU won its first six games. Uhrlaub's 18 free throws earned Kansas a 31-17 victory over Grinnell in the sixth contest. But the Jayhawks were only able to break up two four-game losing streaks with a two-game sweep of Washington University. Kansas closed the year by taking a pair of games from Oklahoma, despite a 26-point outburst by the Sooners' Ed Waite, a record total against the Jayhawks.

Missouri, again going 17-1 with their only loss to Kansas State in the final game of the year, won the Valley behind center George Williams, "the sweetest player to perform on Robinson boards this season," according to the archive files. Kansas wound up fourth.

Despite the lackluster 10-8 record— four of the losses coming against Missouri and the other four while playing Kansas State—the Jayhawks looked toward a favorable future.

"Practice started for the 1922 season April 1, and will continue until school is out, to be resumed next fall," the 1922 *Jayhawker* staff wrote. "Such work is bound to bear results in the shape of a great team for 1922. In fact, some dopesters look forward to a season like the old grads tell about—when Kansas

DeBernardi scoring 17 points, beat Kansas 34-32.

Team captain George Rody scored 23 points in the next KU game—a 41-24 victory at Oklahoma—and Kansas rolled through seven opponents heading for the rematch at unbeaten Missouri.

A university newspaper account of the game read, "During the first half the two teams battled on even terms, neither five having any marked advantage. The score sawed back and forth and the period ended with Kansas holding a bare two-point lead.

"With the start of the final session, Endacott opened hostilities with a long field goal and Rody followed with another basket from a difficult angle. During the remainder of the game, the Jayhawker lead was never endangered. The Tiger short pass baffled the Crimson and Blue defense not one whit and the Missourians were forced to take practically all their shots from the center of the court. The game ended 26 to 16, placing the two teams in a tie for first place."

"It was a beaten Tiger," Allen wrote in his 1937 book *Better Basketball*. "At the end of the game the Tigers' tongue hung out so far that you couldn't tell whether it was his tongue or his tail."

Bouyed by the win in Columbia, Kansas posted clear victories in its final three games to earn, along with Missouri, a share of the Missouri Valley title.

Paul Endacott, known for his defensive prowess, earned All-America honors. Four Jayhawks were named All-Missouri Valley and George Rody, who scored 15.2 points a game, was the high scorer in the league. Endacott joined Rody on the all-conference first team. John Wulf and Charlie Black, a sophomore, were placed on the second team and Armin Woestemeyer was given honorable mention.

Phog Allen had two seasons that could be called crucial to his career at Kansas, and 1923 brought the first. After splitting games with Missouri, the Jayhawks earned a share of the 1922 Missouri Valley title. The coach wanted more for 1923.

Endacott, Black, and Wulf formed the core of the Kansas team while Waldo Bowman developed into a starting player

Paul Endacott lettered all three years as a player from 1921-1923 and was team captain for one year. He was named to the All-America and all-conference teams.

and Tusten Ackerman—like Endacott, a Lawrence native—became eligible as a sophomore. Kansas fielded the team-to-beat in the 1923 Missouri Valley race.

Ackerman won two All-America certificates while at Kansas. He and his former high school teammate, Endacott, were the first two basketball Jayhawks to twice earn All-America honors.

Bowman, while not a player of Ackerman's abilities, started school with Endacott and convinced "Endy" to go out for freshman basketball as a way to escape physical education class. Endacott said when the players were awarded their green freshmen "K"s, he and Bowman sneaked into the women's gym in Robinson to take each other's picture. Playing for Kansas gave both men a great deal of pride.

Allen tested his team with a week's work at Creighton, capped with a 29-7 rout of the Bluejays in which Kansas allowed just one field goal. The Jayhawks were never seriously threatened in their first six games. The match at Missouri came up next.

"For eight seasons the Tigers have been drilled in the same general system

"Dick" Black

Charlie Black was an important part of the 1922-1923 season for Kansas. This season resurrected the winning tradition for Kansas. The Jayhawks went undefeated in conference play and lost only one game all season, to KCAC.

of court strategy," Allen wrote in his *Sports Stories*. "With [J. Arthur] Browning and [Frank] Wheat on the forward end of their machine, it seemed probable that it was possessed of the better scoring mechanism. But with Black and Endacott, bolstered by the dependable John Wulf, bulwarking the Kansas five-man defense, it was equally as probable the visiting team would present the better defense. All in all, it was a toss-up to sport followers."

Fate seemed to intervene, however, in favor of the home-standing Tigers. The trip from Lawrence to Columbia on January 16—the day of the game—failed to be a carefree one.

Kansas played three games in as many days from January 11-13 in its annual swing through Iowa. While the games were clear victories, they did not go uncontested. Allen wrote, "Every regular came home a cripple: Black and Wulf had Charley horses; Bowman an injured back; Ackerman a twisted knee and Endacott two badly sprained wrists."

Endacott said Allen's osteopathic background gave him the knowledge to bind the injuries in such a way that the players could play against Missouri.

"I won games on the training table, not as a coach, I always said I wanted Thoroughbreds," Allen often said.

The battered team's route to Columbia took them through Sedalia, Missouri, where the Jayhawks had to change trains. A man approached Endacott and handed him a slip of paper with the message, "To Hell with Kansas." The curse worked. The team bus, which was to take the players from the station at Jefferson City to Columbia, broke down six miles from Columbia and the Jayhawks took off walking, singing hiking songs and "The Crimson and The Blue" and "I'm a Jayhawk."

After covering about three miles, the repaired bus caught up and took the team to the hotel. Allen ordered a special pregame meal, but the hotel could not provide it. And game time was approaching.

Kansas played gamely and the first half ended in a 6-6 tie, but Missouri, as the Jayhawks began to feel the effects of the day's travails, pulled out to a six-point lead. Word was wired back to Lawrence that, "Kansas has broken."

But Endacott scored and so did Black. Endacott again made a basket, tying the score with three and one-half minutes to play. The Jayhawks managed to take the lead on a field goal by Endacott and a free throw by Ackerman. Missouri called timeout.

Endacott, declared the best defensive player in the league, went to work. When the Tigers in-bounded the ball he caused a tie-up and forced a jump ball.

"Endacott, after a tip-off, pounced upon it like a leopard," Allen wrote. "He leaped for it, he dived, he lunged and plunged with no thought of himself. The ball was the thing."

Each time Referee E. C. Quigley tossed the ball up, Endacott grabbed hold of it and forced another jump. There were 16 jump balls in the final three and one-half minutes; each involved Endacott, and the Jayhawk guard won every one to save the 21-19 victory.

It turned, to Endacott's embarrassment, into one of Phog's favorite stories. Endacott, completely spent from the effort and in a self-described "trance," could not catch his breath after the game.

"I discovered," Allen said in several of his books, "upon examination that the intercostal muscles, due to overexertion, had cramped. He had played himself out. It was then that I fully realized what he had given. We worked on him twenty minutes before we could get him comfortable."

Allen was in awe of "this picture of these men who had given their all, bent over their teammate who had given part of his superhuman self."

A season should end on an effort like that, but the Jayhawks had most of the schedule to go. Kansas took a perfect 9-0 record into Kansas City to play Allen's former team, the Kansas City Athletic Club. KCAC, which had won its division's national championship, defeated KU 27-23 with the last two points coming on a shot that was in the air as the final whistle blew.

The return to intercollegiate competition took the Jayhawks back to winning, and Kansas ran its record to 16-1 going into the final game—a battle with 14-1 Missouri in Lawrence.

This match had the drama jerked from it as Kansas jumped ahead and kept the Tigers well behind before settling for a 23-20 victory. More than 2,000 people were turned away at the door of a capacity-filled Robinson Gym. Allen crowned the 1923 Kansas team "ever-victorious" because it was the first to go through the nine-team Missouri Valley without a conference loss.

DeVaughn Francis, writing in the 1923 *Jayhawker*, said: "Machine-like floor work and basket shooting and with its integral parts so perfectly co-ordinated. From John Wulf, lanky center and three-season man, to Tus Ackerman, forward, the newcomer on the team, Doctor Allen's quintet demonstrated that it was the best rounded outfit that the conference has ever seen."

Paul Endacott and Charlie Black

The 1922 team went 1-1 against the powerhouse conference defending champion Missouri Tigers.

were All-America, and Wulf joined them on the all-conference first team. Endacott never considered himself much of a player and admitted to a great deal of unease about the attention that Allen paid to the game in Columbia and the guard's part in it.

"Years later Mrs. Allen told me that Phog told her at the beginning of the 1923 season, 'Now we've tied Missouri and if I can't beat them both games in 1923, I'm going to quit coaching.'

"I never understood why he attached so much importance to that game until I learned about 15 years after I got out of college that if we'd lost that game he was going to quit, he just could be the director [of athletics]."

Allen awarded 11 letters that season. While team captain Paul Endacott, John Wulf, Tusten Ackerman, Charlie Black, and Waldo Bowman played the bulk of the minutes, Phog never forgot the important roles of the other players.

In a letter requesting that the school authorize the varsity basketball "K"s, Allen made special mention of one man who saw little playing time: "Adolph Rupp had worked for three consecutive years, given the best he had in him for the success of the team. It is an unwrit-

The 1923 team was named the best college basketball team in the country by the Helms Foundation.

ten law among coaches that when a man comes out and does his stint without fail for three successive years that man should receive a recommendation for a letter."

Rupp, who joked that he sneaked into the games when Allen was not watching, is the coach who surpassed Allen's record for basketball victories. "The Baron of Basketball" entered the Naismith Hall of Fame in 1959 and piled up 875 victories at the University of Kentucky. No coach at the NCAA level has more.

It should be noted that all the players from the "ever-victorious" 1923 team went on to very successful professional lives after graduation—Endacott, for instance, became the president of Phillips Oil. Those players lived Phog Allen's credo: "I wanted All-Americans who would be All-Americans in the outside world as well."

Sixteen years later, the Helms Foundation gave the 1922 and 1923 teams one last honor when it named them the best college basketball teams in the country for those seasons. The honor is noted by the white "National Champions" banners hanging in Allen Field House.

Allen had restored Kansas to basketball prominence. The Jayhawks, after sharing the 1922 Missouri Valley title with Missouri, won five straight outright titles and did not lose more than two conference games in a season from 1922-1927.

"Tus" Ackerman joined Paul Endacott and Charlie Black as a two-time All-American selection, as would Gale Gordon and Al Peterson before the string of championships ended.

Allen never rested in trying to find the best players on his squad even after the season began. In the first conference game of 1924—against Drake—he played 20 different men, switching whole teams in some substitutions.

Nebraska and Oklahoma experienced basketball resurgences in 1924. An Ackerman field goal "thrown 15 seconds before the gun," according to the yearbook, allowed the Jayhawks to beat the Cornhuskers 19-18 in one of the tightest collegiate games of the season. Oklahoma broke Kansas' string of 34 consecutive league victories with a 26-20 triumph in a game played "literally too fast for the eye," the game report states.

That, however, was the only Valley loss for the Jayhawks as Allen, whose team went 16-3, again awarded his traditional gold basketball medallions symbolizing the league title. Basketball joined in a Kansas sweep in the 1923-1924 school year. Every sport in which the Jayhawks fielded teams for conference play won championships.

The 1925 Jayhawks, with Ackerman back for a final season, also suffered just one defeat—a 40-28 upset by Kansas State which got a combined 29 points from "half-pint forwards" K. R. Bunker and Clifton Byers.

The *Jayhawker* yearbook for 1925 honored Naismith with this frontispiece: "Dedication to Dr. James A. [sic] Naismith. Twenty-six years at the University as director of Physical Education, father of basketball, exponent of clean sportsmanship, believer in the Kansas Spirit, a Christian gentleman, and true friend of all K.U. students."

The 1926 season began slowly but picked up avalanche-style speed within two weeks. Kansas, for only the second time since 1903, opened with a loss, with Washington University posting a 25-18 setback in Lawrence. The Jayhawks came back with victories over Kansas State and Grinnell.

The second defeat of 1926 was a 29-21 loss at the hands of Oklahoma. The game report called it "a neat Dr. Jekell-Mr. Hyde stunt, playing the Sooners off their feet in the first half and being just as badly outclassed in the second frame."

Phog Allen adjusted his lineup for the Missouri game two days later. He put Glenn Burton in Gale Gordon's guard spot and moved Gordon to forward. The Jayhawks responded to the change to the tune of a 24-15 victory over the Tigers. That decision started KU on a winning streak that would encompass the remaining 14 games of the season and rake in a fifth consecutive Missouri Valley title.

"[Albert] Peterson, [Gale] Gordon and [George] Schmidt were too strong a combination for the opposing teams to overcome in the offensive part of the game," the *Jayhawker* said at season's end. "Without question, this trio is one of the smoothest and fastest scoring combinations ever unleashed on a college basket ball floor."

The acclaim for Peterson and Gordon, both from Kansas City, Kansas, did not stop with local press as each was named All-America in addition to All-Missouri Valley.

The *Lawrence Journal-World* asked James Naismith to select an "all Modern KU basketball team" from the players of the previous five years of championship teams. Naismith's choices: Gale Gordon, Charles Black, Albert Peterson, Paul Endacott, and Tusten Ackerman. Each player earned All-America honors twice.

While Naismith recalled the past, the future was being built. Construction continued on Hoch Auditorium, and by May 1926, some of the details were reported in the school newspaper: "As an ornamental feature, four brass Jayhawks, about three feet high, perched upon poles, will extend out at an angle from the front of the building. The poles upon which the Jayhawks will roost will be about twelve feet in length and the base of the poles will be thirty-five feet above the ground."

"At the front of the floor level will be an orchestra pit, but it will be constructed in such a manner that it can be eliminated when the floor is needed as a basketball court."

Kansas opened the season with four road games, winning a non-conference game at Creighton and then taking Missouri Valley tilts at Drake and Washington University. Allen took his team to the Convention Hall in Kansas City, Missouri, and found several familiar faces playing for the Kansas City Athletic Club. Among the "foes" were former Jayhawks Tusten Ackerman, James Mosby, Herbert Proudfit, and William Wilken. The Jayhawks didn't treat their

Adolph Rupp, a player for Allen, is the coach who first broke Phog Allen's victory-total record. Rupp won 875 games at Kentucky.

lettermen any different, however, than a regular team of foes and posted a 27-21 victory.

Kansas went home and was immediately dumped twice at Robinson Gym, the first a 15-12 defensive tussle with Iowa State and the second a 27-24 loss to Nebraska, which was coached by former Kansas star Charlie Black. The game marked the first Nebraska victory over Kansas since Allen returned as the Jayhawks coach in 1920.

KU played a nonconference game with Hillyards Chemical Company of St. Joseph, Missouri, and commenced a winning streak. The Jayhawks used a free throw by George Schmidt, after Kansas State called too many time outs, for the difference in a 35-34 victory.

Kansas built a nine-game winning streak before heading home to close the season with two games in Robinson Gym. Peterson broke a 26-26 tie with a pair of field goals and two free throws to give Kansas a 36-29 victory over Missouri and clinch a sixth consecutive Missouri Valley title for the Jayhawks. Peterson totaled 22 points in the game.

The Jayhawks capped their 15-2 season with a 29-24 victory over Kansas State as Peterson, en route to a third all-conference selection at center, ended his career with a 10-point game. Peterson led the defensive-minded Valley in scoring in both 1926, at 9.0 points a game, and 1927, with a 10.5-point average. The Kansas State victory allowed Peterson and the class of 1927 to boast a 48-5 record over their three years of eligibility. Peterson and Company would be missed more than anyone thought.

The following year marked the end of an era. Old Robinson Gym quite literally was overshadowed by the building

that was erected to the west. What was state-of-the-art when designed by James Naismith and opened in 1908, would be replaced by Hoch Auditorium—"The Opera House."

The 1928 season proved to be one of less than fitting good-byes.

The Jayhawks' final game in Robinson was a rare December game and even rarer home loss as Kansas State closed the old building with a 20-13 defeat of Kansas. Robinson had been a good home. Kansas boasted a 148-38 record—a 79.6 winning percentage—from 1908 through the 1928 opener.

Dedicatory ceremonies for Hoch Auditorium, built for $350,000, were staged October 14, 1927. The basketball team first played there January 6, 1928, and notched a 29-26 overtime triumph over Washington University. Harold "Dutch" Hauser, taking Albert Peterson's place at center, scored all three points in overtime to help Kansas to the victory.

Victories were even harder to come by the rest of the season, as the Jayhawks sagged to a 9-9 record. All of its games that year counted as Missouri Valley conference games, giving Kansas more conference losses in that season than in the previous six seasons combined.

Kansas left the Missouri Valley Conference after the 1928 season. The 9-9 record and fourth-place finish were hardly typical of the team that won or shared 13 of the 21 Valley championships from 1908 through 1928. Several schools felt the need to move on, and Kansas, along with Iowa State, Kansas State, Missouri, Nebraska, and Oklahoma, formed what they called the Big Six Conference.

Kansas played in Robinson Gym for 20 years, amassing a 79.6 winning percentage.

Previous page, top: Tus Ackerman, here showing his dribbling prowess, was an integral part of the legendary 1923 team. He was also selected to the All-America teams of 1924 and 1925.

Below: The 1928 team was the first to play in Hoch Auditorium, built to replace the already outgrown Robinson Gym. It was also the last to play in the Missouri Conference as Kansas left it to form the Big Six Conference in 1929.

Master Motivator

Hoch Auditorium, named for former Kansas governor Ed Hoch, was a beautiful basketball arena, but it proved to be far from perfect. The wooden basketball floor sat directly on the concrete deck of the building. The resulting lack of "give" caused painful shin splits.

Space limitations prevented designers from including a home-team locker room. The basketball team was not the primary tenant in the building. It was shared with various University functions. Only a lasting friendship between Coach Phog Allen and Donald M. Swarthout, dean of the School of Fine Arts, kept the time-sharing conflicts at a minimum.

Hoch Auditorium became the athletic equivalent of the formal living room from which parents bar children. Robinson Gym, the family room, still served for every other contingency.

"We practiced in Robinson, but we played our games in Hoch," said Bob Allen, Phog's son who played for Kansas from 1939-1941. "If you practiced there a day or two, there's no way you could play a game. So we never did practice at Hoch, except the day before the game. We'd go over and shoot free throws and run a few plays and get used to the lighting.

"A visiting team, if they had a game the next night playing elsewhere, they frequently found they didn't do well because their legs were dead. There was no resilience to the floor at all. It was just wood on concrete."

The Kansas team dressed for games at Robinson and, after final pregame remarks by Phog Allen, headed over to Hoch. The jaunt was no little trip, especially in the cold and wind and snow of January and February.

"You ran through the slop and the snow if there was snow on the ground," recalled Bob Allen. "It wasn't bad. After the game was over you were perspiring and hot but it was such a short run that you'd never feel it."

The players' problems with Hoch didn't compare to those of some of the fans. Hoch Auditorium received the nickname "The Opera House." Situated on the floor of the building, the basketball court was a long way from the seats in the upper balcony. While seating increased with the move from old Robinson, the viewing did not improve.

"The biggest problem in Hoch was that there were few [good] spectator seats and they were poorly constructed for a basketball arena," said Bob Allen. "The only good seats were on the lower floor. There were two other decks above that. You got so high that they couldn't really tell what the heck was going on down there as far as play-making. You could just see a bunch of ants down there.

"They put chairs along the goals, behind the goals at either ends. Especially on one end they were really quite close, so if you had a driving layup they might really knock you on your rear."

The younger Allen recalled a game in which a Kansas State player "took my feet out from under me and deposited me in the second row of seats. I remember that very well as being a very unpleasant thing."

Allen hit chairs with an elbow and neck and spent the rest of the game in the hospital.

"It wasn't really a good place to play. Nobody liked to play us there," he said. "We won most of our games. I think Henry Iba at Oklahoma State called it the 'House of Horrors.' It was a poor place to play.

"But Hoch was friendly to us because...it was a poor place to play and we were more used to it than they were."

The first full season in Hoch quickly dissolved into one of the most forgettable in Kansas basketball as the Jayhawks finished with a 3-15 record and tied with Kansas State for last place in the Big Six Conference.

KU opened the season by helping Washburn dedicate its new basketball arena, losing to the host Ichabods 25-24—one of only three Kansas losses in the history of the 28 game series between the neighbors. The Jayhawks dropped a 38-31 decision to Missouri in Kansas City before being beaten twice by Notre Dame.

A semester-break trip to Berkeley,

California, resulted in two losses to the California Golden Bears before Kansas earned its first win of the season. Russell Thomson and Floyd Ramsey each scored nine points and Forrest "Frosty" Cox played his usual strong defensive game in helping the Jayhawks to a 24-23 victory over Cal-Berkeley.

The triumph did not signal a turning point. Returning to the Midwest, Kansas dropped four consecutive Big Six games. The close scores of those games show just how frustrating the season became: Oklahoma defeated KU 27-25, Missouri posted a 34-30 victory with the last two baskets of the game,

Nebraska took a 30-29 decision, and Iowa State won 27-24.

Kansas broke the losing streak with a 31-24 victory over Kansas State, but another four games passed before the Jayhawks won again. The game report states, "Reversing their usual style of fading out in the closing minutes, the Jayhawkers came from behind to nose out Iowa State 33 to 32 in a thrilling finish."

The season closed with the Jayhawks, who led 30-25 in the second half, dropping a 36-35 game at Kansas State despite 18 points from Russell Thomson and 14 from Tom Bishop. The decision dragged KU into the Big Six cellar with the Wildcats.

Allen substituted relatively freely throughout the season but the team still had the bulk of its troubles in the second half. The 1929 *Jayhawker* inferred the poor record resulted from conditioning.

"Lack of sufficient stamina to carry their scoring tactics into the second half was fatal to the Jayhawker basketball team this year, and caused them to suffer one of the most disastrous seasons in history," wrote the yearbook staff.

"With a coach as efficient and popular as Dr. Allen, together with the stars who will return next year, it is not improbable that Kansas will get on the right track and regain the proud position it formerly held in Valley basketball."

Allen tried to find a path out of the morass for the Jayhawks, and as a result, those duties kept him from home. Bob Allen said a series of speaking engagements kept his father on the road but added, with a smile, "I was one of six children and maybe he got home late on purpose. I know that Mother and he usually ate after feeding us.

"It was usually a very light meal. He was under a lot of pressure and tension, so he didn't eat a lot of food. I remember one of his favorite meals when he would come home late was merely bread and milk. He would float some broken-up bread in ice milk and that would be his evening meal."

Phog Allen responded to the pressure and, according to the 1930 *Jayhawker*, "changed his style of play this winter and developed a powerful team." The new Kansas game plan featured a "slow-breaking attack and a modified zone defense."

KU began the season with 13 victories, never allowing more than 30 points in any game in the streak. During the Missouri game in Kansas City on December 21, 1929, the Tigers scored just 12 points, four in the second half. The defense the Jayhawks played reminded the official game reporter of the "Allen team of 1923 when Paul Endacott and Charles Black featured a Mount Oread defensive machine that held down opponents."

Kansas opened conference play against Oklahoma, which had gone undefeated in the final year of Missouri Valley competition and the first of the Big Six. With Russell "Rub" Thomson scoring 12 points and James Bausch getting 10, the Jayhawks posted a 34-22 victory, breaking the Sooners' conference winning streak at 29 games.

Injuries began to mount for the Jayhawks, who had four of their last five games on the road. But KU owned a game and a half lead over second-place Missouri when the teams met for the first of two games. The Tigers sliced a game off its deficit with a 29-18 victory.

Jack Roadcap scored 16 points helping Iowa State to a 30-27 victory that dropped KU into second place. After a non-conference loss at Creighton, Kansas kept within striking distance of front-running Missouri with a 36-35 triumph at Nebraska as Tom Bishop scored 23 points for the Jayhawks.

A crowd of 4,300 showed for the final game of the season, which sent Missouri to Lawrence to decide the Big Six Conference championship.

The *Jayhawker* reported: "Flashing a dazzling offensive to pile up a commanding lead in the first half, the Tigers

relied upon their superior height to stave off a maddened Kansas team in the second period, and although a Kansas rally appeared in the closing minutes the final gun spelled *finis* upon a valiant attempt."

The 23-18 loss kept Kansas one game back of Missouri for the Big Six title, but 1930's 14-4 record showed that the 1929 season had been an aberration. "Frosty" Cox earned All-America honors. He and Bishop were both named all-conference and would be back for 1931.

Ted O'Leary, then a junior, later reminisced about Phog Allen, writing, "Somehow he convinced you that when you played, you played for Kansas, you were supposed to win. If you didn't it was a fluke. He was a very enthusiastic positive man and he made you share his enthusiasm."

The introduction to the basketball section of the yearbook took its usually buoyant enthusiasm to even greater heights: "Kansas is the mother of basketball, and her sons have kept pace through the years. Coached by one of the game's closest students and inspired by its inventor, the Jayhawkers have always been amazingly successful on the court."

With sophomore center Bill Johnson joining the already strong varsity, Kansas expected to perform well in 1930-1931. The Jayhawks, a typical Allen team, were based on defense. They did not allow Washburn a field goal in the first half of the season opener and again showed that KU could play that half of the game.

The Jayhawks kept opponents to no more than 29 points as they progressed undefeated in their first eight games. Their fate turned when they met Nebraska. Cornhusker G. Sheldon Davey's free throw in the final minute of overtime clinched a Nebraska victory, 31-30.

Kansas improved to 11-1 with a 31-29 victory over Oklahoma A&M—coached by former Jayhawk George Rody—with O'Leary's 17 points leading all scorers. Oklahoma came next on the schedule and roared back from the 20-8 halftime deficit to post a 33-30 victory, the highest point total against the Jayhawks all season.

KU worked itself back into a first-place tie with Nebraska—coached by

former Jayhawk Charlie Black. Tom Bishop had 14 points helping Kansas to the 34-29 victory at Lincoln, Nebraska.

The Kansas defense held Kansas State to 26 points. In fact, defense clinched the Big Six championship by limiting Iowa State to 16 points. The Cyclones led 12-10 at halftime, but KU scored the first 12 points of the second half.

Kansas dropped a 26-19 conference decision to Missouri and closed the year by beating Creighton for a 15-3 overall record. The league title was the first since 1927 for the Jayhawks, but allowed Allen to continue his boast of at least one conference championship for each class. Bishop and "Frosty" Cox claimed their second all-Big Six Conference awards.

Above: During their 1936 drive for the Olympic playoffs, the Jayhawks defeated Nebraska 34-29 in Lincoln.
Bottom: The 1936 team won the conference and made it to the Olympic playoffs, losing to Utah State.

KU pulled into a first-place tie with Oklahoma by beating Missouri 24-16, with only a home game against the Sooners remaining on the schedule.

The Oklahoma game provided Phog Allen with a story he would use for many seasons, and one almost as popular with the coach as Paul Endacott's 1923 effort at Missouri.

"Each story was selected at an *apropos* time in the season or at a game of some kind," said Jerry Waugh, who played for Allen from 1949-1951.

"[Bill] Johnson was from Oklahoma City, his father had died and so he returned home to be at the funeral. They were playing again for the championship and it was Oklahoma, this time in Kansas. And Doc, he said the team was upset as they took the floor. They were uncertain because Johnson wasn't playing with them this night and they were hoping he would return.

"Then he would pause and he would say, '...as they listened for the drone of the airplane to bring Johnson back.' He would dramatically put his hand up to his ear as if he was listening for the plane right then."

Johnson showed up, although probably not as late as Allen indicated, and scored eight points to back Ted O'Leary's 14 points—"O'Leary rained baskets on the Oklahoma heads from all angles of the floor," reported the yearbook staff—in a 33-29 Kansas victory.

Allen not only had a good story with which to motivate future Jayhawks, he had his 10th conference title in 15 seasons of coaching at Kansas.

O'Leary, who tied for the league scoring championship with an 11.0 point average, made All-America. O'Leary, Lee Page, and Bill Johnson took all-Big Six honors. More important to the staff of the *Jayhawker,* however, was the dominance over the cross-state rivals. "It is interesting to note that over the three-year period that O'Leary and Page served the Crimson team, the Kansas Aggie Wildcats have gone without a morsel of Jayhawk meat in eight vigorous attempts."

That quickly changed as Kansas opened the 1932-1933 season with two games against the Wildcats and Kansas State won both by four points, although neither game counted in the Big Six

With Bill Johnson, Ted O'Leary, and Leland Page back for 1932, Allen's core team returned to the favorite's role. The Jayhawks staggered to a 2-3 start in conference play. Kansas lost 31-26 in overtime to Oklahoma and, after defeating Nebraska and Kansas State, fell to Iowa State and Missouri.

O'Leary and Johnson each scored 17 points as Kansas evened its Big Six record with a 40-27 victory at Iowa State. The Jayhawks wormed into the league race with triumphs over Kansas State and Nebraska.

standings. The Jayhawks quickly turned things around and won seven consecutive games. Included in that string was a three-game sweep of Stanford—coached by former Jayhawk John Bunn.

KU lost a four-point game at Oklahoma, picked up three victories, and then lost a four-point contest at Missouri. Three clear victories completed the schedule. Kansas was 13-4, with its 8-2 league mark worth a third consecutive Big Six Conference title.

The final game marked another match with Oklahoma. Although the Jayhawks owned at least a share of the league title, the Sooners could grab half with a victory. But Kansas rolled, leading 18-8 at the half and by 15 points in the second half before the game ended 35-26.

Bill Johnson was voted his second all-conference and first all-America honors after the season. The Jayhawks had a 41-12 record—22-8 in the Big Six—and three conference championships in his tenure.

On the freshman team that season was Milton "Mitt" Allen, the first of Phog's sons to play for Kansas.

Bob Allen said neither he nor his brother felt pressured by being the son of a famous coach. "I don't believe Dad would have used either of us, if we weren't the best at our positions that he had available."

Basketball was a big part of life at the Allen household. When very young, Bob Allen said, he and his siblings would choose which KU players to cheer for every year, and when he became big enough to play: "I don't remember anything but playing basketball."

"We had a pair of basketball goals in our back yard and we played constantly," he said. "We'd come home after school and we'd have a game. There'd be guys who would just plan to be over there and we'd play. I was five years younger than my brother [Mitt] and I remember getting into some of his games. Usually he would guard me and that was usually rather brutal. The only shots I got were those back over my head. I had a position on the court where I knew, I had practiced shooting it back over my head like a backward free throw. I got so I could make them very frequently. That was the only shot I ever got."

Allen said the court was dirt but, even if it rained or snowed, the game would go on after the players threw sand on the mud.

"Years later," said Bob Allen, "when my Mother dug it up to make a garden out of that thing, there was over two feet of hard sand just packed tight over the period of years."

While the Allen backyard court became popular with the neighbor children, Phog Allen couldn't find the time for that level of the game. "He was pleased we were out there playing, and he would supply the balls for us," Bob Allen said. "We wore out many of them."

Mitt Allen's first varsity season was with the 1933-1934 Jayhawks, who completed a 16-1 record and marked the best season for KU basketball since the 17-1 record in 1925. Kansas won its first four games in solid fashion but dropped a defensive battle at Nebraska, 24-21. The score was 1-1 after nine minutes of the game in Lincoln, and the Cornhuskers led 9-8 at halftime.

Ray Ebling, a sophomore, had 13 points as Kansas came back after the loss with a 27-25 triumph at Missouri that was sealed with free throws from John Wells and Gordon Gray. The closest Kansas came to a loss the rest of the season was against Nebraska in Lawrence.

The Jayhawks jumped into control in the Nebraska game and led 20-6 in the second half and 22-10 with 10 minutes to play. The Cornhuskers charged back, however, and pulled to 24-18. KU's Francis Kappleman hit a free throw, which became very key after Nebraska's Rollin Parsons made two baskets, and Kenneth Lunney scored to make the tally 25-24 for Kansas just before the final gun.

Ebling had 14 points in that game and a season-high 24 in a 39-25 victory over Oklahoma that wrapped up the 1934 Big Six title. He closed the season with 12 points, with his last basket the clincher in a 23-21 triumph over Missouri. Ebling tied the conference record for points in a season, set when Oklahoma's Tom Churchill scored 124 points in 1929.

Phog Allen opted to try one of his long-time passions in the 1934-1935 season-opener. He had 12-foot baskets brought into Hoch Auditorium for a game with Kansas State. Allen said Naismith never meant to lock the goal in at 10 feet, that it was just a handy distance from the floor of the gym to the raised running track in the Springfield, Massachusetts, YMCA Training School, but the distance "for some strange reason became as sanctified as motherhood."

Kansas went 1-1 with the 12-foot baskets. Since the taller baskets were worth three points, Ebling became KU's first three-point shooter. Although the idea never caught on, Phog Allen's passion for the 12-foot basket continued for the rest of his career.

Iowa State, fielding one of its best teams in many seasons, pointed to Kansas as the team to beat in its rematch. The Jayhawks won in Lawrence, 35-18, but the second game claimed a 32-20 Iowa State victory.

That loss dampened Kansas' hopes for a fifth consecutive league title. They swept a two-game series with Kansas State, but a pair of contests at Columbia doused the chances of the Big Six championship. Ken Jorgenson held conference scoring leader Ray Ebling without a point in a 23-21 Missouri triumph and limited Ebling to two free throws the next night in a 21-18 Tigers' victory.

Kansas closed the year with two wins over Oklahoma. The Jayhawks went 15-5 overall and 12-4 in the Big Six for second place behind Iowa State.

Ebling, an All-America and all-conference choice, scored 22 and 18 points in the Oklahoma games to grab his second Big Six scoring title with 188 season points—a 13.4 point average. Team captain Dick Wells also pulled in all-conference mention.

The second-place finish did not change the yearbook plans to run a story about Allen.

Written by Ted O'Leary, a letterman from 1930-1932, the story mentioned the coach's strength in fundamentals, particularly passing the ball and conditioning.

"Dr. Allen has installed in his basketball teams the idea that they are the royalty of the games," wrote O'Leary. "John McGraw did that for the New York Giants, Knute Rockne did it for his football teams and, William T. Tilden believed it about himself.

"The feeling of *noblesse oblige* enjoyed by Kansas teams is a potent factor in their success... Kansas teams step on the court with a feeling that they have a tradition to uphold and nine times out of ten they uphold it."

The yearbook deemed Allen a "moulder of champions."

Between the 1935 and 1936 seasons, Phog Allen worked diligently to get basketball into the Olympics in time for the XIth Olympiad in Berlin. Once he accomplished that, he wanted to find a way to send the game's inventor, James Naismith, to see the game played in the Olympics.

Allen conceived a plan that had each high school and college withhold one cent from the price of each admission to one game played during the week of February 9-15 to finance the trip to Germany for Naismith and his wife. The idea became a huge success and, although Naismith's wife could not go to Berlin because of illness, James Naismith saw the first Olympic basketball competition. He called it the greatest moment in his life.

The entire Kansas team nearly went, too. The Jayhawks rolled through their regular season 18-0, completing the conference schedule 10-0 with 51-26 and 51-29 routs over Oklahoma and Missouri. Ray Ebling led the conference in scoring for the third consecutive season and was again an all-America choice. Fred Pralle and Francis Kappleman joined Ebling on the all-conference team.

KU advanced to the Olympic playoffs and dispatched Washburn, 33-30, and Oklahoma State, 34-28, to set up a best-of-three series with Utah State.

The Jayhawks beat Utah State in overtime, 39-37. The second game saw Utah State battle from a 31-23 deficit in the second half to win 42-37. The Utes, two days later, eliminated the Jayhawks with a 50-31 decision. Noble left that game very early, leaving Kansas with just three regulars on the floor. Utah State ran off 16 consecutive points in the second half to put the game away.

Victories and conference titles mounted, but Allen still constantly tinkered with his game. He had certain preconceptions about basketball and did not waver from those, but improvements could always be made.

"The year I came here, in 1936, he changed the offense to the anterior-posterior screening offense," said Dick Harp, who played for and coached with Allen. "That was his offense for the rest of his coaching career, really.

Harp was a freshman in 1937, coming from Kansas City, Kansas. He received a solid education in the basics of basketball while at Rosedale High School, but admits the real learning came at KU.

"For each of the parts of the game he had fundamental skills, whatever it was and that was something new that had not been true in my experience in basketball," Harp said of Phog Allen. "He had a technique for performing those, which he taught you, which was not as common in those days as it is now.

There was nothing really complicated about the Allen method, and the coach wanted to keep it that way.

"I would be advocating something," said Harp, "and maybe it was something on offense to do differently that might be a little more complicated or a little sophisticated or a little different. He would say, 'Yeah Dick, we can do that but remember we need to do the ABCs if we're going to be successful.'

With Fred Pralle back, and with Allen further imprinting his simple but effective style of play into the Jayhawks, Kansas dropped right back into the favorite's role. KU ran up a 12-2 record before losing its first game in the conference—a 33-32 defeat in overtime at Kansas State.

The Jayhawks also lost at Nebraska, 37-32. When both Kansas and the Cornhuskers won the final game of their seasons, the two old rivals were left in a tie for the Big Six championship, just as they were in 1912 and 1914.

The Kansas record for the season ended 15-4, and Allen, who had coached at the school for 20 years, had amassed a 295-87 record and 14 conference titles. Pralle became the latest Kansas star to earn both All-America and all-conference honors.

To think that Allen's career was nearly at an end was a mistake. Francis "Jay" Plumley, a former player who handled the freshman team, at the end of a radio show just prior to the start of the 1937-1938 season said, "Well, good

luck, Doc, we'll see you in church at 7:30 tomorrow night."

To which Allen replied, "All right, Jay, I'll be right there in the front row." And he would be for another 19 years.

That season marked the first for Dick Harp as a player, but he was green. All Allen had going for him was Pralle— no mean starting place—and, of course, the Phog Allen mystique.

"By then Doc had had, if you just look at the won-and-loss record, significant success and he was recognized na-

Top: Ray Ebling came to KU from Lindsborg, Kansas, and earned All-America honors in 1936. *Bottom:* Fred Pralle earned All-America honors during 1937 and 1938.

tionally," Harp said. "He had established the fact that Kansas had a great basketball program and he was then recognized as an innovator in the game of basketball and as a great coach."

Not even a great coach can win without players, and Allen was lucky to have Pralle around. Behind his leadership, Kansas won its first eight games. The Jayhawks lost 34-29 at Drake. After winning the next game, KU lost for the second time of the season, this time to Oklahoma, which proved itself a challenger for the Big Six championship.

Neither the Sooners nor the Jayhawks lost again until the conference rematch on February 18 in Norman, Oklahoma.

"Oklahoma that year had some people named [Jim] McNatt and Marvin Mesch and Bill Martin was the captain of the team," recalled Harp. "They were a fast-breaking team and to this day I look on them as having as good a fast break as I ever saw in basketball."

"We lost the opening game to them here," Harp said. "And when it came down to the season's end, we played there, and it was really the game for the championship. When we went to Oklahoma, we always stayed in Oklahoma City and bused down to Norman. Usually we would have an alumni luncheon on the day of the game and Doc would speak. This particular game he spoke, probably because we were not favored to win the game, and I always felt the inspiration of what he said."

Doc fired the team up and the Jayhawks came away 41-38 winners. Victories over Iowa State, Nebraska, and Missouri completed the 18-2 season and another conference trophy. Pralle scored 22 points in the Missouri game to take the Big Six scoring championship— 12.1 points a game—and collected his second All-America certificate and third all-Big Six honors.

Allen said, "Squad morale won the Big Six basketball championship for 1938." In truth, it was more Fred Pralle.

"I was a freshman and Pralle was a senior and actually the team was pretty bad and yet they were winning the championship," said Bob Allen. "When we went 18-2 I can tell you that Pralle was the one-man team. A bunch of nobodies, little guys. Those guys actually played and scored points and made goals. They won the championship with a bunch of no-names and Pralle, who was an absolute great. In my personal opinion, he was the greatest guard that KU ever had."

Unfortunately, Pralle graduated, but another fantasy was fulfilled that season as Dick Harp played for Phog Allen.

"Playing for Doc Allen was the culmination of a boyhood dream," Harp said. "About the eighth grade, it was my ambition to be able to go to Kansas and play basketball for Dr. Allen."

Harp met his boyhood idol when Rosedale played at Lawrence High School. Since Bob Allen played for Lawrence, Phog Allen watched the game. Afterward, Phog Allen was introduced to Dick Harp, the man who would succeed him as the basketball coach at the University of Kansas.

Kansas won or shared seven of the eight titles—coming in second the other year—from 1931 through 1938. But 1939 started out rough. After topping Warrensburg Normal to open the schedule, Kansas dropped three straight games. A four-game winning streak failed to prepare the Jayhawks for league play, and they lost the Big Six opener 43-31 at Oklahoma.

KU next defeated Kansas State at home, but with a tough 33-29 decision, Allen felt his team had been outnumbered.

The coach wrote to Earl Falkenstien, the financial secretary of the athletic department, about a game official who had been censured for "chiseling on the expense account."

"[It] didn't do [us] any good in the game last night," Allen wrote. "I have never seen a fellow as biased and prejudiced as this fellow was last night."

Phog Allen generally did not give officials that rough a time since he had more important concerns in his locker room. Allen developed into a master at getting his teams ready to play.

Said Bob Allen, "Basically he would concentrate pretty much on what we had to do: You had this guy and you had this guy. Now this guy is great, but you can outplay him. He would say, we're going to do exactly what we're going to do. We're going to play our game and they're going to have to make adjustments to us. Because we're as good as anybody and better than most of them. He said, tonight you guys are going to play a great game.

"Then if it came to halftime and you weren't playing a great game he did a lot of different things. Sometimes he would say nothing. I remember one time, nothing. We kept expecting him to say you didn't cover so and so, you didn't run your offense, you didn't do this and that. Nothing. He just sat there.

"One time he didn't even sit there. He just never came in and we were thinking that we're going to have to go back out on the court and we haven't even seen him. And then he finally came in and said, 'What do you think about it?' He said, 'I don't even want to see you. Get out of here.' You go out there and say, hell, I can't embarrass myself any more. You'd just go out and play your tail off."

The younger Allen had other instances—such as the time Phog Allen grabbed a rickety chair and, telling the players they stink, bashed it against the wall. More likely, however, there would be the appeal, about how the players were representing Kansas, Bob Allen said, "like it was something airy, something ethereal, something unheard of. Like you're lucky to be here. You don't want to disgrace them do you? This is the greatest university in the world. He really believed it.

"He made you feel like you owed something and it was up to you to produce. You were giving something back to your school. It's harder than hell to repeat what he tried to infuse in you, but he did really feel it and made the kids feel that."

"Allen demanded, in his coaching, that you give the effort to be the very best that you could. That was the part of motivation and his teaching and coaching that was important because the best you can do is to get the player to do what he can do with the very best of his ability and energies and he was very good at that," Dick Harp said.

Even a master at motivation like Doc Allen could not turn the 1939 season into a complete success. Kansas lost four Big Six games—the most since 1929— and finished one game behind conference co-champions Oklahoma and

Missouri. The Jayhawks lost to and beat both teams during the season.

Oklahoma became the first Big Six representative in what would become the NCAA Tournament. The Kansas players, with the NCAA champion getting a shot at playing in the 1940 Olympics, looked on with envy and started to plan for next season.

A Promise

Phog Allen was one of the instigators among the National Association of Basketball Coaches in the development of a postseason tournament. The tournament, now lucratively run by the NCAA, underwent tough beginnings, and the coaches, many of whom made a pittance anyway, balked at the idea of having to support a money-losing event.

"Our junior year was the year after the tournament was started in 1939," said Bob Allen. "Dad was a prime mover in getting a basketball championship sponsored by colleges, rather than having Ned Irish and the Madison Square Garden and the [National Invitational Tournament], which had gotten to be very big, get all the money that he felt should go legitimately to the colleges and universities.

"So he, in '38, had organized the concept that the National Association of Basketball Coaches should run its own tournament along with a guy named Harold Olsen from Ohio State and Dutch Lonborg at Northwestern. That first one [in 1939] was held at Northwestern. Dutch Lonborg said he thought he could make a go of it."

But the tournament lost money the first year, and the coaches became skittish. They turned to Phog Allen, and the Kansas coach agreed to stage the tournament in Kansas City, Missouri, in March 1940.

"We knew that this tournament was going to be held in Kansas City," Bob Allen said. "It kind of hung up in everybody's mind that it would sure be great to get to play in that. So our junior year, after a poor year in '39, [Dick] Harp and [Don] Ebling and all of us were kind of dreaming."

Kansas started the season like a team on a mission. Outside of an overtime loss to Phog Allen's former team in Warrensburg, the Jayhawks were perfect through their first 10 games.

After a loss at Oklahoma State gave Kansas its third loss of the season, the Jayhawks went to Manhattan and found themselves trailing Kansas State at halftime.

"Dr. Allen was quite the capable motivator and there wasn't anything he wouldn't try," said Ralph Miller. "We were up at Kansas State and he lined us up and told me to slap Bobby [Allen]. We stared at each other and he told me to slap him again. We did it.

"We were seven or eight points behind at halftime and came back and won. I don't know what that had to do with it, but we won."

KU opened the March portion of its schedule with a 42-40 victory over Missouri that gave the Jayhawks at least a share of another Big Six championship.

After a non-conference loss at Creighton, Kansas traveled to its final regular-season game at Norman. Missouri completed its league schedule at 8-2, with the loss to Kansas costing the Tigers the outright title. Kansas went to Oklahoma with an 8-1 league mark while the Sooners were 7-2.

Oklahoma played for two teams, since Missouri needed a Sooners' victory to drag Kansas into a tie. When Oklahoma posted its 47-36 triumph over the Jayhawks, the Big Six had half of its teams tied for first place. The other three were all 2-8 and tied for fourth.

There had been conference co-champions before, but now the possibility of playing in the NABC Tournament was at stake and the league could have just one representative.

"We knew there was going to have to be some kind of a playoff and they decided to go to Wichita with that playoff," recalled Bob Allen. "Up in the Muehlbach Hotel [in Kansas City] they met and the man who flipped the coin was impartial. He flipped the coin and Oklahoma and Missouri had to play the first game. Both of those teams were physically much stronger than we were. We did not have anybody bigger than [John] Kline, who was 6-3.

"And Missouri got beat [by Oklahoma, 52-41]. They had the biggest team. We were kind of glad to see them get out of there because they were big, too big for us. So we were glad to see them get beat."

Between the two playoff games there was a dance on the arena floor.

"They had thrown this stuff that makes the floor slick. We went out and shot goals on it and Dad said there was no way we can stand up on this thing,"

Bob Allen said. "Oklahoma had shot goals on it, too, so they must have realized it, too.

"Dad sent Dean Nesmith out to get some boot soles that make your boots stick—it was gum substance and it was black like tar—for our shoes. We came out on that court and we were able to stand up very well, really. All our shoes were black soled but there was nothing said. The officials didn't comment on it, but the floor was marked up horribly. And we stood up better than Oklahoma did and beat them [45-39]."

Ralph Miller said he approached Phog Allen during the season about installing an offense with a post man. Miller said the coach did not jump at the suggestion, but, after a lecture on offense, had Miller play post in a scrimmage against the traditional Allen offense. They scrimmaged for two hours, with Miller's post team winning. Allen, according to Miller, didn't say anything at the time.

Miller was called to Allen's room on the train during the ride back from the Oklahoma loss and was informed that Allen had decided to switch to a post offense.

"We hadn't practiced it all season," Miller said, "but we used it the rest of the year."

With the tournament field limited to 16 teams, however, Kansas had to go through further elimination games, with Missouri Valley Conference champion Oklahoma State at Oklahoma City up next.

Miller remembered that Kansas was still using a ball with laces on it while Oklahoma State had changed to the no-lace ball. There was a discussion on how to handle the discrepancy and officials decided to play with the Kansas ball the first half and the Oklahoma State ball the second.

"They outscored us using our ball and were ahead at halftime and we outscored them in the second half with their ball and beat them," Miller said.

Bob Allen said, "They knew we would play our control offense. There was no [possession] time limit. You could work as long as you wanted to, with screens and picks and screens and picks, the same thing until somebody just happened to slip away and scored. It was

two teams that were built on the same kind of control game.

"Well, the game ended in a tie and we won it in overtime. Dick Harp made the winning goal and we beat them 45-43. That got us into the NCAAs and we had to play Rice Institute, which had won the Southwest Conference. That

Phog Allen and son Bob, *shown above*, made basketball a family affair.

Ralph Miller helped the 1940 team to the finals in the NABC playoffs, but the team got away from the control game in the championship game against Indiana.

sively. Harp used to cut paper clippings out of the paper and show Engleman in a great photo in perfect defensive position. Unfortunately his man was already dribbling in for a layup. He was never known to have made a pass to anybody for a goal. He was a great shooter but a liability defensively."

Southern Cal, which had won the NIT that season, also advanced to the semifinals. Phog Allen called Stanford Coach John Bunn, a former Kansas player, for a scouting report. Bunn said USC was "an absolutely great team with no weakness, but they'll just play hard enough to win. They'll ease off and then they'll blow you out and then they'll ease off."

Phog's plan was to stay close enough to the Trojans to knock them off late in the game.

Bob Allen completed a three-point play that put the Jayhawks up 41-40, but USC pulled back ahead with a field goal as time was running out.

The younger Allen relived the moment: "We don't score on the next move and they bring it down and they're kind of stalling and Engleman's trying to, as you frequently do, steal the ball, and he's down with his head. Jack Leopard sees him go by and thinks the pass is open, and I steal the ball. I pass it to Engleman, and he goes down and scores. We beat them in the last 15 seconds of the ballgame, 43-42."

"The gun went off as the ball came into my hands," John Kline wrote to Allen in 1942. "In that moment I had the greatest feeling of complete joy that I have ever experienced in my life. I could have thrown the ball all the way to the 'moon' at that moment."

"They're the fightingest, most courageous bunch of boys who ever played on a Kansas basketball team," said Allen on the radio after the USC game.

As strongly as Kansas had played to this point—the Jayhawks took a 19-5 record into the title game—the team sagged against Indiana.

"We get off to an early lead," said Bob Allen. "I think we were ahead 10-4 against Indiana and then Engleman and Miller each shot a couple of shots that were uncalled for. In our particular style of play it was control, control, control."

"In those days the coach couldn't

was the first game in Kansas City."

Phog Allen was looking for more offense as the tournament began. He played John Kline at one guard but "Kline was no scorer," according to Bob Allen. "They didn't even guard him." The coach wanted to have Don Ebling and Howard Engleman at forward, moving Ralph Miller to the middle. Dick Harp was a guard and Bob Allen handled what Phog Allen called the quarterback spot.

"He had a great night against Rice," said Bob Allen. "I think Engleman made 20-some points and the headlines. But Engleman was notoriously poor defen-

have the team come over," Allen explained. "You had to send in a substitute with anything you wanted to say. So Harp is the captain and he called time out and really read them off. He read Engleman and Miller both off, saying, 'What the hell is this, some kind of shooting contest?' They both kind of had their heads down.

"Indiana just went on and just kind of kicked our butts over the next few minutes and went up something like 18-12 and that's a big lead in those days."

The Hoosiers won 60-42, a score that would stand as the most lopsided NCAA Tournament title game until Ohio State beat California 75-55 in 1960.

"The only game I forget is the Indiana game—the 1940 game for the national championship," Dick Harp said. "We didn't do very well. We had played well through the tournament and didn't play well then. Maybe we were tired. We played tired. We just didn't play well and got beat badly.

"We had the victory over Oklahoma in Wichita and the victory over Oklahoma State in Oklahoma City and our games with Rice and Southern Cal. They were really fine victories. Then to play for the national championship and not play well was a great disappointment. And it still is."

As rough as losses are for the players on the court, coaches are left on the bench with little control of what happens in the game. Losses often eat at a coach, who then questions himself. Phog Allen, a master at preparing his team for a game, understood that he had to let the losses go.

Off the court the game did not—at least outwardly—bother Phog Allen. On the court, however, even in an era when coaches rarely stood up from the bench, the players always knew that Doc was watching.

"He let it be known he was there," Harp said. "It wasn't his nature not to let it be known that he was anywhere. Bench coaching was not then what it seems to be now. He might think about bench coaching now as over-coaching, I don't know. Doc was a commanding presence, so he was always significant."

Allen was practical, too. He knew that Bob Allen wanted to attend medical school at the University of Pennsylvania, so the coach scheduled a game in 1941 at Temple after a swing through New York. While the younger Allen looked into the medical school, the coach took the team on a self-guided tour of historic Philadelphia.

Bob Allen said, "Dad would frequently be deflected from what he was going to say by something else he wanted to say. So he told them, 'That's where Ben Franklin did so and so.' Dad made all the players on that trip write their experiences and what they remembered. And [Howard] Engleman had a big laugh about how he knew that's where Ben Franklin was but he didn't know what he ever did because Dad never finished the statement. He never told them what Ben Franklin did there."

Bob Allen described the 1941 team as "mediocre" but even with a late season slump that resulted in losses to Iowa State and Oklahoma, Kansas again tied for the Big Six title. The Jayhawks were 12-6 overall and 7-3 in the league. Iowa State also went 7-3. Instead of a playoff, however, the league decided to flip a coin for the right to try to get into the NCAA Tournament, and the Cyclones won.

Bob Allen is among the top guards in Kansas history. With Allen pulling the trigger—and playing defense—KU went 44-19. Allen was a two-time all-conference choice and passed the ball enough to Howard Engleman, who led the conference in scoring as a senior, to help the forward win two all-conference and one All-America mention.

The Jayhawks missed Ralph Miller, who decided to give in to his balky knee and undergo surgery in 1941. He returned for the next season, and Kansas tied for the Big Six championship. Oklahoma defeated KU 63-51 to finish the league season 8-2, and the Jayhawks grabbed their share of the title by closing with victories over Kansas State and Missouri.

With no Big Six playoff, Kansas won the coin toss and moved into post-season play, beating Oklahoma State 32-28 in the Fifth District Playoff before being eliminated by Colorado—coached by former Jayhawk "Frosty" Cox—46-44. A consolation victory over Rice gave Kansas a 17-5 record.

Ralph Miller said the team felt good about its NCAA chances when the tournament started, although "I really don't know if we could have beaten [eventual champion] Stanford."

Especially since Miller was ill. The football and basketball star participated in a fraternity swim meet and took some water on a turn. While in Kansas City for the NCAA Western Playoffs, the water in Miller's lungs developed into pleurisy. After returning to Lawrence, Miller spent 31 days in a hospital.

The 1942 Missouri game marked 25 years of coaching at Kansas for Allen. A scholarship in Allen's name was announced, and he was given, among other things, a huge scrapbook of letters of remembrance either about big games or the coach himself.

Chancellor Deane Malott wrote, "You have also demonstrated your ability to take anything from a bunch of star athletes to a collection of buggy whips and year after year produce a championship basketball team."

The 1942 season marked the 19th conference championship either won or shared during Allen's 25 seasons. Kansas had a record of 374-113, a 76.8 winning percentage.

The following year Allen sent out his "Iron Five" in Charlie Black, John Buescher, Ray Evans, Otto Schnellbacher, and Armand Dixon. With World War II on, the Jayhawks played nine games against military teams and those teams, with more experienced players on them, accounted for four of Kansas' six losses of the year.

The other two losses were to Creighton, leaving the Jayhawks with a perfect 10-0 Big Six record and a healthy 22-6 overall. Four of the "Iron Five"—all except Dixon—made all-conference, and Evans and Black were All-America.

Four of the 1944 losses were to military-base teams, but the war had deeper impact on KU basketball as players left campus for military service. Evans and Schnellbacher, for instance, did not return to school until 1946. KU slumped to 5-5 and third place in the Big Six, losing twice each to co-champions Iowa State and Oklahoma.

Kansas recovered some in 1945, going 12-5 and having a shot at the Big Six Conference title until Iowa State, the eventual champion, beat the Jayhawks 61-39 in the season's final game.

By 1946 the war had truly ended as far as Kansas basketball was concerned. Black and Schnellbacher returned from military service, and the Jayhawks celebrated with an explosion in scoring.

The normally total-defense bent that marked Allen's team turned around. While KU still made it difficult for the opponents to score, the Jayhawks were shooting like never before. Kansas averaged a school record 55.7 points a game, including 62 points a game at home. Charlie Black set a KU record with 173 points.

The fans liked the high-scoring Jayhawks, too. A total of 26,500 crowded in for the eight games in Hoch.

Henry Iba, however, never let go of his ball-control ideas of basketball, and a 46-28 regular-season loss to Oklahoma State and a 49-38 setback to the Cowboys in an NCAA playoff marked the only defeats in a 19-2 season.

Phog Allen always found himself involved in more than Kansas basketball. He served on the city council and on a number of community projects. During the war, he helped with the Lawrence draft board, and after the war, he was chairman of a committee to help returning veterans adjust to civilian life. There was at least one veteran whom the coach made his own special case.

"Otto [Schnellbacher] was kind of a personal product of Dad's," said Bob Allen. "Otto didn't have any money so [Phog Allen] would have Otto wash his car every day just so Otto would have some money. I don't know what the NCAA rules were in that era, but Otto would come down and wash Dad's car and Mother's car. I don't think he got over a quarter. It was nothing.

"But Otto said many times just what it meant to him."

Black and Schnellbacher returned for a final year of eligibility. Both were all-conference, and Black picked up his fourth All-America certificate.

Tickets at the 4,000-seat Hoch Auditorium were in such demand that students had to alternate games, with those holding odd-numbered tickets going to one game and the even-numbered tickets good for admission to the next.

Despite the high hopes, the season did not turn out that sweet.

Kansas opened with a large non-conference schedule going 8-4. The last loss in that group was a 52-50 overtime decision to Colorado on January 2. The Jayhawks began Big Six play five days later and dropped a 39-34 decision to Missouri. It proved to be the final game that Phog Allen coached that year.

Allen put his team through its usual paces. Jerry Waugh said practices always meant a lot of hands-on work by Doc Allen.

"I could remember his statement of, 'Damn the dribble. Damn the dribble,'" Waugh said. "He'd get started in practice: 'Damn the dribble. Pass it. Pass it.'

"He talked in terms of ABC basketball—pass and cut," said Waugh. "He made a great to-do about the theory of a perfect offense. He writes in his book when a man with the ball in a guarded position passes to his teammate in an unguarded position and he himself moves to an unguarded position. He made a big deal about passing and cutting, which are philosophically pretty general and loose, but it made a lot more sense later in my life."

Waugh happened to be at a practice after the Missouri game. Allen, demonstrating his theories, suffered a concussion when he was knocked to the gym floor. Physicians ordered him to stay away for the rest of the season. Howard Engleman, a former player, then a law student earning extra money coaching the freshmen, took over the varsity.

Without their usual coach, the Jayhawks lost five consecutive games—the longest Kansas losing streak since 1929. KU finished 16-11 overall and 5-5—third—in the Big Six. It was a very tough season. Nine of the 11 losses were by five points or less.

Allen, convalescing in California, never had basketball far from his mind, but he likely needed to be physically away from the game.

"That was an important time," said Dick Harp. "He hadn't been away from basketball for all those years. I'm not sure he needed the break, but I think he came back refreshed. Just seemingly in our conversations after that happened that he came back with a great deal of enthusiasm."

One of Allen first actions upon his return was contact Harp about joinging the team as KU's first full-time assistant.

Charlie Black was a four-time All-American at Kansas.

The Kansas basketball program was getting another rejuvenating shot, this one coming from the Kansas Legislature. Topeka Representative Alfred B. Page, in February, introduced a measure for a new field house.

"Kansas has enjoyed national fame for its proficiency in basketball," Page said. "On completion of the contemplated field-house at Kansas State college in Manhattan, and this proposed building on the university campus, the state finally will be giving its proper recognition to the sport."

Allen, recognized as one of the great motivators of the game, had a genuine concern for his players. They became part of Allen's family, whether they were a starter the magnitude of Charlie Black—either one— or the last man on the bench.

Phog Allen had his own order of importance and the way the team went about things before tipoff was certainly one of them. Waugh said before home games the team would meet at the Eldridge House at 3 p.m. "You could study but he preferred that you take your clothes off and get into bed and rest for two hours," said Waugh.

Dean Nesmith would call the players for a 5:30 meeting in the lobby when Allen would lead the team in a brisk walk. The team boarded a bus and headed for the Jayhawk Cafe for a pre-game meal of "Ovaltine and toast and celery because that was supposed to be good for your nerves," according to Waugh. "Just something very light. That's all you had. Then you went to Robinson where you prepared for the game."

After a quick warmup, the chalk talk began with the starters' names listed on the blackboard along with defensive assignments. Allen would give a short scouting report.

"Then Doc would come up to each player and he would take them by the hand and look them in the eye and shake their hand and say, 'Are you ready?'," Waugh said. "It was dramatic. It was quiet. You're going into competition right now and he was building this on us. And he goes to each player, 'Are you ready?'"

Allen would look deep into each of his players' eyes and, at times when he was more mystical than usual, would say he could see "the victory light" shining in the eyes of the starters.

Some players began to feel that the coach's actions were just a motivational trick.

Waugh said, "There was a guy named Gene Peterson that played at that time who was a Phi Beta Kappa, later a doctor. He comes to Pete, and Pete's 6-7, our big man at that time. He shakes Pete's hand and says 'Pete, are you ready?' Pete says, 'Not really, Doc, I've kind of got a headache.' Doc dramatically said, 'Maurice Martin take off your warmup.

I never play a sick man.'

"And so Pete doesn't start. Maurice Martin starts in his place. We go out the door and all of us say Pete for crying out loud tell him you're ready. Pete in his own way liked to make fun of that kind of situation. He'd put Doc on and the rest of us would kind of go along.

"This was not funny to Doc because this is where he prepared everybody to play the game, emotionally. Although you knew what he was doing to you, you felt that sense of getting yourself emotionally ready to play and you sensed these things happening to you. I sat through it for four years and watched it."

Allen and trainer Dean Nesmith personally saw to the health of the basketball team. The coach's osteopathic background helped. According to Jerry Waugh, Allen knew just how to rub a foot to take all the tension out of an athlete.

"I'm not sure he had any mystical manipulative ideas that were beyond what anybody knew normally anyway, but he could talk players into thinking they were better or well," said Waugh. "He had that ability to make the person feel that his arm was better. He was good at the psychology of healing and took great pride in his ability to perform those feats of healing."

The post-game routine carried into the following day. The players would report to Nesmith for a rub down.

"And it really felt good," Waugh said. "You were hurting a little bit because when I played in those days you were on the floor more. I had 'strawberries' on both sides of my hips. My knees were skinned from diving for balls. You were always sore and hurt all over.

"If you played hard, Deaner gave you a good rub. The 'rubberoo' he called it. But if you didn't do too well or he didn't like the way you played, you were short lived in there."

While the coach put his team through the usual routines, Kansas basketball went through one of those unrecognizable seasons in 1947-1948. Phog Allen's teams had always been noted for defense, but three times that season scoring records were set against Kansas, including 70 points allowed to Nebraska and a 77-point total run up by Colorado

in the season's next-to-last game.

And this from a team anchored by Jerry Waugh, known as "the Sheriff of Sumner County" for the way he "put the handcuffs on opposing high scorers," the *Jayhawker* yearbook said.

Waugh said, "I remember [Allen] used to say, 'It takes so little to squeeze

Top: Phog Allen congratulates Ralph Miller after the NCAA playoffs.
Bottom: Kansas, with Ralph Miller back as captain, tied for first in the Big Six in 1941-1942.

Top: The 1945 Jayhawks finished second in the Big Six Conference. KU finished first in 1946. *Bottom:* Gib Stramel, left, and Owen Peck, right, helped the Jayhawks to a 19-2 record and a conference championship in 1946.

head. When game week came up and you were playing Kansas State there was not much good about Kansas State. He really indoctrinated you against Kansas State, and the players. He belittled them. He did all those things to get you emotionally ready to play.

"And Missouri also represented that. There was a great rivalry, as far as Doc was concerned, with both Missouri and Kansas State. Those were the big rivalries that we had and Doc fostered that and perpetuated it."

The 1948 season belonged to Kansas State. The Wildcats went 22-6 overall and won the Big Seven Conference— Colorado joined the Big Six prior to the season—with a 9-3 record. Kansas limped in at 4-8 (9-15 overall), including a 10-game losing streak that ended with a final-game 61-54 triumph over Iowa State.

Said Jerry Waugh, "We were going through a team that was having tough times and complaining. That one year was a bad year to me because we didn't pull together as a team and that bothered me.

"Doc called me in, I recall it was in the spring of the year, and said that he was going to recruit this team. And he said, 'We are going to get some players who can play with you. We're going to have a good team before you leave here.'"

Kansas won 22 consecutive meetings with Kansas State—a streak that ran from January 11, 1938, until February 20, 1947. In the 1947-1948 season, the Wildcats won all three meetings with Kansas and only the final game was close. Second-year Kansas State Coach Jack Gardner made a quick impact on the rivalry.

Allen belittled Gardner when the Kansas State coach complained about a perceived advantage for the Jayhawks. "If a postman kicked at every dog that barked at him, he wouldn't get the mail delivered," Allen often said. But, in fact, Jack Gardner had Phog Allen's attention.

"Jack came along and had success at Kansas State," said Dick Harp. "Doc was not about to stand still and let that happen without giving that his full shot. He determined that he was going to get together a group of players that would be competitive for the national championship.

above mediocrity. To stick your head up there and be more than average. It takes so little to squeeze your head up through the crowd and be more than that.'"

Outside of Waugh, Kansas failed to do that. The Jayhawks failed to beat either Kansas State or Missouri—the two big foes in Allen's eyes—that season.

"Doc promoted that rivalry between schools, boy, listen," said Waugh. "He and Jack Gardner used to go head to

"He determined—and this is another part of his greatness—that things were going to have to change and maybe I'm going to have to recruit differently. We're going to have to get the players now. The players are not going to come by letter or a telephone call, they're going to have to come from what had been given the term recruiting. So he had determined that he was going to get the players to get the team to be good enough to win the NCAA.

"That was an entirely different focus for him. All those years of the success of the Kansas team certainly made most of the basketball players in Kansas, who were good basketball players, have the desire to come to Kansas."

"That was one of the first things he told me when I came in June of '48," continued Harp. "He asked me to visit Bill Hougland, Bill Lienhard and Bob Kenney. He said I want you to tell them and their parents that we are not only going to win the conference but we are going to win the national championship and go to the Olympics. I said you really don't want me to tell them that and he said you're damn right I do.

"Nowadays you start off with the goals. You have the goal to win the conference, win the conference tournament, the goal to win the regional. All those goals. He just said we're going to win the national championship."

Hougland, Lienhard, and Kenney—all Kansas natives—became integral parts of KU basketball. But the biggest and most important prize still had to be won and that was Clyde Lovellette.

"I know Dad said this was one man we've got to have," Bob Allen said, "and if we get him, he says, we'll be building toward the idea that by the time these kids are seniors they can win the NCAA championship and be a part of the Olympic basketball team. He went after Clyde

The 1946-1947 Jayhawks are shown here against Iowa State, one of their victories in Big Six play that year.

Although Allen's emphasis on training remained the same, the 1947 Jayhawks had a hard time putting the techniques into practice. The Jayhawks went 16-11 to finish in a tie for third in the Big Six.

hard. He spent more time recruiting Clyde than any player we had at KU."

Lovellette, however, thought about staying close to his Terre Haute home and attending Indiana to play for Branch McCracken. But Phog Allen made a left-end recruiting move, going to Lovellette's mother and convincing her that Clyde would be better served at Kansas.

"He sold Mrs. Lovellette," said Bob Allen. "He really worked hard on her in getting Clyde interested in coming to Kansas. She actually came out during that time and wanted to see the University of Kansas. She wanted to know where Clyde was going to be. She felt very sacrificial that she was not going to be able to see all of his games like she'd always done. Then she got an idea of the big picture and what it all could mean."

"I don't know if Dad bragged about it," Bob Allen said, "but he was very happy about the future he could look forward to with Clyde.

"Now, why would a big man like that come out to the University of Kansas? Dad loved to throw out these little things

like Clyde had asthma and he wanted to be where the atmosphere was conducive to his treatments—Mount Oread. He loved that."

In the end it wasn't Phog Allen who sold Kansas, it was the University itself.

"Knowing what Phog was all about, that didn't enter the picture," Lovellette said. "When Phog came to talk to me, it was about the tradition at Kansas as far as the basketball was concerned. What I would vote mainly for was the reality of Phog was a human being who I could associate with and feel comfortable being around. And the people of Kansas, the state of Kansas, I liked the people. There were really down-to-earth people who I could enjoy being around and associate with. Family, more so than a number.

"I didn't want to go to a school that was sort of I just want you for the basketball team and manipulate you in any way and try to make you feel bigger than you're supposed to be by all the accolades they'd throw at you. These people were just down to earth and I enjoyed

that. From every person that we met in Lawrence from the college campus to the guy on the street, it was all the same."

There were several reasons Lovellette chose Kansas—the "altitude" of Mount Oread and the benefits for an asthma sufferer notwithstanding—he liked the size of the school, Allen's interest must have flattered him, and it was Jayhawks basketball that he was joining.

"Of course, Kansas had a tradition of real good solid basketball," Lovellette said, "and I wanted to go some place where I knew I could play. I feel that I could have played anywhere I went coming out of the high school.

"Also, Phog sort of made a couple promises, that he was getting a team together to challenge for the national title and he wanted me to be a part of that. He wanted to go to the Olympics and the national championship of the NCAA. He was going out and getting ball players. He was confident that he would win the national title in '52 and also be part of the Olympics. And he said if he could recruit me to fill in that spot in the middle there, he said I think I've got me a winner here."

Allen's 1948 team suffered through one of its few losing seasons.

Prophecy Fulfilled

Kansas basketball suffered a post-war depression that carried into the 1948-1949 season. Other colleges put teams on the court mostly consisting of veterans from the military, often resulting in an advantage in terms of maturity and size.

"A lot of people, like Kansas State, had taken advantage of players who had been in the service and so forth," said Dick Harp. "They played Kansas State here and Kansas State had a good team—they had [Clarence] Brannon and it was the beginning of [Jack] Gardner's [tenure]. Kansas had them beat the whole way, I think, and lost the game right at the end."

Harp attended the KU-K-State game while Phog Allen tried to convince him to join the staff as an assistant. Harp took the assistant coach's position, making the 1949 team a special one to him.

"A number of them were fine basketball players," he said. "We had maybe 15-17 kids who could play basketball, but not much size. We had kids like Dale Engel and Buddy Bull and Maurice Martin and [Charles] Penny. They were all good kids who could play and played hard. I've often thought that we didn't do well by them.

"Doc was never great for playing a whole bunch of people. In fact people didn't do that as much as they do now. There wasn't a rotation, but that would have been something you could have done with them, you could have had a rotation and you could have grouped them. They had some unique abilities and played their butts off."

While that quality endears a player to a coach, it does not show up as well as talent. Kansas opened the year with victories over smaller schools—Rockhurst and Trinity—and then hit the road.

Allen never lost sight of the present team's need, but he stayed acutely aware of his four-year plan. The recruitment of Clyde Lovellette was such an important part of the great plan for 1952, that Phog Allen was not going to jeopardize it. The coach scheduled an early season game for December 1948 at Purdue. Lovellette, playing in the days before freshmen could play on the varsity, did not make the trip. But Allen made sure he invited Clyde's mother to the team's post-game meal.

"Doc was always good with the mothers," said Jerry Waugh, a player on that season's team. "That was his forte. He recruited the parents. He recruited the mother, long before anybody recruited the mother. He was a master at that.

"Doc called us all together and said Mrs. Lovellette will be there tonight and I want each of you to go up and say something nice about Clyde. It was, 'Mrs. Lovellette, it's nice to meet you. We really enjoy having Clyde back there and we're really going to have a good team when he's ready to play next year.'

"It was something to make her feel good. And Doc set that whole thing up. And the mother walks away and thinks, 'Oh, those nice boys, I'm glad my son is there.' And Doc set it up."

Allen made sure that Lovellette was well tended to in Lawrence, too. He still joked how the altitude of Mount Oread helped Lovellette's asthma.

"I have asthma, that part was right," Lovellette said. "I don't think the height of the hill would have any effect, though. He liked to tell that story and I went along with it.

"One thing he did," said Lovellette, "because he was an osteopath, he worked with the spinal column. He kept us in shape that way. He kept us loose, manipulated in the back. He worked on all the ball players and kept the sacroiliac in position. All these things sound kind of funny but I never had a cold in my four years I was at Kansas. I never missed a ball game because of my asthma. I never was injured in a game at Kansas. He kept me in physically good shape."

Jerry Waugh explained Doc Allen's teaching methods. "He used animals to demonstrate and explain bodily movements." said Waugh, "He had an old film about the mongoose and a cobra. There is a film of a mongoose who does battle with a cobra and subdues the cobra by getting it in the back of the neck."

Allen showed that film—"Killing the Killer"—once a year, using the mongoose as the perfect instance of defensive position and how continuous movement allowed it to kill the snake.

Waugh continued, "Then he would talk about playing with your dog and when you try to catch your dog notice how the dog drops his weight for balance and how difficult it is to catch that dog because the dog has lowered his center of gravity and maintained his balance so he can move in any direction and you can't get him.

Phog Allen had basketball down to a precise science. Waugh said the Jayhawks had to run down the sideline six feet from the sideline "because that gives you margin to field an errant pass. That's how he'd say it."

"That was part of the teaching," said Waugh. "And he would say that you must tell a player 7,642 times and then you tell him once more."

Colorado joined the Big Six to create the Big Seven Conference, which staged a Christmas tournament in Kansas City, Missouri. The Big Seven invited a non-conference foe to round out a tournament field of eight. Kansas finished fifth in the first holiday tournament in 1946 and played well enough to take second in 1947, losing the title game 52-49 to Oklahoma.

The Jayhawks opened the regular season at Oklahoma and were again beaten, dropping them to 4-4 on the season. KU hovered around the .500 mark all season. The final bright spot was Gene Peterson's 34-point game against Creighton on January 29. Kansas won three of its next five games and was 12-8 but lost its last four games. For the second consecutive season the Jayhawks, 3-9 in the league, finished tied for last in the Big Seven.

Phog Allen suffered his concussion at a 1947 practice and missed about half of that season recovering. That, however, did not change his hands-on method of coaching.

"Phog would come out in his sweat clothes," said Clyde Lovellette. "He was 62. He would show us passing, dribbling position, and things like this. Now he wasn't doing this as quick and agile as a man half his age, but he was getting in there and showing you that he was dressed and ready for practice. Although he was 62, he was ready to play."

And to coach. Allen and Dick Harp

worked extensively with Lovellette in an attempt to move his game from the high school to major college level.

"Clyde was a great player. He was a very competitive player," Harp said. "In his high school career he had mostly scored right around the basket. He had never developed offensively much. He had never developed many skills, other than the opportunity to get the ball in under the basket, not an insignificant skill. He could do that very well.

"But he did not have any other shots. So Doc wanted him to learn to shoot the hook shot. We spent a lot of time his freshman year and in the summer actually learning to shoot the hook.

"And Clyde was a good learner," said Harp. "Clyde had good touch on the basketball. And actually when he was here he could shoot the ball out on the court some. And later, in professional

Dick Harp joined the team as an assistant coach in 1949. After years as Allen's right hand man, he moved up to head coach when Allen retired.

basketball, he became an outstanding scorer from outside."

"The freshmen year you're playing against the same-aged kids, the same maturity factor," said Lovellette. "But once you step up the sophomore year you were running into guys who were senior and juniors. It was a growing process."

Phog Allen put together another tough non-conference schedule in 1950. The Jayhawks played their first 10

The starting five for the 1950-1951 Jayhawks included, *from the left,* Jerry Waugh, Bill Hougland, Clyde Lovellette, Bill Lienhard and Bob Kenney.

games away from Lawrence. A sixth-place showing at the Big Seven tournament proved to be as poor an indicator of KU's strength as the previous year's second-place finish.

As the season progressed, the Jayhawks found Lovellette an ever-more inviting target in the middle.

"[Allen] always told us," said Lovellette, "that if I've got a ball player who is a couple feet from the basket, and I've got another ball player 10-12 feet from the basket, I sure want to get the ball to the guy who's closest to the basket."

"The offense was geared around me," Lovellette continued, "but the supporting cast we had was tremendous. As far as our guards and wing players were concerned, we all knew our roles in Phog's offense and the defense. We knew what

we could do and what we couldn't do. He'd preach that to us."

But even with the big center scoring at a record clip, Kansas settled in at 9-9 after a 55-50 loss at Kansas State, and the pressure was beginning to show on some of the players.

Lovellette remembered Allen pushing the entire team by promising support no matter the outcome. "He used to tell us, you do what I say on the court, and I'll back you 100 percent. You don't do what I say on the court, I'll leave you out to dry.

"That was his philosophy. As long as we did what he said on the court, if we lose that's fine. He was 100 percent out there on the court, if we ran the offense and ran and played the defense the way it was supposed to be played, he had no complaints, but you start going free lancing and things like that, he said I'm going to come down on you." And he proved it time after time.

"[Allen] was not a great 'X' and 'O' man," Waugh said. "He was at one time, I'm sure. But to the day he retired he was always a great motivator. He could manipulate people to succeed.

"I injured an ankle midway through the season and it took a long time for me to recover. It was a bad injury. I was having a tough time recovering and therefore I would start and then he would substitute for me. I wasn't playing very much. And the more I didn't play, the tighter I became as a player. I tried harder. I felt the pressure and really didn't play well and played even less.

"So I make an appointment with him. I'm mad at him by that time because he's not treating me fair, like any disgruntled player thinks. I can remember walking into his office in old Robinson and he stands up and shakes hands. Doc was always so dramatic and smiling and gripping your hand and looking you in the eye.

"I got the grip and we sat down and I said, 'Doc, I made this appointment because I really need to talk about my play. I'm concerned about my performance.' He said, 'Jerry, I want you to remember one thing before we get into this. There's nobody who thinks any more of you than I do.'"

"Of course, he completely disarmed me." said Waugh, "I was ticked when I went in there and was going to be mad at him and I was going to get this thing out in the open and we were going to straighten it out. And he completely disarmed me.

"So we talked and I said I knew I could do better and I felt pressure and we went over all these things and dramatically again he says, slapping his hand on the table, 'You will start the next game.'

"And I did. We probably had five games left in the season, four or five games. I started every game and played every minute of every game the rest of the season and exceeded my season average in scoring."

After the loss to Kansas State, Waugh led the Jayhawks to four consecutive victories, with an avenging 79-68 triumph over the Wildcats, which capped a perfect season at Hoch Auditorium, putting the Jayhawks into first place in the Big Seven. Only a three-point loss in overtime at Oklahoma allowed Kansas State and Nebraska to share the conference title with KU.

Bradley won the Missouri Valley title that year and earned the right to face the Big Seven challenger for an NCAA Tournament berth. The Braves beat KU 59-57 but it had still been a good final month. Harp said the strong finish was very important to the development of the program.

"The thing that was crucial here was how we were going to recover from the year before," he said. "Bradley beat us in the [Fifth District] Playoffs in '50 but it was a game we could have won. Jerry [Waugh] had a great game.

"That was a year I really wanted for my own personal crusade. I was anxious for us to win because the seniors, they were good young people there. They were the first group that had come back after the war."

After consecutive ties for last place and a third-place finish in 1947, the 1950 Big Seven championship came right on pace for Allen.

"I can recall a statement Doc made," said Waugh, "that a young man never comes to the University of Kansas without winning a gold basketball emblematic of winning a championship. In those days he gave a gold basketball when you won a championship.

"He made a big deal out of the conference championship. Today a lot of people say the conference championship doesn't mean anything, it's the NCAA, it's money, it's this, that, and the other. Not to Doc. The most important thing a team can do is to prepare itself to play in its league play. And he preached that. These are your peers and your neighbors and you must recruit against them. You must be the best in your neighborhood."

"It's a miracle," Allen wrote, "if a team jumps from the bottom to championship contention in a single season."

The miracle was fed by Lovellette's league-leading 23.0 point-per-game scor-

The Jayhawks' 1952 appearance in the NCAA Tournament proved to be Phog Allen's only national championship in the annual event that he helped establish.

ing average. The Jayhawks center scored 39 points in a game with Missouri. He collected the first of three All-America and all-conference honors and amassed nicknames nearly as quickly as points. Lovellette was known as "The Monster of the Music Hall," "Cumulus Clyde," "The Terre Haute Terror," "The Leaning Tower of Kansas," "Peerless Percheron," and "Mr. Highpockets."

Allen, however, didn't want to take chances and went in search of a backup for his center. He found one in Medicine Lodge, Kansas, named B. H. Born.

Born, however, almost went to Bradley. He saw the team take second in the NCAA Tournament and traveled with the Braves to New York to see them play in the NIT.

Born said, "I called the principal in my school and asked if it was okay if I went on and spent three more days with Bradley and go to New York. He said, well, you'll probably learn more in New York than you would in Medicine Lodge."

But while Bradley showed Born what it could do in 1950, Allen told him what was in store at Kansas.

"The way Phog Allen recruited me was he said we're going to have one of the best teams in the country and we think we're going to win the NCAA," Born recalled.

Born said he never played with the freshmen at KU, that his job from the the time he walked on campus was to give Clyde Lovellette some competition during practice. In return he became two things, the butt of many of Lovellette's pranks and, more important, an All-American.

"Lovellette was a bit of a character," Born said. "He did some things that I'm not really proud of. He used to do stuff like put gum in my socks. He used to ask me, 'Is your Mom coming up this week?' I said, 'No Clyde, why do you ask?' And he'd say things like 'I was trying to figure how much you are going to play tomorrow.' "

Phog Allen hated to play at off-campus sites such as Madison Square Garden, but he allowed the games to be scheduled—under his terms. The Jayhawks had an early season game against St. John's in New York, just before the great point-shaving scandals of the era broke. He also liked the chance to use the media to berate gamblers and others he felt were damaging college basketball.

"I remember sitting in the Muehlbach Hotel in Kansas City," Lovellette said. "We were supposed to play St. John's in New York and they were going to use two eastern officials. Phog said, 'I'll tell you what you can do, you can fill that Madison Square Garden and we won't be there until we have a Midwest or Big Seven official.' They wouldn't agree to it. We sat in the Muehlbach for

quite some time.

"We just sat there until they decided that these guys aren't coming unless we get another official. Then we flew out of Kansas City to New York. And we played with a Big Seven official. Phog got his way. He called New York the snakepit of basketball. He wasn't going to go in there without some kind of official we were accustomed to."

Allen knew the highly visible games could be used for other purposes, such as pushing his pet peeves involving the rules of the game. One that particularly bothered the coach was what he called "fouling for profit," when a team behind late in the game would foul in an attempt to get the ball. The ploy remains standard practice today.

Allen felt the way to defuse the fouling was to take the ball out of bounds, which was an option teams had in that era.

"For Doc to make his point that year we never shot a one-shot foul. We took it out of bounds every time," said Jerry Waugh. "We get down to the end of the ball game and St John's is one point ahead of us and Bill Hougland is fouled and Hougland is a good shooter. There must have been six, seven seconds left in the game so in our own minds we think maybe Doc will shoot it and tie it up and take it into overtime and win it in overtime. Well, he says, take her out of bounds.

"So we take her out of bounds, pass it around a couple times. Somebody puts her up from the outside. Lovellette, who never moved in a lifetime, happens to move across the lane. The ball comes off right into his hands, and he puts it in and we win by one. Man, did Doc hold court then."

"The writers came to me," said Waugh, "and wanted to know what I thought and I wasn't going to say that Doc's crazy or anything and I say, 'Well, you can't criticize success. We won and it was a smart move.'

"Doc was this kind of a coach. He always made right moves. It always turned out right for Dr. Allen. He seemed to do the things that bred success and that was just another one of the things that happened in Doc's coaching career that turned out right. There are some people who are winners and Doc was a

winner."

Allen also used his time in New York to rail against the influence of gamblers on the game. His charges proved to be exactly right, although some longtime friends in the coaching ranks, whose players were involved, were dragged down in the process. The Kansas players, with Lovellette the ringleader, tried to trick Allen into believing that they were also involved.

"We tried to perpetrate ourselves," Lovellette said. "Photographs and such

were taken. We'd give them to Phog to try to get him upset and tell him we were on the take."

After the victory at St. John's, the Jayhawks headed for Lexington and a game with a powerful Kentucky team. Allen reached rare form in his pregame motivations.

"We went out to play Kentucky for the first time," said Waugh, "and he had the room dark. Doc had us sitting on the training table before we played Kentucky and had the lights turned down except for one set of lights over the table. He talked to us about how you five men tonight sitting here wearing Kansas across your chest are the only five men who have been chosen to represent the University of Kansas and the great state

Clyde Lovellette was a powerful player from the time he joined the varsity. He was the conference scoring champ as well as an all-conference and All-America selection all three years at KU.

Dean Kelley played a significant role in leading the Jayhawks to the 1952 NCAA title.

of Kansas against Kentucky. He built up all that—how important you were and you were the five chosen to go out and be the representatives.

"All of it was ritual. All of it was part of a family. All of it was devised, thought out as to how a team becomes a team. How traditions are developed and lore gets passed on from year to year about the great teams of the past and the team of '23 and the team of such and such.

"He repeated those stories like the old Indians who sit about the camp fire and tell of past victories in battles. It was the same concept that he developed. The warriors who tell the stories and the young men who sit and listen."

Motivation was not enough against Kentucky, however, as the Wildcats came away 68-39 winners. Kansas won six of its next seven games but then lost five of seven before ending the season with three consecutive victories for a 16-8 record.

Kansas State locked up the Big Seven championship on February 24 with a 65-51 triumph over the Jayhawks, making the bus ride back to Lawrence very long— except for Coach Allen, who used the time to catch up on his sleep.

Jerry Waugh said, "I can remember him getting on the bus and unbuckling his belt, untying his tie and [Waugh snaps his fingers] he was asleep.

"I asked him about that one time. My stomach was upset. I couldn't eat. I felt the pressure of leadership and the responsibility of success.

"But for Doc, game's over. It didn't make any difference if we'd won by one point or lost by 100. I asked him about it and he said if you're going to survive in this environment of coaching, you've got to be able to put it away when it's over and not carry it home with you.

"I caught him in the twilight of his career but I'm sure when he was a young man he went home and kicked the chair and the dog and raised hell with every-body and did it differently."

Kansas State opened Mike Ahearn Field House for the 1950-1951 season and next would be KU's turn for a new large building for basketball. Jerry Waugh said the only thing Phog Allen wanted to be sure about was that the Jayhawks' new home ended up larger than the building in Manhattan.

History intervened in the form of the conflict in Korea, which escalated to such a point that officials rationed the steel needed for the building's support beams. Construction halted.

"They had to sell this concept that it would be an armory or used by the ROTC unit—to this day they parade out in the grounds there—so it was masked so to speak in order to get the steel," said Jerry Waugh.

A field house space-use report dated August 8, 1951, listed five proposed uses for the field house, including "increased facilities for the physical condition of units of the armed forces in case of mo-bilization," and to "enable three units of the ROTC to carry on drills and inspec-tion parades regardless of the weather."

Back up the hill in Hoch, Lovellette again won the Big Seven scoring title in 1951, scoring 23.8 points a game.

"We felt we finished strongly," Lovel-lette said. "We just kept improving. You could just see the improvement in the squad. We didn't lose anybody. Nobody dropped out, everybody came back and we added a junior college player in John Keller.

"We just grew steadily, and, I think, at the pace that Phog wanted. He wasn't disappointed, or he never let on that he was, because he had his goals set. He had his mind set. And we had ours set that in 1952 we were going to take it all. He was a prophet on that end."

Thirty-one years earlier, Phog Allen hit a crossroads in his career, and he told his wife that if his team didn't beat Missouri both times in the 1923 season, he was going to quit coaching. The Jayhawks, even though they were not aware of the importance of the game, came through.

After Allen suffered a concussion in 1947 and, perhaps more important, after Kansas State became a basketball force under Jack Gardner, Phog Allen wanted one very big season. He targeted 1952 where the NCAA title would also lead into the Olympic playoffs.

"He was an individual whom I enjoyed," said Clyde Lovellette. "He was a strong individual. He was person who was bone-headed to the point of 'I know what I want.' But he was a caring individual. We all had the most respect for him and what he was trying to do."

Kansas roared to a 13-0 start. Only twice over that span were the Jayhawks ever threatened—a one-point victory at Southern Methodist and a 90-88 triumph over Kansas State in the semifinals of the Big Seven tournament.

Lovellette said, "It was a game-by-game situation. We'd already played together for three years. We knew everybody, what everybody else did. It was more like a family.

"It was if you play every game, go out and have fun and do your best, we'll win. It was never a game of going out on the court where we were afraid of our opponent because if we do our thing right then everything else would fall into place.

"Phog had instilled that in us from the first time he started recruiting us for '52. Really it was sort of like a predestination that we were going to do this. We didn't really think about it."

The Jayhawks, Lovellette admitted, felt pretty good about themselves until a solid 81-64 thumping at Kansas State followed, four days later, with a 49-45 loss at Oklahoma State.

"Now [Allen] didn't take those well at all," said assistant coach Dick Harp. "He was really upset. He was disappointed at that time because we really didn't play well and got beat pretty good.

"Those two losses were important to us because he really did get mad about it. We did change some and that was important to the rest of our success to win the championship."

Lovellette said, "When you have a run like that, everybody is going to gun for you, number one, because they'd like to knock off the undefeated team and number two if you're not up for the ball game, you're liable to get knocked off, which was the case. It was just complacency on the team and not working hard and getting beat.

"That brought us back to the reality that, hey, this is the last year of our

Former Oklahoma State head coach Henry Iba congratulates Phog Allen on his 700th career victory in 1952. Respected as two of the greatest college coaches ever, both are members of the Naismith Hall of Fame.

tenure at Kansas and if we're going to do what we're supposed to be doing we'd better get back on the right track."

"[Allen] took us to a classroom in Robinson and there was no chalk talk. There was no other kind of talk," Lovellette recalled. "He said I want to read you a story. He read us two stories, 'Casey at the Bat', and he would cry, and 'The Return of Casey' and he had us all crying. Then we went out and practiced."

It was classic Phog Allen, using Grantland Rice's sequel to the Ernest L. Thayer poem 'Casey at the Bat', in which Casey returns and wins a game for Mudville. It was also exactly what a great team needed to hear—that there were still games to be played that season. The championship hopes did not end in Manhattan and Stillwater.

"He was just a master of getting you to the pitch that he needed to get you to sustain you for the next 20 minutes of basketball at halftime, or 40 minutes if before the ball game," Lovellette said. "You'd come out of the dressing room and could have bitten nails in two. But it was with a subtlety, not screaming and hollering and ranting and raving."

The Jayhawks returned after the semester break and whipped Iowa State 86-68. Five games later they posted a 66-46 pay-back victory over Oklahoma State for the 700th victory of Allen's coaching career. Lovellette scored 27 points and Bob Kenney added 23.

On March 7, KU topped Kansas State,

78-61, passing the Wildcats for the lead in the Big Seven race with a game to go. Lovellette closed the regular season with a record 41 points against Colorado, with the Jayhawks sealing the league title in the process.

Only Danny Manning and Wilt Chamberlain scored more points in a season for Kansas than Lovellette did that year.

Going into the NCAA Tournament, Kansas was 22-2—11-1 in the Big Seven. They were paired against Texas Christian in the first round of the 16-team tournament. The Jayhawks led by as many as 17 points late in the game against the Horned Frogs before settling for a 68-64 victory. KU dispatched St. Louis and Santa Clara by identical 74-55 scores. Lovellette scored a tournament-record 44 points in the St. Louis game.

As lopsided as the final scores were, Lovellette said the games were won with second-half rallies by the Jayhawks.

"We'd be down at halftime and come back and plug away and come back," Lovellette said. "Phog would talk to us at halftime and keep us focused on what he told us. He told us this is the year we can't be beat. And we'd go back out there and whip on them the second half."

That advanced Kansas to the NCAA title game—just as Phog Allen had envisioned five years earlier—against St. John's, which had upset top-ranked Kentucky and second-ranked Illinois for the right to face third-ranked Kansas.

"We came out of that dressing room and here was the final game staring us in the face, that this is either it or not," said Lovellette. "This was the year that he said he was going to do all of this with us and this was the game. We could either be the national champions or be the runnerup. And he told us that we were not going to be the runnerup.

"We came out of that dressing room and that was on our minds. Again we came out to the point of being loose enough that when St. John's came out on the floor—we had heard so much about the giant killers—that we were going to jump on them and jump on them quick and hard and they wouldn't have the opportunity to kill the giant.

"There was no doubt from the tip off that we were going to win. I don't think it was even a contest, It was a pretty easy win as I can remember."

Lovellette, the most valuable player of the tournament, scored 33 points and Bob Kenney and Bill Lienhard had 12 points each in the 80-63 victory. Outside of the Kansas loss in the 1940 final, the 17-point victory was the most lopsided in NCAA Tournament history.

But there was still one more item on Phog Allen's shopping list—he wanted to win the Olympic playoffs, which would make him the coach of the United States team and his Kansas players the bulk of the squad.

That involved some traveling. Four days after winning the NCAA championship in Seattle, Washington, the Jay-

Above: The 1952 NCAA championship was played against St. Johns. Lovellette scored 33 points and was named MVP for the tournament.
Opposite page, top: The Jayhawks dominated Santa Clara in the NCAA semifinals in 1952, 74-56, as Dean Smith showed his determination in diving after a loose ball.
Bottom: Phog Allen's prediction to Clyde Lovellette came true in Seattle, Washington, four years later.

hawks had an Olympic playoff game in Kansas City, Missouri, with NAIA champion Southwest Missouri, which was discharged 92-65. The next day, KU flew to New York for a semifinal game with La Salle, the NIT winner. The Explorers were eliminated 70-65, leaving only the Peoria, Illinois, Caterpillars, who were the AAU champions, between the Jayhawks and the Olympics.

NCAA Executive Director Walter Byers presents the 1952 NCAA championship plaque to Phog Allen.

Emotion carried KU well, but the traveling and the tension of so many big games in succession weighed on the Jayhawks.

"Dean Kelley, I remember his face just got longer and longer," recalled Bob Allen. "They were so darn tired. We won the NCAA in Seattle on Saturday. We came to Kansas City and had to beat the NAIA champions and then we had to go back and beat the NIT winner and that was La Salle and Saturday we had to play Peoria, the AAU champion. Even

then they were going to school in between there."

Peoria went out ahead early and led by 15 points in the first half.

Bob Allen and his brother Mitt had seats not far behind the Kansas bench and, it turns out, near some gamblers.

"They were ahead by 15 or so and this gambler sitting on the adjacent row to us, he was blowing hot air, 'Oh, this is not a game. They are blowing these guys out of here,' the gambler said. 'They'll beat them 25.'

"Mitt said, '25 what?' He said they'll beat you by 25. Mitt said I'll take that for whatever you want to make it. The guy said I'll bet you $100 they beat them at least 20. Mitt said I'll take that and I want the money placed right here where everybody can see it. So they put up a $100, each of them, on the back of a chair and some guy had some tape and taped it right there.

"Mitt was just so mad about that guy saying that Kansas shouldn't even be playing Peoria."

While Phog Allen would have fainted at the thought of his son's betting, it was a smart wager. Kansas worked back in the game with Lovellette taking control.

"And Clyde, I think he made 35 or 40 points against them," Bob Allen said. "With the game winding down and the score tied, Peoria had the ball and threw it in to their big center, and he was bigger than Clyde.

"Clyde was not real agile, but this time he stepped around and deflected the pass, goes out, recovers it and dribbles down and blows the layup. They throw the ball the length of the court to a guy from Purdue named [Howie Williams] and he beat them."

It is probably the one regret in Lovellette's playing career, but he felt worse for Phog Allen than himself.

Lovellette said, "I stole the ball, and I was out in front. There was a Kansas boy on my right, I can't remember who, and going down the court. Seconds were ticking off the clock and I took off too far back and on my left side was coming one of the Peoria boys. I put the ball off to the left and he got it and one pass up the center and the other boy fired it and it went in and we got beat by two.

"If I had given it to one of the Kansas boys on the break, he could have laid it

in. I think that I was driving down there with the anticipation that, 'Here I am I can win the ball game for us' and I should have been more team-minded.

"Phog never said a word to me [about that play] but I felt that he could have been the Olympic head coach with just a little more team-oriented thought."

Although the 62-60 loss to Peoria cost Allen the main Olympic coaching position, he was invited to go as an assistant. Seven Kansas team members—Lovellette, Bill Lienhard, John Keller, Bob Kenney, Dean Kelley, Bill Hougland, and Charlie Hoag—earned spots on the team that won the Gold Medal in Helsinki.

Phog Allen had made good on his boast of winning the 1952 NCAA title and having Kansas represented in the Olympic Games.

Lovellette's collegiate career covered 77 games during which he scored 1,888 points and averaged 24.5 points a game. A three-time All-American, he was the conference scoring leader three seasons, with his 28.0 average in 1951-1952 still fourth best in league history. No conference player averaged more than 20 points a game until Lovellette turned the trick in 1950 and only Oklahoma's Wayman Tisdale, in a 1983-1985 career, has been able to match Lovellette's three scoring championships.

His name still dots the NCAA's Final Four record book, with his 66 points in the final two games the fifth-best total, with every other Top 10 mark coming after 1952; his 35.3-point tournament scoring average is sixth-best and again the oldest mark listed.

"Even considering [Wilt] Chamberlain, Lovellette was the most dominating player we ever had," said Bob Allen. "He absolutely won the NCAA by himself. Look at the record. He made 30 points or more every [tournament] game and those were days when people didn't make 30 points all the time. He was fantastic.

"Lovellette could hook, he could jump shoot. He shot two-handed overhead shots and made them. In critical times when he was looking for a pass he could just turn his hands up and knock it in the hole. I've seen him time after time make 10 in a row from out there. Not just one-handed but two-handed, anytime. And that hook shot was just lethal.

"He was a smart player. And he was a competitor. I watched him many times practice around the circle," said Allen. "Clyde had that agility. He was marvelous when he got a guy on his hip. He knew how to hook, just a momentary hook [of the other player] to get position and just make the quick step. There was no way to stop that guy."

Clyde Lovellette was MVP of the 1952 NCAA Tournament.

Return to the Title Game

Phog Allen delivered another big season in 1952-1953. Starters Clyde Lovellette, Bob Kenney, John Keller, and Bill Lienhard graduated in 1952—along with key reserves such as Bill Hougland and Charlie Hoag—yet Kansas still produced talent on the court. The big dilemma was replacing Lovellette and the points he represented. That task fell to B. H. Born.

"But when we started off the season, [Born's] junior year," said Dick Harp, the assistant coach for that team. "I think we played at Tulane and Rice and my goodness, they had him off the court more than he was on the court. They were knocking him around some. He was not equipped to fight back that kind of basketball.

"Dean [Nesmith] said to me at some point during the game, 'How are we going to win with B. H.?' I didn't answer him but I guess maybe I was wondering that. Doc [Allen] never said anything. He just would shake his head."

Born, however, had spent two years dealing with Lovellette every day in practice. The older, bigger player was anything but gentle with Born, but the younger man never backed down.

"He literally tried to kill me," Born said, recalling practice sessions with Lovellette. "He broke my nose one time. He bloodied my lip. He knocked me out one time; these are all in practice. I put him on my all-opponent team one year. But he toughened me up and made me a better player from then on. As far as positive aspects, he probably prepared me for the next year."

After the first two games, Harp said, "B. H. started to improve. When we came back, he never quit improving. B. H. was a lot quicker than people realize and he had his own way, but B. H. became an aggressive competitive basketball player."

Kansas went 5-1 over its first six games and then lost consecutive matches with Kansas State and Oklahoma. The 93-87 defeat by the Wildcats came in the championship game of the Big Seven tournament while the Sooners' 76-61 victory put KU at 0-1 in the league.

Phog Allen always had his team prepared, and during this time, he had some of the best help imaginable for that chore in Harp and a reserve guard named Dean "Smiles" Smith.

"Dean was a tactician, even in high school," recalled Born. "He was on Topeka's team and he was the quarterback on that team. He was the brains. They had a good team there and he controlled the ball and how things went.

"So he talked his way into a scholarship at Kansas. But when he got there, three things were a problem. One was that he was slow. The other was that he is short and the third was that he wasn't a very good shot. Those three things tended to keep him out of the games because we had the national championship team there and we were playing in a pretty fast league."

Born said, "Everybody had to do something for their scholarship, you either had to hand out towels or helped coach the freshmen. So [Smith's] second year he coached the freshmen. He coached the junior varsity when I was a sophomore rather than handing out towels. That's how he got started. He went on and he would help Dick Harp."

Harp and Smith scouted upcoming opponents, checking scouting reports and studying film, if available. They would take what they learned to the practice floor, with Smith directing the opponent's schemes against the Kansas starters.

"We were never surprised, because he had it down," said Born. "What ever the other team did, we'd already seen in practice.

"I think that's what helped him become such a good coach. He knew all these offenses from all the teams in the conference, and we were playing some pretty good non-league teams, too. I think that gave him a good start."

Harp said Smith entered KU with the idea of becoming a coach and never wavered from that goal. In the 1990-1991 season, Smith's North Carolina team gave him coaching victory number 700, just the sixth coach to reach that milestone.

With Harp and Smith preparing the

team for the opponent, Allen did the rest. The Kansas coach even found another motivational tool, one he discovered in his mailbox.

People used to write letters to him," said Born. "He'd bring these letters out and say, 'It says here that Born works well on defense but he can sure use a better shot than he's shooting.'"

It is not clear how much store Allen put in the letters, it's possible the coach just wanted the players to know someone was watching, but it became something of a routine, Born said.

"He'd read portions of these letters. He had them from little old ladies from Centralia and alums from all over the country," said Born.

The preparation and outside "coaching" paid off, and the Jayhawks won 11 of their next 13 games, with one coming against non-conference foe Oklahoma State. After that game, Born matched Lovellette's school record with 44 points in a 78-55 victory over Colorado.

"I set the Big Seven [single game] scoring record in there against Colorado and when I scored about the 40th point, they high-lowed me," said Born. "I fell over one of them and broke my thumb.

"After the game I suppose I had about 300 people come up and shake hands with me and fraternity brothers, you know, squeezing as hard as they could squeeze. Finally, I starting shaking with my left hand. It was bringing tears to my eyes, it hurt so bad."

Two games later, a 69-60 victory over Missouri on March 9 allowed Kansas, 10-2 in the league, to claim the Big Seven title by a game over Kansas State.

Just as in 1952, KU posted clear victories in its first three NCAA games, winning 73-65 over Oklahoma City, 61-55 over Oklahoma State and 79-53 in the semifinals against Washington.

As usual, Kansas used an aggressive defense to take control of the game. "In the semifinals against Washington, we had eight points before they ever shot the ball. We kept stopping them at the midcourt," Born recalled.

Washington finished as the second-rated team in the country, but the only team ranked higher than the Huskies, Indiana coached by Branch McCracken, also advanced to the 1953 NCAA Tournament title game in Indiana.

B. H. Born, a 6-9 center from Medicine Lodge, Kansas, was named the outstanding player in the 1953 NCAA Tournament.

Kansas kept with Indiana, even though Born suffered an illness that caused a problem with his equilibrium, and he said it affected his balance on rebounds.

"At the half I was dead tired and I went over to Dean Nesmith and said I need to get my throat cleaned out," said Born. "So he got some alum water, which was one of Doc's things. Alum water is not the most pleasant stuff to try to gargle.

"So I'm standing there trying to gargle that stuff and Doc saw me there. Here we are in the finals of the NCAA, 20 minutes of basketball and we're either the champion or the loser. Doc spent half that halftime teaching me how to gargle. I got so mad. Maybe that's why he was doing it. He was a great psychologist. He'd say, 'No, no, no take some more of that, then throw your head back and do it this way.' He'd take some of it and throw his head back.

"Finally Dick Harp grabbed some chalk and over the last three minutes of the halftime said, 'Here's what you're doing wrong. I want you to do this and Al Kelley put your press in a little quicker and the third guy has to cover the man who's going to receive the ball.'"

The quick chalk talk behind them, the Jayhawks went back onto the floor. During the second half, Born committed his fourth foul, leading McCracken to begin what has become a tradition among Indiana basketball coaches.

"They ring the bell or blow the whistle

Dean Smith lettered for the Jayhawks in 1952 and 1953.

or something and they say that's five [fouls]," Born said. "I fouled out quite a few games, so we keep pretty close track of those things. They stopped the game and polled the press. All the sports writers sitting there had me down for four. So the official scorer changed it to four.

"Branch McCracken goes up there and he's pounding on the desk and said, 'I don't give a damn what the press says, it's the official scorer who keeps track of how many fouls.'"

McCracken lost that battle, and the Kansas team grabbed a much-needed 10-minute rest while the Indiana coach argued. The Jayhawks pulled ahead; but Born committed another foul and

this time there was no doubt as to how many he had. Born scored 26 points in that game, and his disqualification left KU without a major scoring threat.

Jerry Alberts replaced Born, but the Hoosiers' Bob "Slick" Leonard "shot a shot up there he shouldn't have," according to Born, and put Indiana ahead. Alberts had a chance to win the game for Kansas only to have his shot "skip across the top" of the basket, said Born.

Indiana won 69-68.

After the game, it was announced that B. H. Born won the voting for Most Valuable Player of the tournament. By out-polling Indiana's Don Schlundt, Born became the first player from a losing team so honored.

Huge crowds at KU greeted the returning national champions in 1952 and another turnout of more than 2,000 people welcomed the 1953 runners-up back to Lawrence, which Born said meant a lot to the team.

Winding up second, however, often whets the appetite for first-place.

"We thought we were going to have a good team that year," said Born. "The problem was we had lost Dean Kelley [who graduated] and Gil Reich had gotten hurt along with some other players. We just were never able to fill the guard positions."

The lack of leadership showed in the 1953-1954 season-openers in Louisiana. Tulane beat the Jayhawks 69-65, and two nights later Louisiana State, led by Bob Pettit, defeated them 68-63.

The Jayhawks returned home and defeated Tulsa before sweeping through the Big Seven Conference tournament. Victories at Hoch Auditorium over Oklahoma and Missouri ran the KU record to 6-2. Playing close to home gave the Jayhawks a big boost.

"Hoch was a good place to play with the crowd sitting right down on the floor," said Born. "When you'd take a ball out of bounds, you'd have to stand right between the feet of the students surrounding the place. It was like playing in a jar and the place was so loud."

Born said Phog Allen had black "flags" placed behind the goals to help make the baskets easier to see. That added to the Hoch mystique, however.

"They used to call them the pirate flags," said Born. "All the people would be moving around in there and those flags would flutter back and forth. They called them pirate flags because of what was probably going to happen to you."

On several occasions the power went out in the building and the game would be delayed 15 or 20 minutes before it could be restored.

"Hoch wasn't the best place to play in the world, but we had a hell of a tradition there," Born said. "We won every game I played in there, I believe. I know we had won every game when [Clyde] Lovellette was playing in '52. I think we continued that on. I never lost when I played at Hoch my three years."

The Jayhawks were 27-0 at home with Born on the team, but 0-3 in Stillwater, Oklahoma, and Oklahoma State broke the team's six-game winning streak with a 54-50 decision. Kansas won twice more before losing at Colorado.

"That is the one I fouled out before the half," Born recalled. "That's the first time I'd ever done that and I've never done that after that. They threw money on the floor. It took them five minutes to sweep up the money after that last foul."

The Jayhawks rattled off eight consecutive victories, ending with an 83-62 victory over Colorado, which had been the last team to beat them. That assured KU of at least a share of Phog Allen's twenty-fourth conference championship, since it put the Jayhawks one game ahead of the second-place Buffaloes with one game to play.

However, a share was all Kansas was going to get, since Missouri handed KU a 76-67 defeat, and Colorado dumped Kansas State 79-76. The Jayhawks completed the season 16-5.

"[Missouri] hit maybe 20 out of 22 free throws and just out-played us and beat us," said Born. "That threw Colorado and us into a tie for first. In those days they drew straws [for the NCAA berth]. We got the short straw, so we didn't get to go to the NCAA. But we had tied for the conference or won the conference all three years."

In addition to the usual Allen gold basketball "emblematic of the conference championship," KU further honored its Big Seven titlists.

"We also got jackets," said Born. "In those days you didn't get rings or any-

Gene Elstun served as team captain in 1956-1957 and also earned all-conference honors.

thing. They gave you "K" jackets with conference champs on them. That was always a big deal."

The conference title gave the Jayhawks an edge in the all-conference voting where Born and Al Kelley each became two-time all-Big Seven players and Harold Patterson and Dallas Dobbs also made first team in 1954.

The 1955 season started out well, with four consecutive victories. The Jayhawks lost two close games and had to settle for seventh place in the Big Seven tournament. Three consecutive losses, including two at Hoch, shoved the Jayhawks into a league standings hole from which they never emerged. They ended up 11-10 overall and 5-7—fifth—in the Big Seven. All-conference selection Dallas Dobbs, worth 15.9 points a game, led the team in scoring.

Without the success of the basketball team to generate excitement, the *University Daily Kansan* sports staff created some of its own. The new field house being erected on the south part of the campus was still, at least officially, without a name. After unabashedly proposing that the building be named for

The 1955 season was the last at Hoch Auditorium. Unfortunately, the "Opera House" did not go out in style. Kansas went 11-10 overall and ended up fifth in the conference. Hoch burned in a lightning storm in 1991.

named for the inventor of the game.

It turned out that the Regents had already decided to honor Allen. On December 17, 1954, the *Topeka Capitol* reported the Board christened the building "Allen Field House" during its October meeting, but wanted to unveil that fact at the scheduled March dedication.

"It makes the Christmas cheer rise in my heart," Phog Allen told the *Kansan*.

"Dad never did say anything about it," said Bob Allen, Phog's son, "but I'm sure that he felt it was a nice recognition for his length of coaching and experience there. Coaches in those days were not paid like they are now. I don't know what his highest salary was as a coach, but I don't think it was more than $11,000."

The building had a name, but construction had yet to be completed, so the Jayhawks made their game-day jaunt from old Robinson to Hoch nine times in the 1954-1955 season. Unfortunately, they could not send "The Opera House" out in style. The final game in Hoch turned into a 66-55 loss to a mediocre Nebraska team.

Hoch Auditorium served as the home for the Jayhawks for 28 seasons. There were complaints about the floor, the seating, the accommodations, and the lack of a home-team dressing room. But it had been good to Jayhawk teams. KU went 204-38, a 84.3 winning percentage, in Hoch.

The building remained a reminder of those glory days until lightning struck it on June 15, 1991. The resulting fire gutted the building, leaving only memories.

But the basketball program, which started on a court with posts down the center and an 11-foot ceiling before moving to a $100,000 gymnasium and then to a $350,000 auditorium, had a new home.

Built at a cost of $2.65 million, Allen Field House stood as the second-largest basketball arena in the country. Constructed, of course, of native limestone with a rigid steel frame, the field house measured 344 feet by 254 feet. The 60-foot sidewalls sloped 25 feet to the peak in the center. Only the University of Minnesota, with a hockey rink in one half of its building, boasted a larger structure.

Forrest C. Allen, the *Kansan* ran a campaign in which readers had a chance to voice their feelings through a vote.

Every day in early December the vote totals—and a cut-out ballot—ran in the student paper. Allen received far and away the bulk of the support, with James Naismith coming in third behind a movement to name the field house after both the father of basketball and the father of basketball coaching.

The final tally read: Allen 924, both 30, Naismith 10. The lack of support for Naismith probably stemmed from the fact that in November, the four-lane street in front of the field house was

Allen Field House was dedicated March 1, 1955, with a crowd of 17,228 on hand. The Jayhawks, winning their only home conference game of the season, dumped Kansas State 77-67.

"That was important," Dick Harp said of winning that game. "Doc made his halftime speech, they had the skit and everyone thought that was a nice occasion. It came off well and we thought he was magnificent. Yeah, we needed to win that game. That would have been a downer."

Although it is doubtful that much could have dampened the dedicatory party. The fans quickly learned they could cause a thunderous din by stomping their feet on the metal flooring of the balcony. The Jayhawk painted on the middle of the scoreboard was wired so that it would "wink" each time Kansas registered a point. A total of 103 lettermen representing teams from the first year of Kansas basketball through 1953 ringed the court and Allen was formally honored at halftime.

The Kansas Jayhawks moved into their big new house and now Phog Allen wanted a big man to fill it. And the biggest man on the recruiting circuit that summer was Wilt Chamberlain.

The Kansas coach treated the Chamberlain recruitment much like that of Clyde Lovellette. This time, however, Allen did not go out with the stated plan to win the national championship. He just wanted the best player in the country to be wearing crimson and blue.

B. H. Born said he played a part in getting Chamberlain to Kansas. Just out of high school, Chamberlain was playing the Borscht League circuit in the Catskills under coach Red Auerbach. Born joined the league to get in shape for professional basketball.

"Red Auerbach told Chamberlain that this fellow Born was All-American and was the NCAA Most Valuable Player and he'll probably just eat you up, so just do the best you can and you can live with it," Born said. "Of course, I couldn't figure why Chamberlain was so mad and was trying to hard. Red Auerbach had sicced him on me.

"I decided that if there were that good of high school kids around that part of the country, I wasn't going to make it in the pros for very long.

"He's why I'm working for Caterpillar. If it wasn't for him I probably would have taken a pro contract instead of coming to work here."

Allen Field House was the second-largest college basketball facility in the country when it was dedicated in 1955. The first game, above, was a 77-67 win over rival Kansas State.

Chamberlain, too, made a decision and opted for Born's alma mater—the University of Kansas. When he was told of Wilt's decision, Allen reportedly said, "Well, I hope the young man comes out for basketball."

The biggest game the next season doesn't show up on the Kansas record. Over football homecoming weekend, the Jayhawk varsity basketball team scheduled its annual scrimmage with the freshmen. More than 14,000 people packed Allen Field House for the game that marked Chamberlain's debut as a Jayhawk. He responded with 42 points in leading the freshmen to an 81-71 victory over the regular team.

Kansas, without having to play against Chamberlain, had slightly better on-court success in 1955-1956 than the previous season, with three three-game winning streaks marking the bulk of the victories in a 14-9 season.

The Jayhawks' title hopes remained until the final two games when a 79-68 loss to Kansas State and a 75-67 defeat by Colorado knocked Kansas down to 6-6 and fifth place in the Big Seven. Dobbs again paced the Kansas scoring attack, but Maurice King, the number-two scorer on the team, passed him for all-Big Seven mention.

After the final game came perhaps the biggest battle of the season. Phog Allen would turn 71 years old before the next season and 70, as he said many times, "is the age of mandatory senility." Allen reached the age of mandatory retirement.

Dick Harp, a former Kansas player and the coach Allen tabbed as his successor, said he never believed that Allen truly wanted to return for the 1956-1957 season.

"A lot of people said he wanted to coach Wilt Chamberlain just one season," Harp said. "But he never told me that. I think it was a case of some people wanted him to do it and he got caught up in it. He was flattered and so let it go on."

But the University administration did not yield. Phog Allen, who had coached 46 years and won or shared 31 conference championships, retired. Allen coached at Kansas for 39 years, amassing a 590-219 record and 24 league titles. His official NCAA record is 746-264.

He owned the record for victories until passed by Adolph Rupp, one of his former players, and will remain in his current number five all-time position until passed by Dean Smith, another of his former players. Ralph Miller, also a former Jayhawk, coached 657 victories, which is eighth on the all-time NCAA chart.

In September 1974, Dr. Forrest C. "Phog" Allen died at the age of 88.

"Doc will go down in history as the greatest basketball coach of all time," Rupp told the *Topeka Capitol* after Allen's death. "What I did was just an extension of what I learned from him."

Allen was attracted to Lawrence just after the turn of the century because of its paved streets and impressive store fronts. Over the next seven decades he played an important hand in keeping the city up to date.

There is no doubt that Allen is primarily known—and rightly so—for his contributions to college basketball. Even Dr. James Naismith, the man who invented the game, declared Allen "the father of basketball coaching." According to the NCAA, Allen's teams won 746 of the 1,010 intercollegiate games he coached.

But there was a great deal more to this man. He was one of the founders of the National Association of Basketball Coaches and among the group that gave us what is today one of the great spectacles in all of sport—the NCAA Division I Men's Basketball Tournament. He was the driving force that made basketball an Olympic sport.

While athletic director at Kansas, Allen started the Kansas Relays—making him the "official cause of rain" for one spring weekend each year. Kansas Memorial Stadium was built after he decided the school needed a new site for football games. The Kansas Memorial Union was also Allen's idea. As was, of course, the building that bears his name—Allen Field House.

Away from campus, Allen was the president of the Lawrence Country Club, secretary of the Douglas County Selective Service Board, chairman of three war-loan drives, the Community Chest, the Infantile Paralysis Fund, and many other charities.

"Doc had a great perspective about intercollegiate athletics and he didn't believe that it was the only thing on the block," said Dick Harp. "He believed that young men had an opportunity to do something great for themselves and for the university and that's what athletics should be about. And primarily after you won or lost the game it was on to the next one."

Allen's motivational techniques vary over his 39-year career at Kansas—he could invoke the ghost of Jayhawks past or look deep into the players' eyes searching for "the victory light." But the one he pushed the most—the one he seemed to believe the most—was when he would talk to his starting five and preach to them about how proud they should be to be the representative of the University of Kansas for that game.

"I still believe the coaches who come after Phog, Phog is always kind of looking over their shoulder," said Clyde Lovellette, who played on Allen's 1952 national championship team. "I still believe the coaches today, even though they say 'I'm a new thing,' if they'd stop and really be honest with themselves, they really think of Phog. The legacy that he has laid down for them to continue."

"Even though they win a lot of games," said Lovellette, "by the time they leave there, they will be talking about the legacy of Phog Allen, the teams that played on that floor before them, and what it means to be a Kansas Jayhawker."

The game held great importance to Allen, but he tried to impress on his players that basketball was only a small part of living.

Harp said, "The experiences of competition and the people you meet and the opportunities you have from that should be instrumental in your life as an athlete and not just the winning and losing of the game, he taught that in many different ways.

"In the game itself that is when his competitiveness surfaced. As long as you're in the game, you may as well do your very best to win that. But he thought there was more to athletics other than the outcome of the game."

In his office, Allen hung the following motto, one he certainly lived by: "It's a Great World to Live in— But you Can't Live in it for Nothing."

Doc Allen's mark on college basket-

ball is indelible. His mark on the city of Lawrence, the University of Kansas, and the people he knew are maybe even more important.

Wilt Chamberlain was recruited by every major college in the country. He chose to attend the University of Kansas.

Dick Harp was a natural choice to follow Phog Allen as the Kansas coach. He played for KU from 1938-1940—teams that went a combined 50-15 and won two Big Six Conference titles. Harp took the job as KU's first assistant coach in 1948 and worked closely with Allen. But Allen invented basketball coaching and coming directly after him invited comparisons.

"It was perfectly normal for me to be at Kansas and be involved," Harp said. "I never put it in terms of following Doc because that's not possible. It was not possible for anyone to follow John Wooden. It was not possible for anyone to follow Doc Allen. If you knew [Allen] at all, you know that would not be possible. I never gave that a thought."

Being hired as Kansas' fourth basketball coach—the program celebrated its 58th anniversary in Allen's final season—completed a dream for Harp.

"I had always wanted to play at Kansas and I think I maybe even said something in high school about wanting to coach," he said. "When I had the opportunity to come back, I, immediately and without question, wanted to do that because Kansas did then and did when I coached, and does now, mean a great deal to me. In that regards I'm a believer. I believe in the university."

"It was an important thing for me to

be able to do that," said Harp. "I was very fortunate to be able to do that. I was fortunate to get to do that. Then, when it was determined that I needed to leave, I was very fortunate to get to do something else which I wanted to do."

Phog Allen, however, still had his touch on the game. Before he left he had been working with Wilt Chamberlain to "make a sham of the 10-foot basket," said Bob Allen.

"He worked with Wilt as a freshman. And Wilt said, 'Coach, are you trying to legislate against the big man?' Dad said, 'Listen Wilt, as good an athlete as you are, legislation won't affect you. The only thing it will do is make the goal a little higher, and you'll shoot it up there, which you can do just as well as slam it down.'"

Phog Allen had many plans by which Chamberlain could—and did for years—show the basket to be two feet too low in the coach's opinion.

Bob Allen said, "The rule was you cannot touch the floor over the free-throw line until the ball hit the iron. Chamberlain, being a great broad jumper and very agile, there was no rule that he couldn't take two full steps behind the free-throw line. He'd take one-two steps and slam dunk it. The ball hit the rim before he hit the floor. It's a 100 percent free throw.

"It just so happened that there was a Kansas State kid up there watching. He rushed back to [Wildcats Coach] Tex Winter and said 'They've got a 100 percent free-throw there. They've got Chamberlain shooting free throws by dunking them.' So they rushed in the rule that you couldn't do that.

"There were other things," Bob Allen continued, "he'd have them arch the ball over the backboard on out of bounds plays. Just throw it up and Chamberlain would catch it and just throw it down. He was trying to make a farce of the rule of the 10-foot goal."

More than Allen's design to knock the height of the basket, however, all of the coach's schemes only showed just what a factor Wilt Chamberlain could be on the court. The player further showed that skill in his first collegiate game—a 52-point, 31-rebound effort against Northwestern, in which Kansas was victorious, 87-69.

The Jayhawks won their first 12 games, but Dick Harp said there was no pressure on either him or his players, despite the fact that having Chamberlain on the team meant a high ranking and great expectations.

"They were great young people," Harp said. "That was a different experience for them, but they were great young people and they did fine. I always thought they measured up. Obviously their future was not in basketball, except with Wilt and Maurice King.

"So their experience was to be what the other college graduates' was to be— they were going to move on in life in their vocations. I think they enjoyed it and enjoyed the opportunity to play for the championship."

The only regular-season losses came at Ames, Iowa, and Stillwater, Oklahoma. The winning strategy for both Iowa State Coach Bill Stannigan and Oklahoma State's Henry Iba was the same—stall.

Iowa State snapped the long Kansas winning streak with a 39-37 decision at Ames as Ron Medsker hit a basket at the final gun. The Cowboys held the ball for 3:30 before Mel Wright hit a 19-footer with two seconds to play in the game.

"Iowa State and Bill had his better teams in those times," said Harp. "And those were games we should have won.

We lost on last-second shots.

"Those games don't particularly stick out. I would not believe that if we would have played those teams two out of three or three out of five that we wouldn't win the majority of those games. The games were played much the same way and ended up the same way. If there had been a time [shot] clock then, there would have been a great deal of difference."

Kansas completed the regular season 21-2 with an 11-1 Big Seven mark worth a three-game advantage in the standings. Dick Harp joined Phog Allen and W. O. Hamilton as the conference champion in his first season as a coach. Chamberlain, of course, was all-conference, along with teammate Gene Elstun.

The Jayhawks had a slight scare in their first NCAA Tournament game. The fourth-ranked Southern Methodist Mustangs, boosted by playing in their

Two-year starter Maurice King averaged nearly 10 points a game in helping KU to a 24-3 record and the NCAA finals in 1957.

Wilt Chamberlain took the Jayhawks to the Final Four in his first varsity season. They lost in triple-overtime to North Carolina. Chamberlain was MVP of the tournament.

The Jayhawks again advanced to the NCAA title game. North Carolina, coached by the Frank McGuire who directed St. John's when it lost to Kansas in 1952 tournament final. The Tar Heels, unlike the Jayhawks, did not play their best game in the semifinals and needed three overtimes to get past Michigan State 74-70.

The victories made the finals number one North Carolina against number two Kansas. The question was whether the Tar Heels, who were putting a perfect 31-0 season on the line, could recover from their triple-overtime effort in just one day.

The answer became one of the most storied finals in NCAA Tournament history. Not only did it pit the top two teams for the championship, but Kansas' Wilt Chamberlain and North Carolina's Lennie Rosenbluth were the two best players in the country.

The teams battled to an even 46-46 at the end of regulation, and both managed just two points in the first overtime. The second overtime was scoreless, but hardly unexciting.

The Tar Heels' Pete Brennan grabbed Chamberlain around the waist and the Kansas center retaliated with an elbow to Brennan's head. Both benches emptied, and police came onto the court to restore order.

Said Harp, "We finally got some control of the game [in the third overtime] and let it get away from us. We had the game right at the end and we were up one and we had a one-and-one free throw. I thought we had the game won then. We had less than a minute or something.

"We missed the free throw and then they went down and shot and we got the ball. John Parker got the ball down in the corner and we had the game again, but the officials decided to call a foul somewhere and they made both free throws and that was the game."

The Jayhawks led 53-52 in the third overtime, and Chamberlain seemed to have sealed the victory when he blocked a Tommy Kearns shot with 20 seconds to play. But the ball went to North Carolina's Joe Quigg, who tried to drive up the middle. Chamberlain again blocked the shot—with the ball going to Parker—but Maurice King, trying to help out on defense, was called for a foul.

hometown of Dallas, took KU into overtime before Kansas pulled away for a 73-65 victory. The Jayhawks easily eliminated Oklahoma City, 81-61, the next night for their third Final Four berth in six seasons.

Kansas had an easier time in the national semifinals, dispatching San Francisco 80-56.

"That was perhaps the best game we played that year," said Harp. "We played superbly that game and I thought with that kind of momentum... of course many times in tournament play that's not always true. But that was one of the better games we played all year."

Quigg made both free throws for a North Carolina lead.

Kansas still had six seconds, but everyone in Kansas City's Municipal Auditorium knew the Jayhawks would try to get the ball to Chamberlain, and a pass in his direction was tipped away.

"That game has become bigger than life," said Harp. "And when this [1991] Kansas team went to play [North Carolina] in the Final Four, it lifted all that up again. Certainly it's a big game in Carolina's peoples' minds. They wanted to talk to me about it all the time.

"The game has, I think, probably taken its place as one of the great games in NCAA history but principally because of Wilt."

The game was a spectator's dream, but Harp, even 34 years after the fact, said the game was not a lot of fun.

"We didn't play well, so it wasn't particularly fun," he said. "We weren't playing particularly well, although Wilt played very well."

In typical Dick Harp fashion, the coach was not concerned about how the final-game loss would affect his career, and he knew it would have no bearing on the fame that was the fate of Chamberlain, who joined B. H. Born and Temple's Hal Lear in 1956, as Most Valuable Players whose teams did not win the final. Rather, Harp thought about the players for whom basketball was ending.

"Although I think that game meant a lot to him, Wilt was destined to have many successes," Harp said. "But the young men who played with him, that was their opportunity to be national champions and I always regretted more than anything the fact that we didn't win for them."

Wilt Chamberlain, a sophomore, scored 800 points in his 27 games that season, which stood as the Kansas record

Wilt Chamberlain and other "big men" caused many rule changes in college basketball, but never Phog Allen's desired raising of the baskets.

until Danny Manning scored 860 in the 36 games of 1987. In addition "The Stilt" grabbed 510 rebounds, which is still the Jayhawks record. His blocked shot total of 182 is unofficial, but is 109 more than the recognized school record.

With Chamberlain again leading the team in 1957-1958, the Jayhawks won their first 10 games, with no game closer than six points. But Chamberlain suffered an injury midway through the season. The season-opening winning streak melted under two 2-point losses to Oklahoma State—in overtime—and to Oklahoma.

KU won six of its next seven games but saw its Big Seven Conference championship hopes evaporate in consecutive losses at Nebraska and Iowa State.

The Jayhawks finished 18-5, with an 8-4 Big Seven mark—tying KU with Iowa State for second behind Kansas State.

Chamberlain led the Big Seven in scoring and averaged a Kansas-record 30.1 points in his 21 games. He collected his second All-America and all-conference awards, and Ron Loneski also made all-Big Seven.

Loneski, a classmate of Chamberlain's, came back for the 1958-1959 season. Chamberlain did not return, turning professional and joining the Harlem Globetrotters. Before he left, however, Chamberlain made one last mark at KU, clearing 6-feet, 6 and 3/4 inches in the high jump to tie for first in the 1958 conference track meet.

The Jayhawks were 42-8 in the two years Chamberlain played basketball for KU. The eight losses were by a total of 21 points, with three coming in overtime. Only twice—a 4-point loss to Kansas State in double overtime and a 6-point setback at Iowa State—did Kansas lose by more than two points in that era.

Fanning the Flame

Kansas Athletic Department officials counted on Wilt Chamberlain to play his senior year, but when he left school, the team found itself laden with an albatross of a schedule for 1958-1959.

"Faced with a schedule promoted when 'The Dipper' was still an available campus figure, K.U. battled some of the toughest teams in the nation," the 1959 *Jayhawker* noted, without adding the predictable results.

With Chamberlain, Kansas attained national celebrity. Without him, the Jayhawks lapsed into fodder for a great schedule.

KU lost seven straight games early in the season, including consecutive-day losses in Los Angeles to UCLA and Southern California. St. Joseph's and North Carolina State also racked up victories. The Jayhawks dragged into the Big Eight Holiday Tournament—Oklahoma State joined the league after the 1957 season—and only an 84-73 victory over

Missouri kept them from finishing last.

The team showed great promise for the future. The Jayhawks had Bill Bridges, a sophomore voted to the all-conference team, as well as juniors Al Donaghue and Bob Hickman. Kansas finished 8-6—third—in the Big Eight. But the 11-14 overall record marked the first time since the 1947-1948 season that Kansas lost more than it won.

Players often inherit the expectations stemming from the success of the immediate past; coaches are subject to different pressure, that of being measured against previous coaches.

In Dick Harp's case, Phog Allen still loomed over campus as a figure bigger than the building that bears his name. Allen purposely stayed away from practice and kept to his seat in the upper level across from the benches during games.

But even when good times slipped into those of losing records and some people questioned his abilities, Harp never fell into the trap of knocking his predecessor.

"I never ever heard Coach Harp say one negative remark about Doc Allen," Ted Owens said. "He always saw the absolute best in Dr. Allen. I always admired him for that.

"It's very easy to follow somebody, particularly with the expectation level that they had, and to turn on him. But not one time in the four years that we were together, or all the years that we've known each other after that, not one time did I hear him say one critical remark about Doc."

"I'm convinced that everyone who followed a legendary figure like Doc would have to feel some pressure," Owens said. "I think there had to be, even though [Harp] was a very important part of their winning the national championship. If you talk to any of the players, they have a great respect for Doc, but they also have great respect for Dick and the work that he did."

The Jayhawks fared much better in 1960. Instead of battling for last place in the holiday tournament, the improved Kansas team won its way into the tournament finals, losing to Iowa State, 83-70. The Jayhawks won eight of their final nine regular-season games to pull into a first-place tie with Kansas State, giving Coach Dick Harp his second

The 1958-1959 schedule was planned for Wilt Chamberlain. When Wilt left for the Harlem Globetrotters, the Jayhawks were in serious trouble.

conference championship.

Wayne Hightower averaged 21.8 points a game and became the 16th Jayhawk to lead the league in scoring and he and Bill Bridges made all-conference.

The Jayhawks traveled to Manhattan for a Big Eight playoff game and the right to enter the NCAA Tournament. The co-champions split their regular-season games, with KU taking a two-point victory in Lawrence and the Wildcats rolling to a 68-57 triumph in Manhattan. Unlike the first Manhattan game, however, the Jayhawks stuck with Kansas State in the playoff, forcing an overtime before claiming an 84-82 decision and the sixth NCAA Tournament berth in school history.

Staying in Manhattan for the regional games, Kansas eliminated Texas 90-81 but fell to Cincinnati, the eventual third-place finisher, 82-71.

The strong finish impressed the staff of the 1960 *Jayhawker,* which wrote, "Looking back at the 19-9 season record, the Big Eight co-championship and second place in the midwest N.C.A.A. regional, the 1960 basketball season can be remembered as one of the most inspiring in recent Jayhawks annals."

While Kansas had earned national reknown for its basketball prowess, the games closest to home still marked the biggest dates on the Jayhawks' schedule. Kansas State developed into a power of national magnitude and Missouri, while suffering through a series of sub-.500 seasons in the late 1950s and early 1960s, always pointed to the KU games.

The Jayhawks opened the season 3-3—including losses to St. John's and Top 10 North Carolina—but won 12 of its next 14. The only defeats were against Kansas State in the Big Eight Holiday Tournament title game and against Oklahoma State.

Late in that string of games, Missouri headed for Lawrence. The Jayhawks owned a nine-game winning streak over their eastern neighbor.

Bill Bridges, on his way to All-America honors and a third all-Big Eight certificate, fouled out of the game with 10 minutes to play. But Wayne Hightower took over, scoring 36 points and pulling down 21 rebounds in an 88-73 rout of the Tigers. That victory allowed Kansas to

The 1959-1960 team recovered from Chamberlain's departure and went to the NCAA tournament, coming in second in the Midwest Regional.

improve to 7-1 in the Big Eight, tied with Kansas State.

Colorado gave Kansas a one-game lead in the standings by beating Kansas State and losing to the Jayhawks, but that advantage disappeared in an 81-63 Wildcats' victory over Kansas.

About this time Kansas learned that no matter the outcome of the regular season, there would be no post-season in 1961. The NCAA completed its investigation of the recruitment of Wilt Chamberlain and levied a one-year tournament ban on the Jayhawks.

Owens, then an assistant coach, said, "The problem is we had a great team. We had Bill Bridges and Wayne Hightower and Jerry Gardner, who was an excellent guard. And Nolen Ellison and Dee Ketchum and Allen Correll. We had dynamite talent.

"And I'll never forget the day that Dick walked on the court and told them. It was a morale and spirit killer because that was a team that could have done very well in the NCAA playoffs."

KU went 2-2 over its final four games, and Kansas State did not lose again until the NCAA Midwest Regional final in Lawrence—with Cincinnati again eliminating the Big Eight's representative en route to its first national title.

Bill Bridges ranks second all-time in career rebounds at KU with 1,081.

Kansas' 17-8 season ended on a down note, as the 1961 *Jayhawker* noted: "Saturday, March 11, proved to be another grey day for Kansas, as the Hawkers were tripped by a 'fighting' band of Missouri Tigers, 79-76."

The yearbook continued, "When Kansas was 'on,' nobody could stop them; when cold the Hawks were a pushover. Consequently, the Jays bowed to two considerably weaker teams, thereby killing any hopes for a conference championship.

"The lack of team drive at times, as well as the brawl at Missouri, could be in part attributed to the...N.C.A.A. ban clamped on the K.U. basketball team. This ban hurt the attitudes of those holdovers from last year's conference champs, who had dreamed of another N.C.A.A. tournament berth. Moreover,

Missouri Athletic Director Don Faurot has been accused by many of instigating the N.C.A.A. probe—an accusation which has only heightened animosity between the two schools."

The NCAA never discloses who turns in a school, and the accusations against Faurot were probably based more on emotion than fact. More likely, coaches from the East initiated the investigation of Kansas, since they were the most peeved when Chamberlain left Pennsylvania for Mount Oread.

While the resulting sanctions disheartened the 1961 team, the Jayhawks of 1962 felt the hangover. The yearbook section on the basketball team was titled, "KU also fielded a basketball team."

The yearbook staff said, "KU would play as well as most of the teams in the Big Eight—for exactly one half. But during the second period *rigor mortis* usually set in while the opponents were gaining the upper hand."

"In retrospect, Hawker fans can be happy for one thing," the *Jayhawker* staff snidely wrote. "By tying Missouri for the Big Eight basement with a 3-11 record, Kansas maintained its record of having never finished exclusively at the bottom in 55 years of conference basketball history. Every other member of the Big Eight, except for the most recent addition, Oklahoma State, has finished in sole possession of the cellar at least three times."

Kansas lost five of its first six games and 10 of its last 12 in a 7-18 season. The Jayhawks used a 76-71 victory over Iowa State in the next-to-last game of the season to slip into a seventh-place tie with the Tigers.

Jerry Gardner, who averaged 20.7 points a game, took the league scoring title and honorable mention All-America. The other starting guard was Nolen Ellison, who averaged 18.1 points a game and joined Gardner in receiving all-conference honors. The third highest-scoring player on the team was guard Jim Dumas.

The team's problems in 1962 were obviously inside, and that would be cured the next season with the addition of 6-7 sophomore George Unseld to the varsity.

Unseld quickly joined select company, piling up enough points to match the accomplishment of B. H. Born, Wilt

Chamberlain, and Clyde Lovellette of scoring at least 400 points in a sophomore season.

The Jayhawks responded to once again playing a dominant big man, too. They used a 90-88 quadruple-overtime victory over Kansas State to win the Big Eight Holiday Tournament. Kansas dropped eight of its next 10 games, but finished strong with three out of the final four games won.

The end-of-season rally failed to keep KU from a 12-13 record, the first consecutive losing seasons for the Jayhawks since the James Naismith-coached teams of 1903-1904 and 1904-1905.

Unseld had another 400-point season in 1964, and the team started 4-0 although it sagged to 10-12 before closing with a flourish. And while the 8-6 league mark pulled the Jayhawks up to third in the Big Eight, the three-game winning streak enabled Dick Harp to end his Kansas coaching career on an upswing. The fourth coach in the KU basketball history stepped down after eight seasons.

"The winning and losing, that's why you play," Harp said. "I enjoyed the play to see who was going to win and lose, but there came a point in my time here that I realized that I needed to do this other thing. So we made a decision a couple years before I did resign that that was what I was going to do. By then I recognized that for many different reasons, and there were a number of reasons, that I probably shouldn't continue."

Harp is one of those coaches for whom the joy of the game lies on the court. Away from the court, college basketball lost some of its luster for Harp.

"Many of the highlights for me in coaching was when I was an assistant," Harp said. "As time went on, I enjoyed many things about being head coach and some of the things I didn't. Because I didn't enjoy some of those, I felt that maybe I wasn't being as fair to the university as I should be.

"Things like recruiting. I enjoyed visiting young men and their families. I didn't enjoy all the ridiculous extremes you went through and had to do. I kind of laugh because that's actually the way Doc [Allen] thought about it. Doc always thought that recruiting was really foolish. What part of athletics was that?"

Ted Owens, who accepted the promotion from assistant coach to replace Harp, feels his former head coach's role in Kansas basketball has been under-noted over the years.

"Dick Harp made a great contribution to Kansas basketball. He had some years that weren't very good as a head coach but had good ones, too. And he did some great work as Doc's assistant."

Harp's teams combined for a 121-82 record and two conference championships and two second-place finishes, but he is a much bigger part of the picture than the eight seasons from 1956-1964. As a player from 1938-1940 he helped the Jayhawks to a 50-15 record and is one of only five men to have played and coached in an NCAA Tournament title game. He knew the game well enough that Phog Allen asked him to be the first full-time assistant basketball coach at KU, a high recommendation from the "father of basketball coaching."

When he left the head coaching position, Harp left KU and became the head of the Fellowship of Christian Athletes for 13 years. In the late 1980s, North Carolina Coach Dean Smith asked Harp to share his knowledge for his team.

Just as Phog Allen had done when he left, Harp saw his assistant coach moved up the bench one seat. Ted Owens, who played on Oklahoma teams that went 5-2 against the Jayhawks from 1948-1950, took over as the head coach.

"I think when I first came there, [Harp] thought I would do a good job," said Owens. "But he was very honest with me and said we'd just take a look at my work.

"He told me basketball was not everything that he wanted to do in his life but you never know if that means 10 years or 15 years or whatever. I was 30 at the time I came there as his assistant, so I had plenty of time. And it such a great learning experience. He was an excellent teacher. When the time did come close, having his support was really meaningful to me."

While Owens didn't inherit the bonanza that Dick Harp did in his first year as the Kansas coach—Wilt Chamberlain's sophomore year—he did have an abundance of talent for the 1964-1965 season. He also went to the well of tradition to help the Jayhawks forget the recent down seasons and recall the glory days. He ordered the lockers painted with the names of KU greats from the past and added murals depicting scenes of historical triumphs.

The new coach was going to use all the angles since, for Owens, becoming a head basketball coach marked the fulfillment of a dream.

"When I was five years old," Owens said, "I took a basketball and we had an outdoor goal and I had the ball between my legs, I couldn't push it up any other way, had it between my legs and pitched it up and it went in. I've been in love with the game ever since. I've been infatuated with it.

"It wasn't necessarily the shot heard 'round the world, but it was meaningful in my life. I've just always loved the game and always wanted to be part of the game."

Owens' parents raised him with a respect for teachers and coaches. It was important to them that all three of the Owens boys go to college, and all did.

Now Owens was an integral part of a major university and he had the mandate of restoring lost luster to the basketball program.

"There had been a little bit of a drop off," Owens said, "but there was still enough of a spirit there. It was like a flame waiting to be fanned a little bit.

"Coach Harp left me with good talent. We had recruited some good young players, so when I took over the program, even though we had not had a good record the year before, we had good players."

The best of the bunch was "Wonderful" Walt Wesley, who led the Big Eight with a 26.9 point scoring average—the highest average since Wilt Chamberlain's 28.3 in 1958 and the third highest in league history.

After a 3-3 start, Kansas won seven consecutive games. In the heart of that string, Owens became the third rookie coach to win the conference holiday tournament.

Kansas played so well the Jayhawks had visions of winning the conference title. To do that, however, they first had to get past highly regarded Oklahoma State twice in the last three weeks of the season. The first match went through four overtimes before being decided, with the Cowboys taking a 68-64 thriller.

"The killer of the thing is that in every overtime and the regular part of the game, we had possession of the ball and a chance to win it and we didn't convert," said Owens. "We had control and opportunity. It wasn't until the fourth overtime that they had any control of the game at all.

"That was disappointing, because if we had won that all we had to do was go home and win our home games and we had won the race. That coming in your first year as head coach would have been fantastic."

The Jayhawks bounced back, however, breaking an eight-game regular-season losing streak to Kansas State with an 86-66 romp. Victories over Nebraska and Colorado left only Oklahoma State on the schedule.

Henry Iba's famed slow-down version of the game limited possessions. The 64-58 Oklahoma State victory was marked by 12 of 13 shooting by the Cowboys in the second half.

The Jayhawks made some noise, however. Their 17-8 record and second-place Big Eight finish indicated a marked improvement. And Owens and assistant coach Sam Miranda already salted away a franchise player for the next three seasons.

Joseph White, better known as JoJo, graduated Vashon High School in St. Louis at the semester break early in 1965.

"What we were very lucky in," Owens recalled, "is that JoJo graduated at midterm and I don't think a lot of people realized that he was graduating at midterm. That wouldn't happen today. Sam knew that JoJo was going to graduate at midterm so we went over and visited with him."

White said he didn't know "anything about the University of Kansas except Sam Miranda" until he visited the campus. He showed up October 17, 1964, and watched the Kansas football team beat Oklahoma, 15-14.

"The weekend he came to visit," said Owens, "we beat Oklahoma in football and the place went nuts, since that only happens about once every 30 years. But it was a beautiful fall day and 10,000 students ran out on the field and carried the players off. I think Jo looked at that and thought this wouldn't be a bad place to be."

Owens said White graduated from high school one day and enrolled at Kansas the next.

"I knew nothing about the University of Kansas, other than through my high school coach, who was really responsible for me going there," said White. "I had 250 offers to go to school. In measuring out all those different things that I needed to consider, one of them was the radius to where the school was in comparison to where home was. Kansas fell right into that place I was looking for."

He said, "I played football. I played baseball. I played all of them, but basketball was really my love. I always found myself playing that more than other sports. I was good at all of them, but basketball offered more, in terms of what I was looking for—satisfaction of the sport.

"It was exciting. The adrenaline can flow. You can work up a good sweat. It was a fast, up-tempo game. You could force people to play and think, which a lot of people can't do. There's a lot of differences to the challenges to it that I was really satisfied playing the game. And I just loved it. Plus I was kind of good at it."

Kansas fielded a very good team in 1965-1966, with a starting five of Walt Wesley, Al Lopes, Delvin Lewis, Riney Lochmann, and Ron Franz. By the time the second semester started, the Jayhawks were 15-3, having dropped games in Los Angeles to UCLA and Southern Cal and a conference match at Nebraska.

The Jayhawks proved they could play well, but a decision had to be made because JoJo White became eligible to join the varsity at mid-season.

"We had all of the other pieces of the puzzle covered," said Coach Ted Owens. "But he was a great talent who just added so much speed and ball handling and versatility.

"At midterm we knew we had a good team. What we sensed was that this was a team that could win the national championship.

"I asked Jo what he wanted to do and he said I want to play right now. I talked to our captain—Riney Lochmann—and I said 'Riney, we're trying to make a decision about JoJo. JoJo wants to play. He feels we have a great chance and I feel that we have a great chance to win the national championship. But one thing is important, if he plays he will be a starter and that means that you may not start.' Riney said to me, 'Coach, it doesn't matter whether I start or not. We think JoJo can help us to win the national championship and we want him to play.'

"That sealed it as far as I was concerned because in Riney Lochmann and Del Lewis, who were our captains, we had two great young men and two very unselfish players. So with their endorsements and with JoJo's wanting to, we made that decision."

White's first game came against Oklahoma State in Lawrence. "We tried very much to act like we weren't nervous,"

Walt Wesley, a 6-11 center, led KU in scoring in 1965 and 1966.

said Owens. "This was a time that if you lose one more game in the league race, you might be out because Nebraska was not going to lose a lot of games that year.

"But I said we're not going to bring him off the bench, we were going to start him. I didn't mention JoJo in the talk before the game, except for [defensive] assignments. As we walked out of the dressing room he nudged me on the leg and said, 'I'm all right coach.' He got the opening tip and went down and picked it up and shot a 20-footer. The first time he touched the ball. He never played like a rookie."

Kansas rolled to a 59-38 rout of the Cowboys and collected three other lopsided victories before the rematch with Nebraska. The Cornhuskers won the first meeting 83-75, and remained unbeaten in league play.

"Joe Cipriano had a great team at Nebraska that year. They were ranked in the Top 10, and we were ranked in the Top 10," Owens said, calling the second Nebraska game "one of the great games ever played in Allen Field House."

"We had a week to get ready for them," said Owens. "They had a great full court press and we were really well prepared and we just ate their press alive. Instead of having Jo bring the ball up, we put him at midcourt, and we threw over their zone. He took it to the hole. He was getting two-on-ones and three-on-twos, and he handled the ball so well."

The mismatch on the floor led to one on the scoreboard, which read Kansas 110, Nebraska 73.

Owens said, "It was just a great, great night for Kansas basketball and I think that was the first time that our guys realized just how good they could be."

The Jayhawks won their final two league games, and Colorado did KU a favor by knocking off Nebraska, giving Kansas its 32nd conference championship and an NCAA Tournament slot.

KU, 22-3, drew Southern Methodist in the first round and the Mustangs managed to stay within 76-70 of the Jayhawks. It marked the closest game for Kansas since the Nebraska loss. Since White joined the team, the Jayhawks' average margin of victory was 26.4 points.

Kansas advanced to the regional finals and drew Texas Western, later known as Texas-El Paso. For the first time since White moved up to the varsity, Kansas played a tight game, eventually going into overtime. With time running down, and the score still tied, the Jayhawks decided to put their fate in the hands of JoJo White, a sophomore with eight games of major-college experience.

"Here we were at the most crucial play of the year and we were giving it to a rookie," said Owens. "That's the kind of confidence we had in him.

"We inbounded it to him, and he started to penetrate. And as he started to penetrate, Texas Western did a good job of pushing him toward the sideline. He started to the sideline and pivoted on the sideline, and with one second to go, hit a jumper. We were going nuts, and everybody jumped up and grabbed each other."

The jubilation quickly ended, however, as referee Rudy Marich waved the basket off, ruling that White went out of bounds before the shot.

"No KU fan will ever forget the sensation of that moment. Nor will any KU basketball fan soon forget the anguish felt after the official ruled that White had stepped out-of-bounds, forcing the game into a second extra period," the yearbook staff wrote after the season.

White and Owens both said films of the game show the player did not step out of bounds. Owens who "has watched it hundreds of times" said White's heel perhaps broke the out-of-bounds plane but never touched the floor. Given another chance, however, Western took advantage for an 81-80 decision in the second overtime. The Miners went on to win the NCAA Tournament title.

"We would have been better off if JoJo had missed that shot because it was one of those moments of ecstasy where we thought 'We have won it. We have realized our dream of going to the Final Four,'" Owens said. "We were very confident that we could be national champions. It's hard after you think you have it won to get yourself settled back down in the right mental frame of mind. Now all of a sudden we hadn't won and we had a second overtime. We never had control of the second overtime."

Owens called the 1966 team one of the best in school history, and with players like Wesley—who averaged 20.7 points a game—Al Lopes, Del Lewis, and Ron Franz there was a core on which to build. But any good team needs a catalyst to make it great, and White had the ability to push the team several notches higher.

White took the loss to Texas Western and turned it into something positive, something on which to build for the future.

"Losing was never hard for me to take," he said. "Understanding why you lose, that's where the growth comes. Learning how to consistently go out and be able to produce every single night.

"Losing—I could deal with that. I had no problems with losing, as long as I knew that I gave the best that I could give in the performance. If you've done your best, that's all you can do. Being able to always gear yourself to always perform your best each and every time out is where coaches like the players."

White's substantial role grew when All-Americans Walt Wesley, Riney Lochmann, and Del Lewis graduated in 1966. The coaches had a well-stocked freshman team, however, and players such as Vernon Vanoy and Rodger Bohnenstiehl came into their own.

The 1966-1967 Jayhawks again posted rout after rout. Aside from a 62-59 loss at Colorado—the Buffaloes scored three points in the final five seconds for the victory—the closest league game in a 13-1 conference season was a 60-55 victory at Kansas State.

That game marked JoJo White's first taste of the Kansas-Kansas State rivalry in Manhattan.

"There were a number of teams out there that created a challenge, but I didn't find during that time that we had as much of a challenge as we presented," White said of the league race. "I thought we presented more of a challenge. We were the team that was looked up to."

"But it was always a challenge to me

when we played on the road. K-State was Kansas' rival. We played there, and I found out for myself why that was so."

"Regardless of how many times coaches build up the game in terms of its rivalry, it isn't until you are actually there and on the floor that you feel exactly what they're saying. Then your adrenaline starts flowing because the last thing you want to do is to lose there in front of their home crowd."

After wrapping up another 22-3 regular season with a 74-56 victory over Kansas State, Kansas had the honor of staying home and hosting an NCAA regional, with Houston playing the Jayhawks in one game and Louisville and Southern Methodist in the first regional semifinal.

"We thought it would be us and Louisville [in the regional finals]," Owens said of the pre-tournament expectations. "No one knew much about Houston at the time. All our thoughts were beating Louisville.

"SMU upset Louisville and I could see it in our eyes in the dressing room. The guys could see Final Four all over before they ever took the court.

"Now all Houston had was Elvin Hayes and Don Chaney—not bad—and a bunch of studs. But no one really realized how good they were. Houston jumps on us and we get 11 back. We come back and tie the game—the place was going nuts—but we never got control of the game."

As the Jayhawks expected, they did play Louisville, but the 66-53 upset by Houston made the game with the Cardinals worth only third place in the regional.

The Kansas-Kansas State rivalry heated up for 1967-1968. The Wildcats had players such as scoring leader Steve Honeycutt and a big front line consisting of 7-0 Nick Pino, 6-7 Earl Seyfert and 6-7 Gene Williams. Outside of 6-10 Dave Nash, Kansas could not match K-State height, but with JoJo White, Rodger Bohnenstiehl, Bruce Sloan, and Phil Harmon, the Jayhawks comprised a quicker team.

Kansas had just two conference losses midway through the schedule when it ran into games with Kansas State and Nebraska.

One of the KU defeats had been at the hands of the Wildcats, and the Jay-

hawks needed to get that game back. But, the *Jayhawker* reported, Kansas State put on a "display of slow-motion basketball at its best, marred only by infrequent bursts of activity. Then at Nebraska [Kansas] trailed by 17 late in the game and cut the deficit to five before falling by 10 points."

Kansas kept the pressure on K-State, however, and still had a chance to tie, if it got some help from Oklahoma State. The Jayhawks closed the regular season at home against Iowa State, and closed it on fire. Rodger Bohnenstiehl, playing his final game at Allen Field House, hit 10 of 11 shots from the floor as Kansas hit 60 percent for the game in a 91-58 romp.

However, Kansas State squeaked out a two-point victory over the Cowboys for sole possession of the Big Eight championship and the league's invitation to the NCAA Tournament.

Kansas accepted a bid for the National Invitation Tournament and played very well. The Jayhawks hit better than 50 percent of their shots against a strong Temple zone for an 82-76 first-round victory. KU trailed Villanova 31-25 at halftime in the second round, but forced the Wildcats into missing 14 of their first 15 shots in the second period and grabbed a 55-49 decision.

That put the Jayhawks into the semifinals against St. Peter's, which had used a high-powered run-and-gun attack to be cast as the Cinderella team of that season's NIT.

"St. Peter's had beaten Duke," said Owens. "We projected to play Duke in the semifinals. They beat Duke by 29 points. And I'm sitting up there in the crowd and I'm really wanting to play Duke because I'm thinking people back in Lawrence, Kansas, are thinking if you don't beat St. Peter's what kind of a coach are you anyway?

"No one knew how good St. Peter's was. They were really good. They were one of those wild pressing and full court teams. And we could run the ball pretty well and when you have a guy like JoJo you can play an open court game well.

"We decided the best thing to do is just take them out of their tempo all together and we did and it never was a close game in the semifinals. We just walked it up the court and played a half court game

with them and drove them nuts."

As a result, St. Peter's, which averaged better than 90 points a game, managed just 46, and Kansas came away a 14-point victor. That marked the final triumph of the season for the Jayhawks, however, as Dayton, with a 25-2 advantage from the free-throw line won the title game 61-48.

"I ran into a problem during that era of my college career," said JoJo White. "I always felt as an individual that I could make the difference in any game that I played and I approached the game in that way because I was the leader. I always felt that I was blessed with speed and the other gifts that I was blessed with, and developing and using those things, that's what I was driving to to be able to make it automatic on the floor.

"But we always got almost there and could never get over the hump for some reason or another. So in my own mind I was fighting with 'Are you a true champion, or are you a loser?'

"We would win our conference, which was great, but the ultimate was to win the NCAA. The closest we came was my sophomore year.

"I suffered with that personally all the way through. Then we won the gold medal in the [1968] Olympics. During my college career, that was the first time that I had been on the team that had gone all the way. It was like rested in my own mind that, 'No, you are not a loser.'"

White had one semester of eligibility left, but it went virtually unnoticed on campus because the attention was on the Orange Bowl-bound football team.

"The 1968-69 basketball campaign began when oranges were still in blossom at KU, as many fans were getting over their sun tans and hangovers from the New Year's event in Florida, the Jayhawk cagers had rolled up an 11-1 record and No. 4 national ranking and the Big Eight Christmas tournament title," the *Jayhawker* recalled.

KU found itself involved in several races that season. In addition to an anticipated tight Big Eight race, White's career was winding down. Ted Owens approached the 100-victory mark at Kansas, and the Jayhawks had a chance to become the first school to win 1,000 basketball games.

"We were in a battle with Kentucky to

see who was going to be the first team there," Owens said. "We thought we were going to be number-one. In fact we won a couple games at Stanford and Utah State. I told the guys that if you win these two, we are going to beat Kentucky.

"Then just before we were getting ready to win that 1,000th game, we picked up the paper and Adolph [Rupp] and all of them together down at Kentucky, they had a cake and they said they had won their 1,000th game. They figured out that in 1902 or whatever it was, they had beaten the Lexington YMCA twice. We had really built up as a big thing to be number one and be the first to win 1,000 games. We didn't think there was any doubt we were going to be the first. Then they found those [records]."

Actually, Kansas' count was also inaccurate. The Jayhawks celebrated 1,000 victories after a 73-67 triumph over Kansas State, but a subsequent check of the records moved the milestone ahead two games.

The game between, however, did mark Owens' 100th victory at Kansas. It also was White's last game for KU when the Jayhawks hosted Colorado.

As usual, the crowd in Allen Field House was big and boisterous. "We had dust coming out of the seats," White said of home games. "We played with intensity. I know I did, and I was the leader out there. Off of me, it triggered to the point that every time we took the floor we expected that type of game. If the teams that we played against weren't up and ready to play, they were going to get dogged. That's just the way it was. The fans could relate to that. It was like they were as confident in us as we were in ourselves and the way we played."

There was little doubt as to who was the crowd favorite. "JoJo had been to the Olympics that previous summer," said Owens, "and that was the year that we were not picked to win the Olympics and JoJo and that group won the Olympics.

"When Jo came back, he wasn't a Kansas hero anymore, he was a national hero. He and Spencer Heywood had been the top players for our team. Every place we went in the country, when he was introduced the rafters were rocked. It was an emotional thing that whole time."

"JoJo was such a dominating player,

you always had a certain security with him," Owens said. "When you have a point guard who can dominate a game the way he did, you learn to really rely on him.

"The players always had a great deal of confidence in Jo. And one reason they had confidence in Jo was that Jo would get them the basketball. I've always said that the greatest communicator is the pass. If I pass to you I'm telling you that I believe in you and I trust you. If I don't pass you the ball then I'm probably saying that I don't have any faith in you.

"Jo had a unique quality about him. He'd get the ball to the most average

Above: Ted Owens' disappointment shows after the loss to Texas Western. Owens would get many other chances in his career.
Opposite page: Kansas played Texas Western in the 1966 NCAA regional finals. The Jayhawks lost in overtime to the Texas Western team, which went on to win the tournament.

player we had, so it built a level of confidence in that player. He could think, 'If Jo will give me the ball then he must believe in me.' And it had that kind of effect."

Now White's career was ending, but he went out in a very special style.

Playing "in his usual form, White broke

JoJo White ranks as one of KU's all-time great guards.

presses, stole balls, hit his pet setshot, drove the basket flipping up darting twisting layups and scored 30 tallies for the highest point total of his career," the yearbook staff wrote.

Both White and Owens said there was no special plan to have the player leave on his highest point total, the game just flowed in that direction.

"You never want to go out on a bad note," said White. "I was allowed a little bit more freedom offensively. When I was in high school, I carried a big scoring load. When I went to college, my job changed. I became a leader—getting the ball to the right place at the right time and getting the ball to the right people. When it got down to crunch time, I was asked to take some of the big shots and make the big plays. I always could score, and in that last game, I was given more freedom to score. And I did.

"My teammates recognized that, hey, it's your last game, and I was going good. But I was first trying to make sure that we had control of the game before you kind of go off on your own, but things were happening, and my teammates were giving the ball. And I was just shooting them down."

Said Owens, "That was the way the game went, and he was ready. The great thing about Jo was that he would do whatever you asked him to do—if you needed 30 [points], well, he had the potential to do that. If you needed a game where maybe we needed to hurt them inside, he was perfectly willing to do that, too. He was a very unselfish player."

White earned two All-America honors and became a three-time all-Big Eight selection. He averaged 15.3 points a game over his 84 collegiate games, a figure that could have been much higher if his role had been different.

"He was just such a complete player. He could do everything," Owens said. "First of all, he had the great quality that few players had. He would get the ball to the open man. He could do anything. You never saw JoJo dribble behind his back, pass behind his back, that sort of thing, but his fundamentals were good and he just made big plays look very simple.

"He could hit the open man. He could pass the ball so well. He ran the ball club so well. He played great defense. He could score, his highest scoring game ever was his last game. He had 30 points that game, but I remember one of the greatest games he ever played was at Oklahoma State and he had three points. But he ran the ball club that night. He was a great quarterback."

White said, "[Basketball] was always fun for me. I loved it with a passion. I'd go to bed with the dream of being back on

The Jayhawks celebrate in the locker room.

the floor the next day because I was excited about trying to do better each and every time and that included practice as well as the game."

But White's end of eligibility left Kansas without a great point guard.

"He was such a dominant player, and we did not have a dominating point guard coming on to step in," said Owens. "We felt we could be good. We did have some talent. Particularly, we had some good young big players—Robisch and Brown—but they were young."

Kansas won five of the first six post-White games but dropped a 75-67 decision to Colorado that locked up the Big Eight title for the Buffaloes and then fell 64-57 to Kansas State for a second-place conference tie. The Jayhawks again went to the NIT, but were quickly ousted 78-62 by Boston College for a 20-7 overall record.

Illinois Influence

After great success with St. Louis native JoJo White, Kansas recruited a little farther east and found a cache of players that would carry the team to a pair of Final Fours.

"We had enormous success going into Illinois," said KU coach Ted Owens. "In fact, our '71 and '74 teams were dominated by Illinois players. But when you're going after predominantly out-of-state recruits, the competition gets that much tougher. It was difficult to keep it at the level we had it at the time."

"Sam Miranda recruited me," Tom Kivisto said. "Sam was probably as consistent a person and as honest a person as you'll ever meet. For that reason Sam did very well in Illinois. He was from Illinois. He recruited a lot of kids from Illinois—all the way back to Dave Robisch and Rodger Boehnenstiehl. People had a lot of respect for him."

Robisch, from Springfield, Illinois, joined JoJo White on the 1969 all-conference team and became a three-year fixture on that squad. Miranda recruited Bob Kivisto, who started at guard for KU in 1969-1970 as a sophomore. Other starters included Pierre Russell, Bud Stallworth, and Roger Brown.

They made a good team—very good in the eyes of basketball followers.

"That year we were realistic enough to know that we didn't have quite the kind of talent we had before. We'd enjoyed having a couple of All-Americans in JoJo White and Walter Wesley and some other very good players. We knew it would be difficult to keep that level, that quality," Owens said.

The team's problems surfaced early. Over his first five seasons as the Kansas coach, Ted Owens owned a 14-1 record in the Big Eight Conference Holiday Tournament—losing a first-round game in the 1967 event. But in December 1969, KU finished sixth. The team went 17-9 overall—the first time an Owens-coached team failed to win 20 games in a season. Its 8-6 Big Eight mark was good enough for second place, and Robisch led the league with a 26.5 point scoring average.

It was an up-and-down season, but with an evident pattern, as the *Jayhawker* noted: "That's the way it was for Ted Owens' Jayhawks in 1969-70...a perfect season in their 13 home outings and not so perfect the rest of the time."

Bob Kivisto came from a basketball family. His father coached the high school team, where his brother Tom also played. Tom Kivisto became a highly sought prospect, for the way Bob had developed as much as his own talents.

"When I was a senior in high school [Bob] was a sophomore [at KU] and he started every game and they had a really good team," Tom Kivisto said of being recruited by Kansas. "They had all that talent and had a good season. Bob was a great basketball player, and he was happy. He was playing. They had great talent. I could see more young talent coming on."

Kansas offered what Tom Kivisto wanted in a school. He wanted to study medicine and stay in the Midwest. And he wanted to be on a good team.

"My brother was happy," Tom Kivisto said. "The campus was beautiful, and it fit everything I wanted to do. I wasn't particularly all that enamored of following my brother and running into the situation we have today where I run into somebody who thinks I'm Bob, and Bob runs into people who think he's Tom."

But the younger Kivisto decided to take a chance and follow his brother west. Tom Kivisto ended up seeing some of the more amazing seasons ever at Kansas. Even his first college memories bordered on the surreal.

A KU basketball player led a very structured life, and even more so for a freshman, who was trying to juggle a class load, two teams' worth of practices, and adjusting to college life.

"What I remember my freshman year," Tom Kivisto said, "I remember getting up in the dark, going to class, then going to the gym at Allen Field House at 12 o'clock, after cramming down a sandwich on the way over. Leaving the field house about 5:30 so tired I wasn't even hungry. Recovering about 7:30 or 8 o'clock to study until 10:30 or 11. Just to get up in the dark again." But the work was paying off in games.

"One of the big games that year was our opening game and we played Long Beach State and [then-coach] Jerry Tarkanian had a great team," said Ted Owens. "They were ranked fifth or sixth going into the season. At halftime we were ahead 32-8. That is the kind of defensive team we were. We were playing a 1-3-1 zone, and they just had fits with it."

Kansas won the Jayhawk Classic that season with victories over St. Joseph's and Houston. Roger Brown starred in the title game, scoring 23 points and getting 21 rebounds to go with several blocked shots. "I can only say," said Houston Coach Guy Lewis, "we've never been intimidated in the inside like we were tonight since we played against [UCLA's Lew] Alcindor [now known as Kareem Abdul-Jabar]."

"We won the first six games, and I blame myself for the one loss we had that year," Owens said. "It was just poor scheduling. We had a tournament on Friday and Saturday in Lawrence against really good teams. They we traveled on Sunday to Louisville to play on Monday night.

"We full-court pressed all the time and our team was just very tired and emotionally wrung out."

Louisville claimed the December 21 game, 87-75, but Kansas did not lose again until the end of March, running off 21 consecutive victories.

"That team was a great rebounding team and a great defensive team," Owens said. "We only had two extraordinary shooters—Dave Robisch and Bud Stallworth—but we had a great team of athletes. We held our opponents to 37 percent shooting from the field. We only lost one game that year until the playoffs and as a team we only shot 44 percent, so we weren't a particularly good shooting team. But we dominated the boards."

Kansas went 14-0 in the Big Eight, joining the 1959 Kansas State Wildcats as the only teams to go through the eight-team league schedule undefeated. The Jayhawks posted consecutive overtime victories against Oklahoma and Missouri, but every other league game was a clear triumph.

The NCAA Tournament was another thing. The NCAA only invited 25 teams then and the tournament play level had never been more intense. KU went to Wichita for regional play and held off Houston 78-77 before stopping Drake 73-71 to advance to the Final Four.

Kansas had a very good team—average teams do not take 27-1 records into the Final Four—but drew UCLA in the semifinals. The Bruins, who featured Sidney Wicks, Curtis Rowe, Steve Patterson, and Henry Bibby, were rated

Ted Owens, Kansas head coach from 1964-1983, took the Jayhawks to six NCAA tournaments.

number one and had won six of the previous seven NCAA tournaments. And with a similar 27-1 record, UCLA fully expected to make it seven out of eight.

"It was an excellent team but it was a team that could be beaten," Owens said. "We were 13 behind UCLA [at halftime] and they had their famed full-court press. We full-court pressed them and came back and tied the game. Then Dave Robisch hit a shot to put us two up but they called him for traveling, and it kind of cracked our momentum a little bit. I think we had them on the ropes. Anyway we ended up losing by eight."

Kansas dropped the third-place game, 77-75, to Western Kentucky, nearly over-shadowing the victory total that, at 27, came within one win of the

Bud Stallworth scored 50 points in helping Kansas defeat Missouri in 1972.

school-record 28 victories amassed by the 1952 national championship team.

The 1952 team was invited to Allen Field House for a reunion in 1972, and Bud Stallworth really gave them something to remember. Unfortunately for the 1972 Jayhawks, it marked about the only highlight of the season.

Owens recalled, "Bud just had one of those phenomenal days. Missouri tried everything to stop him and Missouri had a very good team. Bud was a great jump shooter and he had great range with it and he could shoot the ball well with someone in his face."

Stallworth attempted 38 shots and hit 19. He also made 12 of 13 free-throw attempts for a total of 50 points, the second-highest scoring game in Kansas history. Only Wilt Chamberlain's career-opening 52-point game against Northwestern in 1957 was bigger.

"He took quite a few [shots]," Owens said. "When you win a big game, the next thing that you do is to get the guys back down to earth and ready for the next ball game. So I called the squad together and said 'Bud I want to congratulate you, you broke two Allen Field House records yesterday.' He was just beaming. And I said, 'the most shots taken and the most shots missed in any game here.'"

"Sitting there, I'm thinking he probably has 30 or 35 and someone came

down later and told us what he had," the coach said. "And it wasn't a matter of just plugging him, but, of course he was the guy to get the ball to that day.

"I don't know that we made any extra effort to get him the ball. The way he was shooting we were trying to get him the ball anyway."

That effort allowed Stallworth, both All-America and all-conference, to end the year with a 25.3 point scoring average, which was almost as much as the other four starters combined.

Kansas defeated Missouri 93-80, but lost its final two games to finish a disappointing 7-7 in the Big Eight and 11-15 overall. Owens, 149-43 in his first seven years, faced his first losing season.

Said Owens, "In '72 our expectations level, even though we lost a lot of those good seniors in '71, we felt we were really going to have an excellent team. We had Tommy Kivisto coming on and then Aubrey Nash and Bobby Kivisto coming back. So our backcourt really looked solid. And Bud Stallworth was back then. We had three freshmen front line guys. So we thought that we had a chance to really be good. Then we lost those [freshmen front line players] and it was just a matter that we had to play a very small lineup and to rebuild so we had not a very good year in '72."

The coach said the freshmen of 1971

had one of the best front lines in his tenure in Randy Canfield, Leonard Gray, and Mike Bossard. But Canfield developed a lung ailment, Gray transferred to Long Beach State, and Bossard left school, one of a series of certification casualities that hit several KU sports.

"We started off the preseason ranked in the Top 10," Tom Kivisto said. "Our problem was that we lost a lot of really good talent. Leonard Gray and Randy Canfield and my brother, he quit after his junior year, and Bud Stallworth, you look at the talent that was there, that was one of the reasons I went to KU. Now everybody seems to have left."

"It wasn't a really good time," said Kivisto. "If you remember, that was also the time of all the Olympic problems, and universities were coming out of their turmoil of the late 1960s and the early 1970s. There was always great support at KU, but if there was ever a time when KU had the least support of any time, it was that time. Maybe the establishment wasn't the thing then and discipline and all those things were kind of on the outs. We were kind of out on the wing."

Kivisto understood why crowds slacked off, "our teams were so bad. You didn't need a reason to come to watch a bad team. We had lost so many ball players. We just never had any continuity. We never knew from month to month who would be on the team, besides who would be playing," he said.

It took some time to integrate new players in the system and 1973 dissolved into a season even worse than 1972. The team was 4-3 early, but managed just four more victories the rest of the season.

"The Jayhawks lacked a killer instinct, which had typified Kansas' basketball teams of the past," wrote the staff of the *Jayhawker,* citing myriad of close games Kansas dropped. "The only way to understand these frustrations would have been to see the games when Kansas was leading by 13 points with five minutes in the game and then to see it taken away from them at the end by Lady Luck."

"In '73 we lost every close game," said Owens. "We lost them by ways you can't imagine. We had a 13-point lead with five minutes to go over at Kansas State and lost the game [67-66]. We

were experimenting with the 30-second clock in those days. We just didn't score down the stretch and probably became a little too cautious."

Ted Owens and assistant coach Sam Miranda refused to sit idly by, however.

"They had great basketball minds," Kivisto said. "We used to hate to see them come to the training table because we knew they'd grab all the salt and pepper shakers and line them all up and get on the table and start running offenses and defenses.

"[Owens] had a great mind for the game. He knew the teams and the offense and defense and the scores of any game, the locations, the date. I think his strength was his knowledge and his second strength was probably his hard work. Those coaches put in extremely long hours brain storming and thinking about offense and defense and things that they wanted to do."

"But sometimes what happens is

Dave Robisch was an All-American selection in 1971.

that you complicate the game," Kivisto said. "My dad came from the 'KISS' method, which is very famous—Keep It Simple, Stupid. What [Kansas] did was difficult to adapt to. We would sometimes change the offense every other week. Some of the players didn't have the playing or skilled background to be able to change offenses every other week.

"The difficulty they had was that the turnover was so great. They didn't have the same people from month to month. Injuries had a lot to do with that. People leaving and coming at semester had a lot to do with that. People transferring. We had a real strong morale problem. I think the intent and the work ethic and the knowledge of the coaches was never at fault for any lack of success we had. It was more a lack of chemistry, which is sometimes beyond the coaches' control. That summed up 1972 and 1973."

Owens also spoke of the team problems, "That team had potential in 1973, but we lost every close game, so it was a team that had no confidence. We had a good nucleus, and we picked up Norman Cook and Roger Morningstar out of junior college. We added them to a pretty solid team that was much better than the team that was 8-18.

"Basically all we had to do was rebuild confidence, but we struggled early in the year. We lost the first round of the Big Eight tournament in Kansas City, and our guys were really starting to doubt themselves.

"It's easy when you're on a roll but when you've had a couple of seasons that haven't been really good, it's hard to get that momentum going again, that confidence flowing."

Kivisto asked for a meeting with the coaches, who he said appeared to have their jobs on the line.

"We sat down and made some decisions. There were two or three players who were really some bad-attitude players who we decided were good quality players but who we decided we weren't going to have back."

"It was my senior year and the coaches, I think they were thinking in the backs of their minds it was their last year. We decided that we're going to go with some kids who at least wanted to work hard. We're going to have a little bit of fun and we're going out and do some things."

Danny Knight started at center with Roger Morningstar and freshman Norm Cook on the wings—the NCAA declared freshmen eligible for varsity play in 1973. Tom Kivisto played point guard, and Dale Greenlee took care of the off-guard slot. Owens turned to Rick Suttle and Tommie Smith when he needed a substitute. Those seven players handled almost every minute that season.

"We decided that we were going to play the kids who worked hard," Kivisto said. "Since we didn't have any other guards—I was the only point guard on the team—I had a standing rule that if you didn't work on defense, we weren't going to run the offense on your side of the court."

Some have called his game blackmail basketball. Kivisto, a high-quality guard who could get the ball anywhere he wanted it, would only get it to the players who performed on the other end of the floor. It was effective. But it was tough, too. College had been a big change for Kivisto, and this became a demand

Roger Morningstar averaged in double figures on conference championship teams in 1974 and 1975.

for even greater sacrifice. Every player wants to score points, and Kivisto, who knew it was only way Kansas could succeed, gave up part of his game.

"I took on a role that was absolutely different than what I grew up in," Kivisto said. "I took on a role where I looked for the shot absolutely last and only because what it did was it instilled discipline with all the other players. They knew I was going to give up the shot and sacrifice all that for them, for those who worked hard.

"That senior year I was criticized a lot for not shooting enough, but we had a standing rule: I would look to pass. I would look to give the ball off rather than shoot, and I demanded certain things from them on hustle and defense. It was a deal we made. And as we got lucky and developed some early wins, which really helped, I think we caught some teams by surprise, and they weren't really ready for the type of game we played and just what we were trying to do with the discipline we had when in the other years we had zilch."

Kivisto described Dale Greenlee and Roger Morningstar as "probably as good as any long three-point shooters today." Tommie Smith and Rick Suttle did not start but gave the team an entirely different look when put in the game. Kivisto explained that it was a passing-game offense with Smith and Suttle in the game "but when they were on the bench we went to the workaholic offense."

Everyone picked Kansas as a second-division team but Kivisto proved that he meant to run the offense his way on December 29, 1973, in the Big Eight Holiday Tournament when he handed out a school-record 18 assists. The Jayhawks, suddenly playing with some confidence, then traveled to Iowa City, for a key inter-sectional game.

"This game is what made our season," Kivisto said. "Winning on the road proved to our people that it took more than talent to win basketball games. The work ethic and great attitude and great chemistry could produce miracles, that the whole becomes better than the sum of its parts."

"[In 1972] we were 7-0 at home and 0-7 on the road," said Kivisto. "Without chemistry, you don't have enough character on the team to win the tough road games. We had a philosophy that we were not going to win on the road. That was just on everybody's mind.

"But when we beat Iowa at Iowa, a Big Ten school on their home floor, we got to thinking that we could rise above this deal. It's not that the feeling is right or wrong or justified or not justified. If

Coach Owens took the 1970-1971 team to the NCAA tournament.

you feel that way, it's reality, and the players really felt that way."

Ted Owens echoed Kivisto's opinion. "What Tommy said is true," said Owens. "We had not won a big game on the road. So we go into Big Ten country and Iowa had a very good team, and we won I think on a tip-in at the last.

"That team could have swung either way. We had come off the bad season in '73. That game really turned it around."

Kivisto said the road woes crept into play at home. The team could not even play relaxed in Allen Field House because they knew a road game loomed a few days away. A 72-71 victory at Iowa—Kivisto recalled that Danny Knight, who had 23 points in the game, scored the winning basket in the final 15 seconds of the game—started one of the great turnarounds in college basketball history.

"We recognized that we were lacking in ability but not lacking in heart, and one road game led to another success and another success and you also get a little lucky," Kivisto said. "Had we not won that game in Iowa, we may have had a different season.

"I think the key there is that after winning two games on the road, we needed to prove to ourselves that we could win. I think in our own minds we were wanting to break the [streak]. We had the confidence to know that if you're ever going to do it, now was the time to do it. Because in those days you didn't get an [at-large] berth to the NCAA like you do today, you had to outright win the conference. Those road games became extremely important."

Kansas won its first three conference games and then was host to number-one ranked Notre Dame in a continuation of a high-profile series started by Owens and Fighting Irish Coach Johnny Dee. Rick Suttle had 23 points in the game, but the Irish won, 76-74. Even with the loss, the Jayhawks knew they could play with any team in the country.

"We just work-horsed some people and played a tough man-to-man," said Kivisto. "We had kind of a slow-down offense, but we didn't really try to get it down the court very much. It was really an interesting year for us. We just kind of decided that we were going to play for fun and just play hard and we all knew each other and we had a certain respect for each other because mostly we were all Illinois kids. Of the seven players who played, six were from Illinois and Danny fit in because nobody worked any harder than Danny Knight."

The hard work made the Jayhawks very competitive, and often victorious,

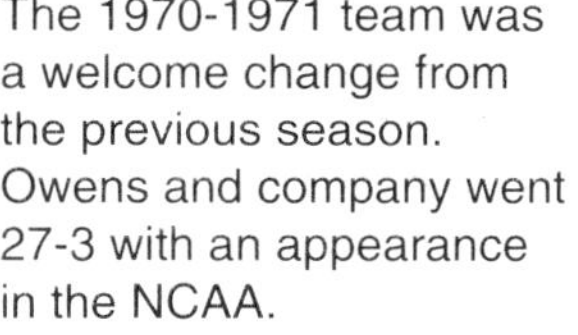

The 1970-1971 team was a welcome change from the previous season. Owens and company went 27-3 with an appearance in the NCAA.

in an exciting fashion. KU trailed Oklahoma by five with 1:25 to play but rallied for a four-point victory as Suttle finished with 31 points. Against Colorado, Norm Cook drilled a 22-footer with 25 seconds left for a 70-68 victory. Six of the 14 conference games were decided by four or fewer points.

The victory at Colorado allowed the Jayhawks to claim a one-half game lead over Kansas State in the league race, with the Wildcats due to visit Lawrence for the next game.

Kansas State jumped out to a 16-4 lead, but Kansas rallied for a 32-20 advantage at the half. Kansas State threatened at 38-35, but Greenlee and Kivisto led a 10-point burst. Suttle had 17 points, 11 rebounds, and eight blocked shots. Greenlee accounted for 16 points and 10 rebounds. Kansas won, 60-55, and claimed another championship trophy.

The cliffhanger nature of the team continued in the NCAA Tournament. After a 21-5 regular season allowed Kansas a first-round bye, the bracket paired the Jayhawks against Creighton, coached by Eddie Sutton.

KU trailed 50-45 with 7:14 to play but took the lead at 53-52 after a Rick Suttle basket and three Roger Morningstar jumpers. Tommie Smith stole a pass, and Kansas stalled until the 1:59

mark. Creighton got the ball back and scored, but Tom Kivisto tossed up one of those patented lobs for Smith, who tipped it in for the 55-54 victory.

In the regional finals, Kansas was down by nine with 4:49 to go against Oral Roberts but scored seven straight points in the final three minutes for an 81-81 tie, an eventual 93-90 victory in overtime.

"After we beat Creighton by just a few points, we watched the game to watch Louisville to find out all the things that they do," Owens said, adding that he figured to play the Cardinals. "But of course Oral Roberts upset them.

"We played them and it was the screwiest game you've ever seen," said Owens. "We jump out and are letter perfect the first few minutes of the game. They were fronting our post players and we were clearing the side and lobbing in to Knight and Suttle, just killing them.

"So we were up 20-5 and it looked like we were really going to bomb them good. But they were too good for that. They came back, and the fact is they moved up nine points on us with three minutes to go. What we did was we hit our last five shots down the stretch and sent the game into overtime. And then we beat them in overtime on their own floor."

Danny Knight, left, a 6-10 center, and Norm Cook, a 6-8 forward, combined to help the Jayhawks to conference championships in 1974 and 1975.

Kansas earned a return trip to the Final Four, the Jayhawks' sixth trip. But, according to Kivisto, instead of being one of the favorites, there was no doubt that Kansas had the fourth-best team in a four-team race.

Marquette, the Jayhawks' semifinal opponent, was anchored by Maurice Lucus, Maurice Ellis, and Lloyd "Speedy" Walton. The other semifinal pitted UCLA—including Marques Johnson, Dave Meyers, Keith Wilkes, Richard Washington, and Bill Walton—against North Carolina State, with Tom Burleson and David Thompson. Those players represented enough All-America certificates to paper the arena in Greensboro, North Carolina. And Kansas barely placed Kivisto on the all-conference team.

"We were a team that believed in one game at a time," Kivisto said. "We could take on anybody who wanted to come, one game at a time, but we knew that we weren't real talented. We knew that we didn't have a lot of great athletes and we knew that we got there through hard work and a little bit of luck.

"Once we got to the Final Four and when we looked at the teams that were there, they were all pretty talented. It was as talented a Final Four group, with the exception of our team, as there ever was in a Final Four. There was the classic semifinal match between UCLA and North Carolina State, a double overtime. There were like three or four college first team All-Americans on that floor at the same time. There was a lot of great talent.

"We did not have an over-powering team," said Ted Owens. "All we were was about seven guys who could score and we had a great leader in Tom Kivisto.

"We did not have a lot of other ball handlers except Tom Kivisto, so what they did was full-court pressed and trapped him. It was good strategy on their part. They trapped him and took the ball out of his hands and put the press of ball handling on other people.

"I remember [Marquette Coach Al] McGuire made the statement you cut off the head and the body dies. That's what they did, they tried to cut off the head. The game was tied at halftime, but their press bothered us in the second half and we went on to lose the game."

Kansas also lost the third-place game, adding a 78-61 defeat by UCLA to the 64-51 semifinal loss to Marquette. The Jayhawks ended the season 23-7. Unlike the previous season, KU did not let the close games get away. Of the seven losses, three were by three points or less and the others were all greater than 10-point differences.

Kansas had two Final Four teams in four seasons, but finished 19-33 in the two losing seasons in between. The 1974 Jayhawks never had illusions of being a great team. It was more just seven guys working hard because winning was more fun than losing. And the coaching staff gave the players all the lead they wanted.

"All the success that happened that year was the confidence the coaches gave us to go do our own thing," said Kivisto. "That is really unique because they were under a lot of pressure. They knew things weren't working. They came off two extremely poor years after having a great '71 year where people got spoiled and they had expectations and got impatient. There was a lot of pressure on them.

"Yet, the thing that I admire about those coaches, they allowed us to dictate a lot of what we were going to be doing. They had the confidence in us to let us do that.

"And they saw it work. Maybe had we come out and been unlucky a couple games and not played very well, they would have put a kibosh to it. But they saw the players were working so hard and the work ethic was there that had not been there for two or three years before that, that they decided to not try to derail things just through an ego.

"I really admire them for that because it would have been easy for them because what coaches normally want to do is control every situation. If I was in their situation as a coach I'm not sure I would have done that knowing what had happened the previous years."

METRO
CO
CATIO

Growing Expectations

While two Final Four teams in four seasons is a great positive to a program, the feat tends to breed expectations of the highest order. And the only thing worse than unfulfilled potential is unwarranted high expectations.

The success of the 1974 Jayhawks can be directly linked to the fact that point guard Tom Kivisto played his coach-on-the-floor role so well. The son of a basketball coach and a player of no mean talent, Kivisto had the knowledge and ability to take a hard-working team further than perhaps it should have gone.

But the nature of college basketball is transience. A player's tenure is limited by legislation. And Kivisto graduated after the 1974 season.

"When I say we only lost Kivisto, that's like the San Francisco 49ers saying, 'We only lost Joe Montana,'" said KU Coach Ted Owens. "It was remarkable to come off the record we had in 1973 and go to the national finals in 1974. We had all of the players back except Tom Kivisto, so all of our efforts in recruiting were to try to fill that void. We never did quite do that. As a consequence we didn't have the dominant leadership that we had had in previous years.

"The expectation level was unbelievable. People would say, 'Well, you were in the Final Four and you only lost one player, that's automatic Final Four again.' It's not quite that easy."

Recruiting is an inexact science. Sometimes, while busy searching for an obvious need, coaches find a player on their doorstep who turns out to be a mainstay. While Owens and his staff sought a replacement at point guard, they had to do very little selling to convince Kansas native Ken Koenigs where to attend school and play basketball.

"In the final analysis, I'd always been a KU man," Koenigs said. "My father went to KU. We'd always go to KU basketball games. I tried to approach it more objectively and see which school had more to offer. Some of it was that KU had more of what I was looking for academically. I always knew that if I wasn't a basketball player I was going to KU. Ted [Owens] made a very good impression on me and my family. He's a good person."

Koenigs broke his four years at Kansas into "three very distinct periods," with the first being his initial taste of major-college basketball.

"As a freshman you are totally intimidated with the way the game is being played," he said. "We were joining a team that had gone to the Final Four the year before and with [Rick] Suttle and [Danny] Knight—Kivisto was gone—but it was a team that had very high expectations."

Owens had put together a strong non-conference schedule that included Indiana, the number-one team 1974-1975 season, and Notre Dame, which finished 1974 rated fourth, and Kentucky, which finished 1975 fourth. The Jayhawks split their first eight games—losing to the name teams—but posted some thrills along the way.

In 1973, the NCAA allowed freshmen to participate in varsity games so in the 1974-1975 season, Ken Koenigs took his place on the Kansas bench.

"Probably one of *THE* best games I ever participated in—although I just sat there and watched—was the Indiana game. It was just before Indiana began its string of about 30 straight and went on to win the national championship the following year. It was just an unbelievable game."

Tommie Smith played one of his best games as Kansas forced Indiana into overtime before bowing 74-70. The games at Notre Dame, a 16-point loss, and Kentucky, a 27-point defeat, were not as thrilling.

Kansas took the Big Eight Holiday Tournament title, winning one-point decisions over Nebraska, 63-62, in the semifinals and Iowa State, 76-75, in the championship game. The tight nature of those games indicated just how close the league race expected to be.

The Jayhawks lost Big Eight games at Iowa State, Kansas State and Missouri but still found themselves among the league leaders as the schedule wound

down to its final four games.

Kansas State owned a one-game lead after the first 10 games of the league schedule, standing 8-2 heading into the February 22 game with KU. The Wildcats had won at home 66-56, and if the Kansas team felt the underdog role, the student body did its part to lift the Jayhawks out of that. Many students camped out through a frosty winter night to make sure they got the best seats when the field house doors opened the next day.

"We came in to shoot some free throws and kids were waiting out in the snow," Owens said. "You just can't let them down. That meant a lot to us."

The Jayhawks, with the faith of the students behind them and their Big Eight Conference hopes riding on the game, roared to a 12-4 lead. Rick Suttle scored 26 points, and Norm Cook had 13 rebounds while Kansas as a team shot 52 percent en route to a 91-53 romp. The 38-point differential tied a 50-12 Kansas victory in 1908 as the most-lopsided in more than 220 games of the series with the Wildcats.

"That game ranked as one of the three or four greatest efforts in my career," said Owens.

After KU slipped past Colorado 78-76 in Boulder in its next game, Owens was handed another game to remember at Nebraska. Kansas and Kansas State were tied for the league lead, with Missouri a game back and Nebraska still within striking distance. The four lead-ers were paired off for the next-to-last Big Eight game, with KU at Lincoln for the final game that year in the Coliseum. The Cornhuskers were going to abandon the building, which had been their home for 50 years, after the following season.

"We were, I thought, really ready to play. They had a great crowd in their old coliseum," Owens said. "Unfortunately, by the time I sat down we were behind by 19, so what followed was the greatest comeback of any team I've ever been associated with.

"We're 19 down. We tried to get them to stay calm and not panic and we cut it to 12 at halftime. We talked to them about things you talk to them about: That it's not impossible; that 12 points is just six possessions.

"In the second half we just kind of whittled away and whittled away. And with 40 seconds to go in the game, we're still five down. Rick Suttle goes to the free-throw line and makes his first one. We call time out. We substituted two big guys Danny Knight and Norman Cook. And we told Rick to bank it off the backboard but to be sure to hit the rim. When we told him to miss the free throw he looked at us like we were nuts."

The strategy was sound. The Big Eight experimented with the 30-second shot clock that season, but there was no three-point goal. Even if Suttle made the free throw, at best Kansas would be down three points with time enough for

Above, left: The 1974 Jayhawks made it to the Final Four for the fifth time in Kansas history with the assistance of Rick Suttle, center, Norm Cook, left, and Roger Morningstar, right, all of whom were returning starters in the 1974-1975 season.
Right: Ted Owens is the second winningest coach in Kansas history, compiling a 348-182 record in 19 years at KU.

The 1974-1975 season saw the Jayhawks capture another conference title as 6-10 center Rick Suttle led the team with a 14.6 scoring average.

just one possession since Nebraska had a good ball-handling team.

Owens continued, "Suttle did it perfectly. He hit the backboard and hit the rim and Norman Cook jumped up and grabbed it and stuck it back in. We had a little deal if you were trying to get in the lane, neat little ways, sophisticated moves to get free in the lane. So Norman Cook stepped into the lane and grabbed it and put it back up and now we're only down by two with 37 seconds to go.

"Good fortune happened to us and they charged us with 17 seconds to go. We go to Rick Suttle. He shoots it in, ties the game, and sends it into overtime."

Kansas trainer Dean Nesmith learned that Missouri upset Kansas State, meaning Kansas could clinch a conference title by beating the Cornhuskers. Nesmith told Owens but the coach withheld the news from the

players, instead telling them they needed to win for a shot at the Big Eight crown.

It still took two overtimes before Kansas claimed a 79-77 victory by consistently going inside to Suttle, who amassed 29 points and 16 rebounds, and Knight, who scored four points in the second overtime.

Kansas took the outright Big Eight championship with a 74-63 victory over Oklahoma, earning all-conference honors for Suttle and an NCAA Tournament berth in the process.

KU drew a rematch with Notre Dame in the first round of the tournament and, while the game did not end up in a 16-point rout like the first meeting, the Fighting Irish still eliminated the Jayhawks with a 77-71 decision.

Recalled Owens, "We fouled out six players. Unbelievable. I'll never forget who was calling the game. We fouled out six guys. That's hard to do."

Donnie Von Moore, Norm Cook, Clint Johnson, Dale Greenlee, Tommie Smith, and Milt Gibson each fouled out. The officiating team of Mickey Crowley and Sturdy Wanamaker called 39 fouls on Kansas and 19 on Notre Dame. The Irish connected on 35 of 50 free throws.

"Their big guy was Adrian Dantley," said Owens. "They had us down 11 but we came back and tied the game. Digger [Phelps, the Notre Dame coach] went to four corners with seven minutes to go and we couldn't handle Dantley. We probably spread out a little more than we should have that early in the game, but the foul trouble finally got to us."

Rick Suttle, Danny Knight, Tommie Smith, Dale Greenlee, and Roger Morningstar all played their final game for KU against Notre Dame. Replacing five men is no small chore but Coach Ted Owens suddenly had to find even more players since Donnie Von Moore came down with pneumonia and missed the season and Reuben Shelton suffered what was termed a "mysterious" gunshot wound in his leg and underwent surgery at midseason.

Even the players available weren't all healthy. Freshman center Paul Mokeski suffered an early season muscle tear and played heavily bandaged.

And at least one healthy player—Norm Cook—was being wooed to turn professional.

"We had practically all seniors," said Owens, "so we lost them. And Norm Cook, the pros started to try to get him to leave. He had played in the Pan American tryouts and made the Pan Am team. The Utah Stars really did get involved, offered him a lot of money and that sort of thing.

"He made a decision to come back to school, but I think even though he made the decision to come back, he always wondered if he made the right decision because here's a youngster from a background where he never had any money. He just never regained the kind of confidence and form that he had had in the previous years. And we didn't have the talent surrounding Norman that we had the previous year."

Cook, distracted or not, averaged a team-high 14.8 points a game in a balanced attack. He also made all-conference.

Owens, according to Ken Koenigs, had Kansas going through a transition. Where his teams had been big-man oriented, Owens wanted the Jayhawks to start to push the ball a little more.

"The system changed a little bit," said Koenigs. "There was a transition coming about in the Big Eight. Some of [Owens'] glory days were in the era where the big man dominated with the halfcourt game. But the Big Eight became so much more up-tempo and the game changed all over the country.

"I think we were actually a transition type of team in that way. Our scoring margin and our point production were fairly high. Actually as far as a breaking team and things like that we were pretty effective with [Darnell] Valentine and John [Douglas] and some of the others."

But Valentine and Douglas were still at other schools in 1976. The move from half-court to an up-tempo game became a tough development.

The 1975-1976 season was a heartbreaker for Owens and the Jayhawkers. KU lost five games by three points or less and three times had victories snatched away by last-second shots. One of the most heart-breaking of those losses came at home to Missouri when guard Willie Smith somehow out-jumped a pack of Jayhawks and tipped in a shot at the buzzer for a 61-60 Tigers victory. That

set off a four-game Kansas losing streak and only a season-ending 55-50 triumph at Oklahoma allowed KU to avoid a losing record at 13-13. The Jayhawks had a 6-8 Big Eight mark and tied Oklahoma for fourth.

The rebuilding continued during the 1976-1977 season, and by late 1976, Owens had put together another talented batch of players.

"Our starting lineup," said Owens, "was Koenigs and Mokeski at the two pivot positions backed up by Donnie Von Moore, who was a good player. We had Clint Johnson, Herb Nobles, and John Douglas, who transferred out of junior college. That was really a good team, plus in Wilmore Fowler and Milt Gibson, we had two other good back court players.

"We were very active. We had big

Ken Koenigs, a 6-10 center, was named All-Big Eight Conference in 1978 and academic All-America in 1977 and 1978.

post players and we had a lot of guys in the 6-1, 6-2 range, who could just fly. That was a great fast-break team. [Former UCLA Coach] John Wooden announced one of our televised games and called it the finest fast-break team that he had seen all year."

Douglas, the junior-college transfer, quickly established himself as a scorer and averaged 19.2 points a game en route to a Big Eight Newcomer of the Year award and selection to the all-

John Douglas, a 6-2 guard, averaged 19.2 points in helping the Jayhawks to an 18-10 record in 1976-1977.

conference team.

The Jayhawks posted a healthy 9-2 record going into the finals of the conference Christmas tournament, where they dropped a 69-65 decision to Missouri.

Kansas went 6-3 during the first part of the Big Eight schedule, then headed to Missouri. Douglas poured in 34 points, including 26 in the second half, but KU still lost 87-79 as the Tigers' Kim Anderson had a 38-point game.

The Jayhawks had a shot at the conference title provided they could get past league-leading Kansas State. The score was tied 83-83 late in the game, and KU had the ball out of bounds. Koenigs handled the throw-in, but had trouble finding an open teammate. Rather than risk a five-second violation, Koenigs asked for a time out. But Kansas had used all of its time outs and Koenigs was assessed a technical foul. Curtis Redding made the tie-breaking free throw, and the Wildcats added a basket on the ensuing possession for the 86-83 victory.

At an Iowa State game, Douglas helped Kansas break out of the slump with a 46-point effort—matching the third-highest game point total in school history. It took a Cris Barnthouse tip-in at the buzzer for the 91-89 overtime victory.

With the expansion of the NCAA Tournament, Big Eight Conference officials sought a way to grab the attention of the committee that selected teams for the event. What they came up with was a post-season tournament, which began after the 1976-1977 regular season.

Kansas hosted Nebraska for a first-round game and won 61-58 to move on to Kansas City for a semifinal match with league champion Kansas State, which had beaten KU twice in the regular season after dropping a preseason tournament semifinal to the Jayhawks. The fourth time the arch-rivals met that season also went to K-State, 80-67. Missouri, also 2-1 versus Kansas, was defeated by Kansas State in overtime, 72-67. The NCAA invited only the Wildcats to the tournament.

The Jayhawks knew there would be no postseason for them, since their 18-10 record was not good enough to be considered for the 32-team NCAA field.

"We were trying to rebuild," said Owens. "When you have a down year or so in recruiting, it takes a while to rebuild. We were in the process of doing that and finally did get that process completed in '78."

A key piece to Owens' rebuilding was a point guard. When Owens found Darnell Valentine, who led Wichita Heights to the state high school title the season before, he found a guard of the highest caliber.

"Darnell was one of those unusual freshmen," said Koenigs. "He was confident but not overly cocky. He was really the man who made that team go. The addition of him to the rest of the people we had really complemented things. He really played an extraordinary role. He was what they call an impact player."

Owens said, "Although they were different, Valentine had some of the same qualities that JoJo [White] did. First of all, they were both enormous workers. Valentine was a tremendous worker. And he not only dominated a game offensively, he really dominated it defensively. He had as beautiful a defensive base as I've ever seen.

"He was such a competitive guy that he, like most players who want to win so badly, sometimes he tried to beat the competition by himself. He grew from that and by his senior year became a player who made his teammates a lot better. That's what JoJo did. JoJo made his teammates better players."

With a freshman playing point guard, Kansas started the year far from the role of the Big Eight favorite.

"We were not even picked in the top three or four in the league that year. We had just come off a so-so year," said Owens. "Kansas State was heavily favored to win the league. They had a great team. They had Rolando Blackman and Curtis Redding, out of New York who was an excellent player, and a backcourt player, Mike Evans. They had a terrific basketball team and they were favored heavily to win the league."

The Wildcats pleased the prognosticators by winning their first six games while Kansas surprised the same predictors with a 7-2 start. The only losses in that run were to number-one ranked Kentucky, 73-66, and at Arkansas, 78-72, against a team that ended up rated sixth in the country.

The Kansas schools each won their first-round games in the Big Eight Holiday Tournament, setting up the first of four battles between the Jayhawks and Wildcats. KU trailed by 12 points at the half before rallying for a 67-62 victory using 20 points from the tournament's most valuable player, Donnie Von Moore.

The arch-rivals' regular-season games were even more spirited than usual. When the Wildcats visited Lawrence, with both teams unbeaten in Big Eight play, a rain of hot dogs greeted the introduction of K-State's Curtis Redding, who exhibited more than a little flamboyance in his style of play. The Jayhawks came away with a 56-52 victory.

KU lost at Nebraska in the next game. Kansas got back to winning, however, and did not suffer another conference loss in the remaining season.

As an answer to the hot-dog bombardment in Lawrence, Kansas State students came up with a dig of their own. Several students showed up in monkey suits and, during the Kansas introductions, pelted the court with bananas and chickens, which had been painted blue. The game was delayed more than 20 minutes while the fruit and fowl was cleaned off the floor.

The fans' actions didn't help the Wildcats team during the Jayhawks' visit in 1978, and Kansas rode the 75-63 victory to a 13-1 Big Eight Conference record, which marked the fourth league title of the Owens era and the 35th since the Jayhawks began league play in 1908.

Kansas improved to 24-3 by dis-

Coach Ted Owens' courtside style was as competitive as KU basketball.

Darnell Valentine, 1978 Big Eight Newcomer of the Year, helped KU to its 35th league championship.

patching Colorado, 82-66, in the first round of the Big Eight Tournament only to run into an all-too familiar foe.

"We beat Kansas State three times," said Owens, "beat them in the [holiday] tournament and beat them two other times. Kansas State finished fourth, they had a very disappointing year for them [18-11]."

"Everything was laid out perfectly for us. All we had to do was win the Big Eight tournament and the first-round game would have been in Wichita and the regional in Allen Field House and then the finals in St. Louis. If there was ever a situation laid out perfectly from a geographic standpoint, from the standpoint of having great fan support, it was that year."

Kansas State had other plans. "They just put a wonderful game together, which they were capable of doing," said Owens. "And we just did not have a great game. We lost, and it was one of those things that you've beaten them three times. It's just tough to beat a good team four times in a year."

The Jayhawks developed into such a good team that, even after the 87-76 K-State loss, they expected to do well in the NCAA Tournament.

"I honestly don't think that we had a cohesiveness as a group as maybe when Darnell came," said Koenigs. "That was probably the most cohesive year. We all got along very well together. This was a team that could have gone far."

The NCAA sorted its bracket differently then. The men's basketball committee placed more weight on winning a conference's automatic berth and even if a team—such as Kansas—had a great record—such as 24-4—it wasn't likely to get many breaks.

"We walked through the Big Eight. We lost that one league game and we lost in the Big Eight Tournament," recalled Koenigs. "Had it been set up the way things are now, we probably would have gotten a Midwest [regional], which was actually in Lawrence, but because then we got knocked out by K-State, we ended up going out west."

"Missouri [which beat Kansas State in the Big Eight Tournament final] had a 14-15 record and they sent them to Wichita and they sent us to the West Coast," said Owens. "Five of the top 10 teams in the country were in the Western Regional—UCLA, Arkansas, North Carolina, New Mexico, and us. It was loaded with great teams."

What Koenigs and most of the people in the Midwest remember about the UCLA game at Eugene, Oregon, was that Curt Gowdy, who was broadcasting the game, mispronounced many of the Kansas players' names in the 83-76 defeat.

"But it was a great year," Owens said. "I think the '78 team and probably the '66 team, even though they didn't make the finals, they were every bit as good as the Final Four teams those years. They were teams, in my opinion, that had a legitimate chance to win the national championship because they were good, and the other thing is because nobody had a [Kareem Abdul] Jabbar or [Bill] Walton at that time."

Koenigs' career at Kansas ended in Eugene. He was never a threat to finish as the all-time leading scorer on the basketball floor, but he was a leader in other ways, such as hard work. And anyone would be pressed to improve on his grade-point average.

"My four years was a great experience," said Koenigs, who along with Darnell Valentine made all-conference in 1978. "Everybody was working for the same goals, we had a fair amount of talent and everything clicked. My career ended on a high note, no doubt about it."

Aside from success on the basketball floor, Koenigs, an academic All-American, bridged a time between two other academic All-Americans in Cris Barnthouse and Darnell Valentine. Barnthouse and Koenigs became medical doctors while Valentine went to the NBA.

"I have told the story of Ken Koenigs many times," Owens said. "Here is a guy who was just so organized that he was a four-point student, he was captain of his basketball team and yet he seemed to enjoy a fairly normal social life. He was just so organized. He was a great leader and a great example.

"The thing I'm really proud of, we graduated players. They ran a poll at one time and I'm not sure that it covered all my time there but it covered maybe a 10-year period that they were checking graduation rates and we graduated over 90 percent of our guys."

One of Owens' problems was that every so often players graduated in bunches. Koenigs, Clint Johnson, Donnie Von Moore, Milt Gibson, and John Douglas all had been seniors in 1978.

"We had Valentine back and we had Paul Mokeski back, who was a senior, and then we'd had a good recruiting year," recalled Owens. "We had Tony Guy and David Magley, who were pretty highly touted young men. So they came in along with Mark Snow.

"But any time you're expecting a lot of freshmen to make a dramatic difference in your team, you're going to be disappointed. Valentine was an unusually mature freshman when he came in, and he was surrounded by a veteran cast so it made his job a lot easier.

"Now, all of a sudden he has to carry more of a load and Mokeski has to carry more of a load. Douglas and Johnson and Koenigs and Von Moore and Milt Gibson were good basketball players. We'd lost a ton and to expect some freshmen to take over was probably not reasonable."

The first thing any staff tries to instill in its players is confidence. Ted Owens had the perfect vehicle for that when he took the Jayhawks to Kentucky, which was coming off an NCAA Tournament championship. Kansas played exceedingly well and had a six-point lead with 40 seconds to play. Enter what Owens called "the most bizarre circumstance you can imagine."

Kentucky had trouble with Kansas' zone defense throughout the game, but scored on a late possession to make it a four-point game. With 16 seconds left, Kansas, having missed at the free-throw line, fouled Kentucky's Dwight Anderson. The Wildcats' player also missed. KU failed to block the shooter, and Anderson grabbed the ball and was fouled again.

That was the fifth foul on Paul Mokeski. This time Anderson made both

Darnell Valentine became every coach's dream, a dominant offensive and defensive player who was a team player and Academic All-America. He was named all-conference in 1978, 1979, 1980, and 1981. He was named All-America in 1981.

Tony Guy was a three-year starter for the Jayhawks from 1979-1982. He averaged a team-high 15.8 points as a junior in 1981.

they won the game."

"You drill and you drill and drill to instinctively with a few seconds to go call time out. Or like in Ken Koenig's case when he had the ball out of bounds and they count, you've got to take the time out. This time it wasn't one of our players. Three or four of them held up their hands to call a time out."

A very young Kansas team had come very close to beating a good Kentucky team in Lexington, Kentucky. Perhaps too close.

Owens said, "It was an absolutely devastating loss. They just sobbed in the dressing room for 30 minutes after that. I couldn't find the words to get them out of it. We were all devastated. What had looked like one of the great victories in Kansas history over a really good Kentucky team ended in a terrible defeat.

"That really hung on with that young team. I don't think that if it had happened to a veteran team, it would have been quite as bad, but we had a couple of freshmen in the lineup, a couple sophomores and maybe one senior. It was a tough loss and I think it had a lot to do with the losses later in the year. I just don't think there was that confidence factor. I just think there were too many young people and sort of the shadow of that earlier loss as Kentucky kind of was a blow to their confidence. "It was a killer to our team."

Kansas finished 18-11, with seven of the losses by two points or less lost in overtime.

The Jayhawks did walk away with the championship trophy in the final Big Eight Holiday Tournament, but none of those games were really close. KU posted an 8-6 Big Eight record and tied four teams for second place before advancing to the post-season tournament final, where an 80-65 defeat by Oklahoma ended the season.

A pattern to the Owens-coached teams had developed. One year after great success the team suffered a slight back-slide and two years after the really good team, KU bottomed out. The 1979-1980 season represented the depths of one of those valleys.

There was another pattern in that the cause of the valleys alternated between the need for a point guard and the need for a strong player in the middle.

free throws and Kentucky crept within two points.

"That was with 10 seconds to go," Owens said. "We call time out. Incidentally, we told them that we were out of time outs. We take the ball out and we were going to run a play that we called 'Crucial Special.' They were double-teaming Valentine, trying to keep the ball out of his hands. So we faked a screen on Valentine and rolled right back to the ball. All we needed to do was to get possession of the ball.

"So the guy who replaced Mokeski instead of rolling straight to the ball, rolled kind of to the sidelines and Anderson gets his hands on it and throws it back into the court where their great little guard, Kyle Macy, grabs the ball and shoots with one or two seconds to go and makes it.

"Our guys instinctively call time out. We don't have any time outs. Macy goes to the line and hits the technical foul and

"We still had [David] Magley and we still had Tony Guy," Owens recalled, trying to reconstruct the lineup for Darnell Valentine's junior season." It was also Kelly Knight's freshman year.

"We never quite filled out, we didn't have the kind of strong pivot play," said Owens. "We lost [Paul] Mokeski. As a matter of fact, Kelly Knight at the end of the year came on and became our pivot man but he was just a freshman and only 6-7. We had fairly good perimeter play but didn't have a good inside game."

The Jayhawks' season had more ups and downs than the Flint Hills. There were two three-game winning streaks, but also two three-game losing streaks. A late-season surge resulted in five victories in seven games and a 15-14 record.

The Jayhawks, with Knight growing into the center's role, showed improvement. An 84-74 overtime victory against Oklahoma State earned KU a first-round home-court berth in the Big Eight Tournament. Kansas defeated Colorado, 75-65, and dispatched league-champion Missouri 80-71 in the semifinals. But Kansas State, which had a 24-9 record that season, ran away with a 79-58 victory in the title game.

Some of Ted Owens' weakest seasons heralded big years the following season. KU went 8-18 in 1972-1973, but went to the Final Four in 1974. A 13-13 record took two years to develop into 1978's 24-5 mark with a team Owens' considered one of his best. Under Owens, the Kansas basketball program lived the "darkest just before the dawn" adage.

The trend prevailed enough to make the Jayhawks look forward to 1981. Darnell Valentine returned for his senior year. He earned All-America acclaim and collected a fourth all-conference honor. Tony Guy, David Magley, John Crawford, and Victor Mitchell were also named to conference teams.

The Jayhawks won their first four league games but slumped in losing four out of five. After a loss in Boulder, Colorado, KU closed the regular season with 26- and 15-point victories over Nebraska and Oklahoma State, respectively, to pull into a three-way tie for second, one game behind Big Eight champion Missouri.

Kansas drew Oklahoma State in the first round of the Big Eight Tournament and posted a more lopsided triumph—96-69. That decision qualified KU for the Big Eight semifinals with Missouri, Kansas State, and Colorado, which had upset Nebraska in the first round.

Coach Ted Owens recalled how well his team played down the stretch, calling the 75-70 victory over Missouri and the 80-68 triumph over Kansas State "two almost perfectly played games."

"The Big Eight had some excellent basketball teams that year," Owens said. "Missouri had Stipanovich and Sundvold, and Kansas State had a really good team. They had just a wonderfully balanced basketball team.

"And we beat Kansas State and Missouri with two almost perfectly played games. In one of the greatest games that I've ever been associated with, we beat Kansas State in the Big Eight Tournament. If I remember right, both of us had less than five turnovers. Kansas State shot better than 50 percent in the game and we shot better than 60 percent in the game. It was just one of the most beautifully played games. I don't think I've had a team play better than we did in that tournament."

The 22-7 Jayhawks were in the

David Magley earned all-conference honors in 1982 as he led the team with a 17.3 scoring average.

KU beat Missouri in the 1981 Big Eight Conference tournament, 75-70.

the Wichita State Shockers.

"We hadn't played Wichita in 25 years," said Owens. When asked if that was on purpose, Owens replied, "Yeah, Kansas had, for the most part, decided that it was not in their best interest to play Wichita, for whatever reason. It was long before my time and of course it continued in my time.

"Oh, there's no question they were fired up, and Kansas over the years had not played them, so we catch them in New Orleans. It was just two good teams playing, each of them with a chance to make it to the Final Four."

Wichita State had a very good team that season. With Cliff Levingston and Antoine Carr, a teammate of Darnell Valentine's when they prepped at Wichita Heights, the Shockers had two of the best big men in the country.

Wichita State spent the five days from the sub-regional upset of Iowa until the Kansas game in New Orleans psyching up for the Jayhawks. "And the Wichita State game, it had one of those crazy endings," Owens said.

"It was one of those things that everything worked out perfectly. We were ahead by three with 50 seconds to go and we had Darnell Valentine at the free-throw line for a one and one. He's the guy you want at the free-throw line. But it rattled in and out.

"They came down and they were having trouble. We were zoning them because we couldn't match up with Levingston and Carr. They brought in a guy off the bench [Mike Jones] and he shot in a bomb with not too many seconds to go. They came back and pressed us and it looks liked they were going to stop us for 10 seconds in the back court when we call time out. We call a play to Valentine, but he got the ball too far under the basket and missed the layup. They get the ball and the guy hits another bomb."

Wichita State grabbed a 66-65 lead but Kansas still had a chance to win. Owens called for "Touchdown"—a play designed to go to Valentine where the guard gets the ball and either gets a good shot or gets fouled.

The coach continued, "It worked perfectly. We get the ball to Valentine and he just gets sprawled out. But they don't call the foul."

NCAA Tournament for the 13th time. The NCAA invited 48 teams that season, but none of the three Big Eight entries earned a higher seed than Kansas' number-seven berth, so all had to play first-round games. The Jayhawks drew Mississippi.

Said Owens, "We had Mississippi, the Southeastern Conference Tournament champions, and then we played Arizona State, who had just beaten the number one team in the country—Oregon State. Oregon State had been undefeated and [Arizona State] beat them in Corvallis, Oregon. They had a bye in the first round. We struggled and beat Mississippi [69-66], which had a good basketball team.

"Then we played Arizona State on national television and just killed them. Arizona State had Byron Scott and an absolutely fantastic team, big front line, great back court. But we played a great ballgame; in fact we had them down 20 at halftime. Tony Guy had a great game."

Kansas eliminated that team of Wildcats 88-71 while in the other second-round game in Wichita that day, third-seeded Iowa suffered a 60-56 upset by

112

Not many officials will call that foul at that stage of the game, and that crew went with the norm and signed off on a 66-65 Wichita State victory. The Shockers ran into fourth-ranked Louisiana State in the next round and were eliminated, 96-85.

Kansas went home with a 24-8 record. It marked the eighth season with at least 20 victories while Owens was the coach, but just the second over the last seven seasons.

The numbers earned Owens a two-year extension on the one year he had remaining on his contract.

The coach knew tough times lay ahead. The cycles spun against the Jayhawks. Darnell Valentine, a four-time all-conference choice and team most valuable player, a 1,821-point scorer and the first Kansas player to amass more than 600 assists, graduated. Again there was a big hole at the point.

Owen believed the contract extension gave him a chance to fill it.

The 1982 season started 9-2, with some impressive showings. But the league season, after KU went out 3-2, went sour under the heat produced by a string of seven losses in eight games. Kansas State stamped an end to the year with a 74-62 victory in the Big Eight Tournament. The Jayhawks went home with a 13-14 overall record after going 4-10—seventh place—in the conference.

The slump arrived earlier in 1983. At one time Kansas, which fielded a very young team, boasted a 7-2 record, but that mark showed more about the schedule than it did the Jayhawks. It had been a period of great experimentation as 12 players had been tested as starters. KU won just three of its next 14 games.

Kansas showed some signs of life, defeating three of its final five regular-season opponents and upsetting conference runner-up Oklahoma in the first round of the Big Eight Tournament. Oklahoma State ended Kansas' run in a 90-83 game, and the Jayhawks, who had finished 4-10 in the Big Eight for the second consecutive season, found themselves saddled with a second straight losing season, 13-16.

Owens went to work searching for additional players to join Kerry Boagni and Calvin Thompson, who each started in 1983 as freshmen. The good end—and the fact Greg Dreiling would be coming off a red-shirt season—gave him hope another turn in the cycle would hit next season.

However, over Spring break Owens was relieved of his coaching duties. Over 19 seasons, Owens compiled a 348-182 record. The Jayhawks won six Big Eight titles and had six other second-place conference finishes under the coach. Now Owens was told the school would honor the remaining year of his contract, but his services were no longer needed.

The 1983 season was Coach Owens' last as head coach of the Kansas Jayhawks.

"It was hard," Owens said. "We had some real opportunities to make a change. We worked so hard and had a great basketball team coming. When you have a couple of down recruiting years, it takes some time to get back.

"We had not done a very good job recruiting but we felt we could bring it back in three years. We had a poor year in '82 but in '83 we had a good team, but we were playing a bunch of freshmen and we'd red-shirted Greg Dreiling. We felt we had the foundation to rebuild back to where we were.

"It came as a complete shock. And it was very difficult."

Carolina Connection

Larry Brown played basketball for Dean Smith, from whom he received a dose of Kansas basketball tradition. So when Brown—then with the New Jersey Nets—heard that Kansas fired Ted Owens, he was immediately interested.

Brown called Smith and asked if he would put in a word of recommendation. Smith, after fending off an offer to take over the Jayhawks himself, did just that. Less than three weeks after Owens was let go, Brown accepted the position as head basketball coach at the University of Kansas.

Brown arrived on campus with a reputation as someone always looking to move on. In his five years in Lawrence he probably answered more questions about his alleged interest in vacant jobs than he heard, "How are you today?" The snide remarks about "Suitcase Larry" were a product of his own doing. Before accepting KU's coaching job, Brown had three other coaching positions—the Denver Rockets of the ABA, UCLA in the college ranks and the NBA's Nets—in four years. But he was a winner, and that is what made Brown so attractive to potential employers.

"He was trying to get us to play the way he wanted us to play," said Mark Turgeon, a freshman at Kansas in 1983-1984. "It was the way he coached his whole life—man-to-man pressure defense, push it, that type of thing.

"But my freshman year we didn't have that kind of team. We ended up playing zone probably 50 percent of the time. We had some good young players in that sophomore class in Calvin [Thompson] and Ronnie [Kellogg], but our backcourt was freshman, sophomore, sophomore. We had some older guys down low, but they weren't fleet of foot. So we played a lot of zone and didn't really run it up as much. We ran a lot of set plays for Carl [Henry] and Kelly [Knight], I remember."

For Mark Turgeon, the chance to play at Kansas was the realization of a childhood dream. He used to play mock games pitting Kansas against Notre Dame and took time to learn to imitate the Jayhawks players of the time such as Paul Mokeski, Ken Koenigs, and Clint Johnson. He idolized Darnell Valentine.

"I used to be Darnell," Turgeon said. "I used to try to shoot free throws like Darnell and do everything like Darnell. We had a puppy and we named it D.V."

The sweet dream was to be at Kansas; the reality wasn't all sweetness, however. The players soon learned that Larry Brown did not take well to losing at all. Trying to switch systems with the parts designed to run the Ted Owens style game did not result in an easy transition. Kansas lost two of its first five regular-season games, including a 91-76 thumping at Houston and a 72-50 setback at home against Kentucky.

"It was a big adjustment," Turgeon said. "We were 3-2 at one point and I remember having big, long meetings that year trying to figure out a way we were going to play."

Turgeon, asked if losses were tough on Brown, replied, "They were sure tough on us. I can't remember any games that we lost that the next day wasn't very, very difficult, except the games that ended the seasons for us. We lost 33 games in my career here. I would say I had 29 unbelievable practices and four [losses] ended the season.

"Coach Brown had a streak there for a while where he never lost two games in a row and that was part of the reason. My sophomore year we just got hammered at Michigan. We had team meetings and all kinds of things and then go to K-State that Wednesday. We played Michigan on a Sunday on national TV and went to K-State and beat them by 18. And it was never a game."

Brown's first season had other growing pains, too. Kerry Boagni transferred out, Cedric Hunter was ineligible for the opening of the conference season, and JoJo White, who had returned as an assistant coach under Ted Owens was let go.

On the court, however, things began to improve. Brown switched to zone play—he may not have liked it but that's the style for which he had the personnel—and the Jayhawks won more than they lost.

"At the start, if for no other reason,

fans came to see the highly emotional Brown pace the sidelines," the *Jayhawker* yearbook stated after the season. "Soon afterward, fans knew that Brown wasn't the only person worth watching."

The Jayhawks swept rivals Missouri and Kansas State but found new antagonists in the process. KU lost at Ames, Iowa, and Boulder, Colorado—places Brown-coached teams always seemed to have trouble—but only one team notched two victories against Kansas that season and ignited a heated rivalry at the same time.

"My freshman year is when the Billy Tubbs and Oklahoma and Kansas controversy kind of got started because they beat us here at home my freshman year to win the Big Eight championship," Turgeon said. "It was a really tight game and Calvin [Thompson] hit the shot at the buzzer to send it into overtime. Then they were up by four with like four seconds to go in overtime and [Tubbs] called time out. Coach Brown sent a player down there to tell him that the world is round, that we'd have another shot at them."

The messenger was Turgeon and he said he didn't want to go, but he delivered the mail anyway. About an answer from Tubbs, Turgeon diplomatically said, "I really can't remember, but it wasn't nice."

The Oklahoma players, who used a string of free throws at the end of the overtime to take a 92-82 victory and the Big Eight title, cut down the nets and gestured at the Kansas fans. The entire series stuck deep in Brown's craw.

"They humiliated us," Brown said after the February 22, 1984, game. "It got ugly."

The Jayhawks came back with a two-point victory over Kansas State before the loss at Boulder. They completed the regular season by beating Oklahoma State, 91-70, for a 9-5 Big Eight record and second place in the conference.

KU drew the Cowboys again for the first round of the league tournament and beat Kansas State for a third time that year to earn a rematch with Oklahoma, which had climbed into the Top 10 of the national rankings. This time it was the Jayhawks celebrating with a 79-78 victory over the Sooners.

"That was a big win for us when we beat Oklahoma in the Big Eight finals," said Turgeon. "It kind of put KU back on the map in the Big Eight because we'd struggled the last couple years. I think it was a sign of things to come. I think Oklahoma was like 29-3 when we beat them. It was a big game for us."

Kansas claimed another one-point game in the first round of the NCAA Tournament, but fell to fourth-seeded Wake Forest in the second. The Jayhawks went 22-10 for the season and Brown, who won 42 games in two years

Larry Brown was named head coach at Kansas in 1983. Brown credits much of his coaching philosophy to Dean Smith, a member of the Jayhawks' 1952 national championship team.

at UCLA, had his third collegiate 20-victory season.

"This team is not as athletically talented [as his UCLA squads]," Brown said after the season. "We're not a great team, but we play up to our potential every night. The style of play would shake you up. They shock me every day."

Brown had shocked the Kansas basketball establishment early in the season by dismissing JoJo White over what he described as "philosophical differences." White was replaced by Ed Manning, who was with Brown in the ABA. Manning happened to have a son who could play basketball a little. A link was immediately drawn, but it should be noted that Brown, four years after he left Kansas, still had Ed Manning on his

Ron Kellogg is regarded as one of the best long range shooters in KU history. He averaged 15.9 points in helping the Jayhawks to a Final Four appearance in 1986.

slowly, however, since Kansas had a nice group of seasoned players already on hand. Carl Henry, the only Jayhawk honored with all-conference accolades in 1984, was gone, but Ron Kellogg, Greg Dreiling, Calvin Thompson, and Cedric Hunter started around Manning, helping him earn the Big Eight Newcomer of the Year award.

The Jayhawks opened Big Eight play with a 76-72 victory over Iowa State to improve to 14-2 on the season. The losses came at Kentucky and to Alabama-Birmingham in the finals of the Great Alaska Shootout.

During the heart of the Big Eight season, Kellogg earned the nickname "Mr. Saturday" for his string of five consecutive Saturdays of 30-point games. That stretch allowed him to finish as the team scoring leader with a 17.6 average, three points better than the freshman Manning.

KU lost two of its next four games, dropping a decision at Oklahoma and getting beat 96-77 at Michigan. Turgeon said that game prompted several long meetings with Coach Brown.

The sessions with Brown put KU back on line for a five-game winning streak, but the Jayhawks, for one of only five times in the tenure of Larry Brown, had lost consecutive games to douse their chances of a Big Eight title. They closed with four regular-season victories, including a vital victory over the Sooners, but were 11-3 in the conference and two games off the Oklahoma pace.

The Big Eight Tournament ended in a semifinal 75-59 rout by Iowa State and even a trip to the NCAA Tournament was short, with 66-64 second-round loss to Auburn ending the 26-8 season.

Twenty-six victories, anchored by two all-conference selections in Kellogg and Manning, is a lot, but the season missed something.

"That was the most disappointing 26-8 year that you could possibly have," said Turgeon. "We didn't win the Big Eight. We lost in the Big Eight tournament in the second round. Greg [Dreiling] was sick, Ronnie [Kellogg] was sick and Calvin [Thompson] was sick. Everybody was sick and we lost to Iowa State and they just hammered us.

"Then we lose to an Auburn team that we should have beaten in the sec-

staff with the San Antonio Spurs.

Ed Manning's son was Danny Manning. The young player announced his intention to play at Kansas shortly after his father agreed to his new job. He was quiet, almost timid, off the court, but he could play basketball and he proved it all the time in pick-up games with the KU players.

"He was [withdrawn], but we all knew he was a player," said Turgeon. "We'd been watching him play, He'd play pick-up games with us. The thing about Danny is he knew that we had some good players in the program and he didn't want to come in and step on any toes.

"A lot of it had to do with him being too unselfish. There would be a lot of times I can remember in games I'd say, 'Danny, you've got to shoot. For us to win you have to shoot.'"

"He didn't know that he was great," said Coach Larry Brown. "He's not like a lot of players with his kind of ability. He's not self-confident."

Manning could be brought along

ond round of the tourney. That was a chance to get to the Sweet Sixteen, which would have been another step in the right direction for us."

Brown wasn't very pleased with it either and responded by instituting an off-season curfew.

"That is almost unheard of," Turgeon said. "We had a curfew until school ended that year, 11 or 12 o'clock, something like that. But it was just almost unheard of. He was just letting us know that we better get our stuff together and next year's going to be our year.

"I remember how mad we were about having that curfew. But it helped. It helped our grades and helped us get better. It helped us win a few games. We worked really hard that summer to get better because we knew we had a chance to be pretty darn good."

Turgeon said the 1985-1986 team had the same feeling as early as 1984. He and Calvin Thompson talked then about how good the team could be when Thompson's class became seniors.

Kansas fielded a team more to Brown's playing style. Tad Boyle was the only player graduating off the 1985 team, meaning all five starters returned.

Brown's methods stayed as steady as his starting lineup. He kept the high-pressure defense on to trigger the unselfish offense. And he treated lord and commoner alike on the basketball floor.

Turgeon described how Coach Brown motivated the team before a game. "He would build you up. Right before the game, he would say, 'We're better than this team. You're better than he is. They can't beat us.' That type of thing.

"In practice he was always breaking you down, trying to make you work harder. That's the way he disciplined players in practice. Then he'd build you up right before a game and tell you you were better, that we were a better team.

"It was successful because I remember at the time you would feel, 'Man, I don't even know why I'm in Division I because he yells at us all the time.' Or you'd be struggling a little bit on the court and he would say, 'Turge,' or 'Danny, you're better than he is.' And that would make you feel like, all right, maybe I am a pretty good player and you would do better in the game. That was his way of getting you pumped."

Kansas lost just three times in the regular season—a six-point defeat by Duke in the finals of the preseason National Invitation Tournament, a three-point overtime loss at Memphis State and a three-point decision at Iowa State, but rolled the rest of the time, beating eventual NCAA champion Louisville twice in the process.

The Jayhawks showed the promise of the season in a December game against Kentucky, which, like the Jayhawks, was in the Top 10 at the time.

Manning—drawing the tough defensive assignment of Kentucky All-America Kenny Walker—scored 22

Carl Henry, left, was a clutch performer for the Jayhawks. He was the leading scorer on the 1983-1984 team, Larry Brown's first squad at Kansas. Calvin Thompson, right, was a four-year starter for the Jayhawks and the third leading scorer on the 1986 Final Four team.

points and collected seven rebounds.

"Danny had been playing so tentatively, but he really came alive out there tonight," Brown said after the game.

The other players on the team knew the importance of Manning, too. "When Danny gets it rolling, watch out," Kellogg said. Manning was always too self-depreciating to accept the role of "star."

"I am not the George Brett of Kansas basketball," Manning said in 1985, referring to the 13-time All-Star of baseball's Kansas City Royals. "Nobody carries this team. In fact, last year I tended to sit back and watch instead of trying to do things myself.

"Setting screens one night, scoring another, rebounding the next—I do whatever needs to be done," said Manning. "I'm the balancer of our team. I complement everybody else. I want teams to say, 'Oh my God. We've got to play Kansas.' And I want to intimidate and make my presence felt."

The Jayhawks opened league play with a 15-2 mark and tore through their first four opponents, including consecutive victories over Oklahoma and Missouri. Kansas, which beat Louisville 83-78 in the semifinals of the NIT, entertained the Cardinals in Lawrence and came out 71-69 winners. Then came the annual trip to Ames, one place where Brown never won.

"What people tend to forget is that [Iowa State] had good teams when Coach Brown was here," said Turgeon. "My freshman year, we just weren't a very good team. We probably should have won—I think they beat us by four. A lot of the reason is that I didn't have a good game. After that they had good teams. They had Jeff Hornacek and Barry Stevens and then Jeff Grayer. They had good teams when Coach Brown was here.

"The year we went 35-4 and they beat us up at their place, they went to the Sweet Sixteen and almost played us in the final eight, they lost to North Carolina State by four points.

"[Brown] was more frustrated about it than anybody. Something like that sticks out. He doesn't have many blemishes on his coaching career—places where he didn't win—and he hardly ever lost two games in a row and that type of thing. It frustrated the players, too. Heck, I wanted to win there. My senior year that was one of my goals. I wanted to win there and we got waxed."

Iowa State came in second in the Big Eight in 1986, but the Cyclones trailed the league-champion Jayhawks by four games after KU closed the regular season with nine consecutive victories. The ninth game in the string was a 90-70

Larry Brown was all smiles when Danny Manning joined the Jayhawk team in 1984.

romp over Iowa State that ran Kansas' winning streak at Allen Field House to 33 games, tying the school's home-court record set in Hoch Auditorium from 1950-1951 through 1954-1955.

The eighth game was played in Norman, Oklahoma, where Kansas broke Oklahoma's 48-game home-court winning streak, 87-80. Brown called that triumph the "best road victory I've ever been associated with."

The Big Eight title ended the longest drought for a league championship in school history at seven years. They did it with a solid batch of players, too. All five starters—Danny Manning, Greg Dreiling, Ron Kellogg, Calvin Thompson, and Cedric Hunter—scored more than 1,000 points in their careers.

Kansas collected three more victories in the Big Eight Tournament, knocking off Kansas State 74-51 and posting two-point victories over Oklahoma and Iowa State to head into the NCAA Tournament with a 31-3 record and 12-game winning streak.

For a change, the Jayhawks, seeded number one in the Midwest Region, and played extremely well in the first round of the tournament, dispatching North Carolina A&T 71-46, and eliminating Temple 65-43. KU earned the right to return to Kansas City for the regional.

Michigan State upset Georgetown to fill the bracket spot beside Kansas while Iowa State dumped second-seeded Michigan. North Carolina State survived upset-minded Arkansas-Little Rock to complete the regional in Kemper Arena.

Kansas, playing before a partisan crowd, led Michigan State 46-37 at halftime. But the Spartans, behind Scott Skiles, worked back into the game and led by two with 2:16 left when a malfunction stopped the clock. Play continued for about 15 seconds before the problem was noticed. In the ensuing discussion, Brown was given a technical foul. Skiles made the free throws and then hit a field goal to put Michigan State up by six with Manning and Ron Kellogg on the bench with five fouls.

Kansas still trailed by half a dozen points with a minute to play, but was able to force overtime with nine seconds left when Archie Marshall tipped in a Calvin Thompson miss for one of his 13 rebounds, tying the score at 80-80.

Thompson, hobbled with a knee problem, took control in the overtime, scoring 10 of his 26 points for the 96-86 victory.

Manning stayed out of foul trouble two days later against North Carolina State and scored eight consecutive points to lift the Jayhawks from a five-point deficit to a 60-57 lead with 8:53 remaining. KU never lost that advantage, finishing off the Wolf Pack with a 75-67 decision for a trip to the Final Four in Dallas.

"I told our kids to celebrate for about 30 seconds," Brown said after the North Carolina State win. "It's a special thing to get there, but you can't be satisfied just getting there. You've got to do everything you can to win once you get there."

Kansas, ranked number two in the country, was paired with top-rated Duke in the national semifinals but suffered through one of the worst outings of a

Danny Manning was an instant star with the Jayhawks. His performance against North Carolina State in the 1986 Midwest Regional helped Kansas to the NCAA Final Four.

Chris Piper, one of Brown's first recruits, was a defensive standout under the basket.

great season. Manning and Greg Dreiling had their playing time cut because of foul trouble.

The Jayhawks still owned the lead, however, when they lost their heart. With 8:10 left in the game, and KU up 59-55, Archie Marshall injured his right knee. Duke, despite Kellogg's 22 points on 11 of 15 shooting, won 71-67 and moved into the NCAA title game. The Jayhawks took home a record 35-4 mark.

"I never remember stepping on the court thinking that we're just going to kill this team," Turgeon said. "I felt that way at home sometimes. But I never thought that when we stepped on the floor against Duke in the Final Four that we should beat this team or we're better than this team. It was kind of like

we feared Duke a little bit. They got a lot of publicity by being in the ACC and they were ranked number-one in the country. And they beat us earlier in the year.

"Now I look back and I think, boy, we had a better team than they did. It just seemed to me that we were deeper and we had Danny, who was young. We had some good players and a great coach. But that was a great year, 35-4."

The loss of Marshall haunted Kansas in 1986-1987. The team was depleted enough by the graduation of Kellogg, Dreiling, and Thompson.

"We'd lost three great seniors," said Mark Turgeon, "but the greatest loss for us right then, it wasn't the three seniors because that's just natural, it was the loss of Archie.

"People don't realize we went to the Sweet Sixteen that year and we were beating Georgetown in the second half. If you give us Archie Marshall, who would have been a pro in my mind if he had never gotten hurt, we're a potential Final Four team. We might not go 35-4, we might lose seven or eight games, but with Danny [Manning], who was the best player, we're a Final Four team again that year. Then we had a lot of problems and we just didn't play the way we were capable of playing in the tournament.

"I thought about red-shirting because of the situation. Coach Brown asked me to red shirt and I thought about it. I just felt loyalty to playing that year and just being with my teammates who I had been with so long."

The season began with the second Late Night with Larry Brown. More than 13,000 people showed up to watch a midnight practice.

Allen Field House was once again a Mecca of college basketball. And the heady atmosphere had a positive effect on the Kansas players.

For Mark Turgeon, who was a senior for the 1986-1987 season, the fans made every home game special, especially during player introductions.

"It's a great feeling," said Turgeon. "It's even better for me because I grew up in Topeka, and that's what I wanted to do. I always thought it was kind of special running out there. The part I always liked is the starting lineup. Our band gets playing that little beat and our students throw the newspapers. I just think the starting lineups are intimidating to the other team, because they are so loud. It's a big, big time."

The rest of the game can be the same way, with the players feeling an energy from the crowd that carries the team.

"My first four years the fans were just unbelievable," said Turgeon. "I remember games we had no business winning and [the crowd] just picked us up with 10 minutes to go and they weren't going to let us lose.

"Our junior year we played Louisville at home and that's the year they won the championship. We just came out dead and did not play well. The [fans] just stuck with us and stuck with us and we made a come back and won by four. That was a game when the fans really helped us."

Kansas again put a veteran team on the court behind Danny Manning, who had won the conference player of the year honor as a sophomore. Cedric Hunter returned at the point and freshman Kevin Pritchard worked his way into a starting role. Chris Piper and Mark Pellock helped Manning down low.

In an interview in late 1986, Manning said, "Whenever somebody on our team is hot, we're going to get them the ball. We have a very unselfish program. That's just the style of Coach Brown's play. Who is ever getting the job done, we just keep going to that person."

From the start of the 1986-1987 season, it was obvious the "hot" player was Manning. In the first three games he scored a total of 79 points on 33 of 45 shooting to go with 35 rebounds. The good numbers continued—he had 26 points and 17 rebounds in a loss at Arkansas—and the Jayhawks took a 7-1 record to the Rainbow Classic.

But in Hawaii, Kansas barely managed to take seventh place in an eight team tournament, beating the host Rainbows 81-80 in overtime with Keith Harris scoring six points in the extra period, after dropping games to Pittsburgh and Ohio State.

Kansas was far from consistent but played well enough to win two close games, drop a tight decision at Oklahoma, and rout Miami [Florida].

Missouri came next on the schedule, and the Tigers, with Derrick Chievous leading the way, were enjoying a banner season. The pairing proved to be among the toughest defenses of the Kansas home-court winning streak.

Chievous had 29 points, and the Tigers led 70-67 with 25 seconds left despite losing possession twice on bad passes. Milt Newton tied the score with a three-pointer. After the second Missouri turnover, Chris Piper was fouled while driving to the basket. Piper went to the line with five seconds left, and the crowd of 15,800 was deathly silent. He hit the first free throw, but when he missed the second, Pellock tipped the

Brown is flanked by assistants, *from the left,* John Calipari, Bob Hill, Ed Manning and R. C. Buford.

ball out to Manning to preserve the 71-70 victory.

The only other challenge to the Allen streak came against Oklahoma when Tim McCalister, who made several similar clock-beating shots in his career, missed a three-point try at the buzzer, and the Jayhawks won 86-84. The home-court streak grew to a conference-record, reaching 48 games by season's end.

Away from home the game was not as easy. The Jayhawks went 15-0 in Allen Field House in 1986-1987 but were 10-11 away from it. That included a 2-5 road record in Big Eight play that kept KU, 9-5 in the league, from finishing any closer than within two games of Missouri.

Manning scored 27 points in the Big Eight Tournament and passed Clyde

Above: Mark Turgeon played with poise as a Jayhawk guard. He played in four NCAA tournaments during his Kansas career. *Following page, top:* Brown led the 1985-1986 Jayhawks to the conference championship. *Bottom:* Greg Dreiling played center for the 1983-1986 Jayhawks. He went on to the NBA's Indiana Pacers.

Lovellette's 1,888-point total as the all-time scorer in Kansas history.

The Jayhawks advanced to the finals of the league tournament to find the Missouri Tigers already there. While Danny Manning, who scored 31 points, and Derrick Chievous, who had 26, did their best to keep the spotlight among the big names, it was Missouri freshman Lee Coward's 12-foot jumper with four seconds to play that supplied the winning points in the 67-65 game.

KU was sent to the Southeast Region and came away with a 66-55 victory over Houston and a 67-63 triumph over Southwest Missouri State, which had jumped to a 16-6 lead early in the game. Turgeon said the Southwest Missouri game was not as close as the score and "one reason is that Danny was scoring at will." Manning scored a career-high 42 points in the game in sending the Jayhawks into a contest with top-seeded Georgetown.

With Reggie Williams dominating the middle for 34 points, the Hoyas eliminated the Jayhawks, ending KU's season with a 25-11 mark.

The NCAA Tournament posed a strange time for Mark Turgeon. He was facing the end of his career. The next Kansas loss would be his final game. Every time he put on the uniform could be the final time.

"I didn't want it to end," he said. "I really thought that even when we're down, even when I knew we're playing Georgetown, I just felt like we could win because we had come so far as a program. I never envisioned us losing my senior year. I felt like we could go on and go on and this was going to be a special thing and we were going to win it all."

While it was known that Turgeon was leaving, the future of Coach Larry Brown, who had amassed a 108-33 record and an NCAA Tournament appearance in each of his four seasons, was again in question. He answered rumors of his leaving with: "I'm happy here and not planning on leaving. My biggest goal at KU is to develop consistency in our program. I don't want us to go through any rebuilding years."

Manning was beginning to get some pressure about turning professional before using all of his collegiate eligibility, but he expressed an interest in playing in the 1988 Olympics and he had a shot at becoming the first player to win Big Eight Conference Player of the Year honors three times.

"I had a lot of friends who said I was crazy to stay in school and that I should take the money," Manning told *The Kansas City Times.* "Then I had other more level-headed friends say you have to look at this, you have to look at that. At one point, I thought about cutting off my telephone receiver because people were calling up out of the blue.

"I had to sit back and just look at the recruiting class we had brought in and see if we had a legitimate shot of winning the national championship.

"And I also wanted to know what Coach Brown's situation was. I didn't want to keep asking him, 'What are you going to do?'"

Brown and Manning both determined Kansas would be the place to be for 1987-1988. And they weren't alone. A packed Allen Field House greeted the team for Late Night with Larry Brown as October 15, 1987, approached and practice could officially begin. The band greeted the team with "Kansas City," because that would be the site of the 1988 Final Four.

But this did not really look like a Final Four team. Chris Piper started the season recovering from arthroscopic surgery on his knee and Archie Marshall, finally rehabilitated from the serious knee injury suffered in the 1986 Final Four, had his career end with another knee injury on December 30. Marvin Branch, the starting center, was ruled ineligible and missed the second half of the season.

KU started collegiate play in 1987-1988 in Hawaii, and just like the previous season, the trip was not that enjoyable. The Jayhawks beat the host Chaminade team but dropped contests to Big Ten foes Iowa and Illinois. Winning ways returned when the team came home, and KU ran its home-court winning streak to 50 games with a 63-54 victory over St. John's before a national television audience.

That was the third game of a seven-game winning streak, which ended in a 70-56 upset by St. John's in New York in the game in which Marshall suffered a knee injury.

Kansas won four of its next five—losing at Iowa State—improving to 12-4 but then suffered the longest losing streak of Brown's KU career. Notre Dame, with David Rivers connecting on four free throws in the final 12 seconds, beat KU 80-76, and then a last-second basket by Beau Reid represented a 70-68 Jayhawks defeat at Nebraska.

On January 30, 1988, Kansas seemed to have broken its problems, jumping to a 22-12 lead over the first 10 minutes of a home game with Kansas State. The Wildcats rallied, and Mitch Richmond finished with 35 points. Kansas led or was close in the second half until Steve Henson canned a three-point shot that set off a 12-5 Wildcats surge. The Jayhawks were forced to foul but got no closer than five points the rest of the way as Richmond was 10 of 10 from the free-throw line.

The home-court winning streak was over at 55 games. It marked the first time the Kansas seniors had lost a home

game and also the first time Brown lost three consecutive games.

Oklahoma arrived four days later and took a 73-65 decision. Kansas had sunk to 12-8, had lost two conference home games, and four straight overall.

Manning put an end to the slump by hitting his first nine shots against Colorado in a 73-62 victory, and the Jayhawks won five straight before losing at home to Duke in overtime after enjoying an early big lead.

Four days later, Manning scored 30 points at Oklahoma and passed the Sooners' Wayman Tisdale as the leading scorer in Big Eight history, but KU dropped the game, 95-87. The Jayhawks lost just once more the rest of the season.

"They had a tough season, 12-8 at one time," said Mark Turgeon, who was a student assistant coach for the 1988 team. "When they were 12-8, we made some adjustments. Coach Brown made some adjustments, I should say.

"We started playing different people. We cleared some people off the team that we felt were negatives and changed their work habits in practices.

Kansas closed the regular season with three consecutive victories, which still left the Jayhawks at 9-5 and in third place in the Big Eight. It hardly seemed like a season of destiny, however, when Kevin Pritchard was injured and did not play in a 69-54 loss to Kansas State in the Big Eight Tournament semifinals. The Jayhawks played a tough schedule and owned a 21-11 record. They felt good about their chances of an at-large invitation to the NCAA Tournament, which all was in the form of a number six seeding in the Midwest Regional.

Turgeon recalled, "Kevin Pritchard gets hurt in the Big Eight tournament, hurts his knee. We lost the next night to K-State. And I believe we're the sixth seed and it's like we're practicing that week and we're not even sure we're going to get by Xavier. The season was going to end that Friday. It was a weird feeling. I'm not saying they wanted it to end, but they wouldn't have minded if it ended at that time.

"Then one of their players said that he was going to stop Danny. That Danny was just an average player. He was over-rated. We had that clipping posted all over our blackboard. We just took it to them and jumped all over them."

KU never trailed in ripping the trash-talking Muskateers 85-72. Manning scored 24 points, and Milt Newton added 21. Both had 12 rebounds, and Xavier was limited to 37.5 percent shooting as a team.

Kansas, while helping itself, got some help down the bracket as third-seeded North Carolina State was upset by Murray State. Kevin Pritchard, playing despite his knee problem, scored 10 points in a 125-second span to keep KU close to Murray State, and Manning and Newton had consecutive baskets to give the Jayhawks the lead at 57-56. Murray State answered with two free throws, but Manning dropped in a hook shot with 37 seconds to play and sealed the game with two free throws with one second showing in a 61-58 game.

"We played Murray State and squeaked by them and basically played the way we played all year," said Turgeon, "not great but just good enough to win. We played good defense and it just kept getting better and better."

The upsets continued on the regional level, Vanderbilt knocked off second-seeded Pittsburgh and "you see Danny's eyes getting a little bigger and everybody's getting a little bigger. Maybe we can do something special here," said Turgeon.

The wide-eyed Manning drilled Vanderbilt for 38 points, including 25 in the first half. Kansas led 19-4 with 10

Cedric Hunter operated as the Jayhawk point guard and holds the school career assist record with 684.

minutes gone in the game en route to the regional final.

Turgeon said, " And lo and behold, K-State beats [top-seeded] Purdue and when we go to bed that night, we're saying to ourselves that we're going to Final Four because we knew we could beat K-State the way we were playing. K-State was a tired team when we played them. They'd put so much into the Purdue game. Milt [Newton] played a heck of a game and everybody came together and played a great game. And our defense, which is what carried us the whole tournament, I feel. All of a sudden we're in the Final Four and you're thinking destiny at that point."

The Jayhawks were paired with Duke, a team that had beat them 74-70 in overtime earlier in the season.

"We're playing a team that we should have beat earlier in the year and know we can beat," said Turgeon. "The eyes kept getting bigger and bigger and working hard and harder. Things are just falling into place. We went out on Duke like 10-0 or something and held on to win."

Kansas scored the first 14 points of the game and led 24-6 midway through the first period. The Blue Devils chipped away and managed to pull within three points before KU posted an 11-4 spurt for a 66-55 advantage with 10 seconds to go. The entire Kansas front line reached double figures, led by Manning's 25 points. Newton added 20 and Piper 10.

Larry Brown became the second coach to take two different schools to the NCAA championship game—joining Frank McGuire who lost to Kansas in the 1952 final while at St. John's and beat the Jayhawks in 1957 while at North Carolina.

This time the title would be decided by old rivals as Oklahoma defeated Arizona 86-78 in the other semifinal. It was the third meeting of the season between the Jayhawks and Sooners, who were playing each other for the 163rd time in a series that began in 1920.

The Sooners owned 73-65 and 95-87

Danny Manning, left, won an unprecedented three consecutive Big 8 Player of the Year titles, 1986-1988, in addition to his Newcomer of the Year award in 1985.
Milt Newton, right, earned a spot on the NCAA All-Tournament Team with his standout play in 1988 in helping the Jayhawks to the national championship.

Manning led KU to the 1988 NCAA championship. He was named Collegiate Player of the Year, Most Outstanding Player in the NCAA Tournament, and was a member of the Olympic team.

victories over Kansas in 1988, but the Jayhawks were glad to see Oklahoma in the finals.

"Down deep we would have rather played Oklahoma than Arizona because of the familiarity," Turgeon recalled. "We'd just lost barely at Oklahoma late in the season, because Danny fouled out with about a minute to go."

The NCAA championship game put Big Eight basketball on the world map. Kansas shot 71 percent in the first half and Oklahoma countered with seven of 11 shooting from three-point range as what had been predicted to be a rout was a 50-50 dead heat at halftime.

Said Turgeon, "Coach Brown just had a feel. None of the assistants knew what he was going to do that game. And I don't think Coach Brown knew what he was going to do. He had an idea what he wanted to do. But he reached down deep into the bench and played Lincoln [Minor] early and played Clint [Normore] a lot early.

"He was reaching way down there and playing guys, knowing he liked the way the game was going and he didn't want to put a stop to that. Because we were scoring at will and he didn't want to put a stop to that."

Kansas seemed to be playing Oklahoma's game, but Turgeon said it was the Jayhawks' game, too.

"We used to pushed the ball, but it was controlled. It wasn't like we were running down there and shooting crazy shots, we were shooting layups and getting good shots and that type of thing. We just weren't stopping them, either. They were on fire," he said.

"It wasn't like we were going crazy and doing things we hadn't done all year. It just seemed that way because it was Oklahoma. Things were just clicking and he didn't want it to stop.

"At halftime we go in and Coach Brown just goes in and starts talking to them right away. He knows exactly what he wants to do. He started delaying in the second half with the big guys out on the floor and things. That was just him having a feel for the game. He coached probably the best game of his career here at Kansas in that championship game."

The Jayhawks tried to turn the pace in their favor. Still Oklahoma led 65-60 with 12:13 left. Then Manning took over.

Some panels had by-passed Manning for Bradley's Hersey Hawkins for national player of the year, citing Hawkins' national scoring championship. Manning did not care. That award didn't matter, there was a bigger trophy he had in mind. He always felt, and always played, as though the team accomplishments outweighed anything an individual could reap.

Manning scored 13 points in the final 11:13. Kevin Pritchard, Danny Manning, and Chris Piper drilled consecutive shots to put the Jayhawks ahead 77-71. Oklahoma, on a Mookie Blaylock turnaround, pulled back within 78-77. Kansas worked some time off the clock before the Sooners fouled Scooter Barry, the son of Rick Barry who is the best free-throw shooter in the history of the NBA.

Barry made his first free throw, but missed the second. Manning rebounded and he was fouled.

The all-time scorer in Big Eight history stood at the line with the biggest free throws of his collegiate career. Later he said all he thought was, "It's over. It's over."

Manning made both free throws for a 81-77 Kansas advantage. Ricky Grace countered with a drive for Oklahoma, and the Sooners took a time out with seven seconds to play and the score 81-79. The Jayhawks again got the ball to Manning, who was immediately fouled. Again he made both free throws, giving him 31 points on the night, and when he pulled down the final Oklahoma missed shot he had a career-high 18 rebounds—and Kansas had another national championship.

"How do you like us now?" Manning asked the postgame news conference. "People said we were lucky. This wasn't a gift. What's luck? It's preparation and opportunity."

Manning joined Clyde Lovellette, B. H. Born, and Wilt Chamberlain as NCAA Tournament most outstanding players from KU. He and Milt Newton, who had a marvelous run through the tournament scoring 89 points with 15 coming in the title game on six of six shooting, were named to the all-tournament team.

Manning's great collegiate career was over. He scored 2,951 points, the sixth highest in NCAA history, and owned the second-highest NCAA Tournament point total at 328. He finished with 43 NCAA, Big Eight, and school records. In his final season he had 11 games of 30 points or more. He won an unprecedented three conference Player of the Year honors and three all-Big Eight awards.

When asked which four players he would like to join him on a Big Eight Conference all-star team, Missouri senior Derrick Chievous did not hesitate in replying, "Manning, Manning, Manning and Manning."

Turgeon said, "He was an unbelievable college player, who played for the right college coach. A man who directed things his way and pushed him and yelled at him like he would yell at anybody else. I just felt like the things that Danny did in games and stuff, as teammates we expected them.

"Like I said, I'd get mad when he wouldn't shoot. It's like we expected him to get 27 every night and 10 boards. There were times his senior year when I'd be shaking my head. He had 39 [points] at Missouri. He had 25 at halftime and probably could have had 50, but started passing the ball at the end

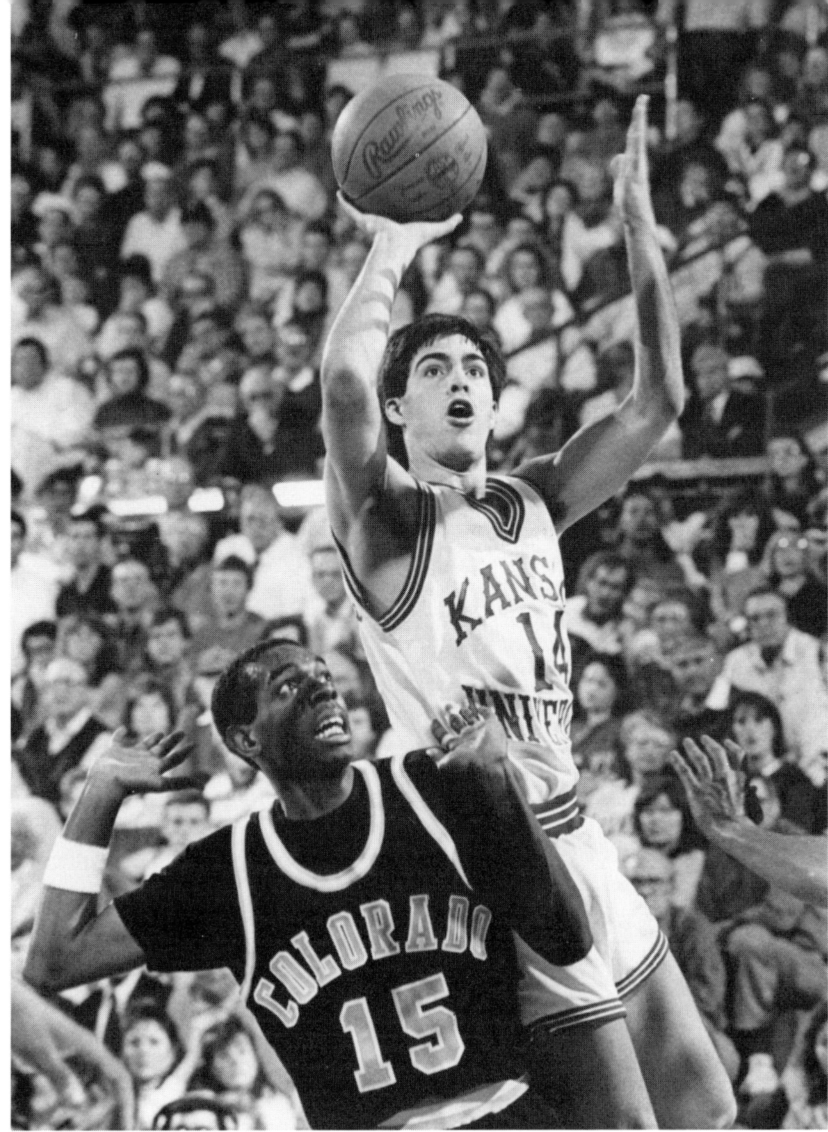

because the game was over. He was just like a man playing with boys out there."

Even before the championship game with Oklahoma the rumors about Brown moving on surfaced. He was going to return to UCLA—in fact the Bruins Sports Information Department had a release ready to hand out. But Brown wanted to tell his Kansas team first and after speaking with the Jayhawks announced his intention to stay at Kansas.

Then the San Antonio Spurs came into the picture and the contract figures reached a level no coach could refuse. On June 13, 1988, Larry Brown announced he would return to the NBA.

"Kansas has been a very special place to me," Brown said in the KU release about his resignation, "and it was a very difficult decision to leave. I can't believe that any college coach in the country has a better situation than I did at KU, and I'm grateful to [Athletics Director] Bob Frederick and the chancellor for that. The offer at San Antonio was simply a once in a lifetime opportunity which I couldn't turn down."

Kevin Pritchard played a significant role in helping Kansas to 101 victories during his four years as a starter.

Full Circle

Larry Brown's departure, even though it had been rumored for so long, still hit Kansas basketball hard. The NCAA would soon be coming down on the program. How would the Jayhawks react having to deal with coming right after a national championship team, a possible probation and now breaking in of—or being broken in by—a new coach.

Not long before Brown's leaving, Athletics Director Bob Frederick attended the Naismith hall of Fame iduction of former Kansas players Clyde Lovellette and Ralph Miller. Frederick was seated next to Dick Harp, who had coached Frederick at KU.

"All Dick talked to me all night long was Roy Williams," Frederick said. "He was saying that if there ever was an opening this guy would be a pretty good coach.

"I listened to him but, quite honestly, I thought the thing was resolved with Larry so it wasn't that I felt any sense of urgency."

But Brown changed his mind when the Spurs called and within an hour of Brown telling Frederick that the coach was leaving, the AD was on the phone to North Carolina, but not to Roy Williams. At least not yet.

"I called Dean Smith and said I'm calling you to ask you if you'd be interested in coming back and taking the job. That's when he laughed and said I don't think it would be appropriate for me to leave after they named the building [the Smith Center basketball arena] after me.

"Then he asked who are some of the names we were considering and I told him a couple and he said well, 'I'd like to talk to you about Roy Williams.' Then it hit me that was who Dick had been talking about."

Frederick met Williams at the Atlanta airport, just before the North Carolina assistant was leaving on a vacation. They talked for several hours and when he returned to Lawrence, Frederick asked permission to bring Williams to campus for a formal interview.

Frederick said Williams did not im-mediately snap up the job offer but "he thought twice during the course of the interview about leaving all that he had been involved with at North Carolina. It was not an easy decision for him but he had heard so many great things from Dick Harp and Dean Smith."

Williams was obviously interested, but then what assistant coach—especially one without head-coaching experience—would not like to take over one of the highest profile coaching positions in the country?

He had also been schooled in the Kansas tradition, playing for Smith at North Carolina and as a member of Smith's coaching staff for 10 years. While Williams assisted Smith, former Kansas Coach Dick Harp helped the Tar Heels for two seasons and provided additional tales of Kansas lore.

Williams was vaguely aware of the Jayhawks before that indoctrination period, having pulled for Wilt Chamberlain in his battles with Bill Russell. Born in North Carolina, Williams knew the Chamberlain-led Jayhawks lost the NCAA title game to the Tar Heels in triple overtime in 1957.

While a student at North Carolina, Williams read an article on Dean Smith recounting the coach's days at KU with Phog Allen figuring in the saga.

Smith kept Williams up on how Kansas fared on the court because the assistant coach, who usually got the first newspaper when the Tar Heels traveled, always had to look up the Jayhawks' score for Smith.

Williams got a first-hand taste of Kansas basketball when North Carolina played the Jayhawks in Kemper Arena on January 3, 1981, and took a 56-55 decision. The following season, Kansas visited Charlotte, North Carolina, for another game.

"Then when Ted [Owens] was no longer the coach and we were at an NCAA tournament, Larry Brown called and told Coach Smith he'd like his help because Larry would like to coach at Kansas," Williams said.

"After Larry got involved I followed it much more. In fact, Larry offered me a job as an assistant. That's when I started looking at it much closer."

Williams finally agreed to take the position. Now Frederick had a harder sell to complete. He had to convince the Kansas fans—who were thinking of getting a very high-profile coach and not someone without head coaching experience—that Williams was indeed the coach for the Jayhawks.

Frederick said, "I knew that there would be a lot of criticism about it initially but there were a couple of things that I thought were really important at that point. I thought we needed, No. 1, stability and No. 2, I didn't want the Kansas job to become a job where we were duddenly going from six coaches in 89 years to a coach every four or five or three or something years.

"I really was interested in trying to find somebody who wanted a family-type program, a program that would last for a long time, who had an appreciation for that kind of thing."

Roy Williams turned out to be a nice fit there. It didn't take long for the new coach to show he belonged, and in just the way Frederick imagined.

"What I see in a guy like Roy Williams is a continuation of the Kansas principles in coaching and teaching. It will have come full circle," said Jerry Waugh, a former Kansas player and a man who has served the athletic department in a series of positions. "I think we will lose less by continuing what Larry taught and it had to do with what I thought Doc taught. And Doc, particularly defensively, I thought, he was way ahead of th times."

Williams quickly disarmed the naysayers and he did it by being Roy Williams and never giving a thought to being Larry Brown, Phog Allen, or Dean Smith.

"I had met [Williams] before because I worked at Carolina in a camp, but my first impression was just how business-like he was and how sincere he was," said Mark Turgeon, who played for Brown and graduated to a spot on the coaching staff. "He was straightforward with me from the very beginning, and straightforward with the team. He said, 'This was the way it's going to be. I know you had a great team in the past and you had a great coach. I respect Coach Brown, but this is the way we're going to do it now.' It was always straightforward and business-like. That's why he's so good."

If Williams ever had second thoughts

about moving to Kansas, they came October 31, 1988, when he was told the extent of the penalties the NCAA handed down. The team was banned from the 1989 NCAA Tournament—the first team barred from a title defense—and, more seriously in Williams' eyes, slapped with recruiting restrictions that the coach felt would echo through the program at least until the mid-1990s. Some people believed the sanctions something of a blessing for Williams, since they removed so many expectations.

Williams said, "Al McGuire, the day

Coach Roy Williams would not let the many problems of 1988-1989 get him down. He went ahead to try to win the conference even though KU was ineligible for post-season play.

Kansas played an aggressive defense and a fast offense throughout 1988-1989. They did well the first half of the season, but lost eight in a row in the second half to finish with a 19-12 record.

we played Temple that year, came to our shoot-around that morning in Atlantic City and said, 'This is great. This is a honeymoon for you.' I said, 'Al, if all honeymoons were like this, no one would get married.'"

"First of all, if it's a left-handed blessing or not, it killed me emotionally to not have that goal at the end of the year, towards being in the NCAA Tournament. It killed me because I was going to be asked to suffer under things for the next three years that I had had nothing to do with. I really, really thought that it was going to put us behind a tremendous eight ball, the recruiting restrictions. We lost kids immediately after it had come. We had kids cancel visits immediately after it was announced.

"It wiped me out and it was a struggle for me every single day to make sure that I kept my feelings from everybody else because I had to be the one who,

more or less, was going to show that we can go on. But deep down inside there was a huge fear there that this is going to be too difficult to overcome.

"At the same time I made the decision that after about 12 hours I decided that was enough, that I have got to go on. The kids are going to follow me, whether I deserve it or not, as long a I'm head coach. So I made that decision but I still had the feelings of insecurity as to whether we could get it done."

Williams swallowed his disappointment and fears and, once games started, had the Kansas fans give him something that helped keep it down.

Two days after Williams was introduced as a part of Kansas basketball, the summer recruiting period began and the coach spent the next month on the road. The first month he was able to spend in Lawrence, however, "I learned just how important basketball was to the people of Kansas."

He said, "I'll never forget my first season, my first game, an exhibition against the Soviet Union and the gym's packed and people are just going crazy. And the opening night practice even before that when all the students were there and when they introduced me that night and the reception I got from the students. At that point I really started understanding how important it was."

The students' affections were not dampened by the Jayhawks' play on the court, either. KU won 13 of its first 15 games and ran its record to 16-4 before hitting the wall.

Williams' style of play demanded a lot of players, all of whom saw a lot of hard minutes playing aggressive defense without relaxing on offense. When Kansas started the 1988-1989 season there were enough players, but when injuries and fatigue began a process of attrition, it was the Jayhawks' record that suffered. An 86-66 romp over Wichita State gave Williams a nineteenth victory, but it would be a month before he saw his twentieth.

The next game, Kansas State outscored Kansas 25-8 in the first 10 minutes of the second half and held off a frantic KU rally, with Steve Henson hitting two clinching free throws with 18 seconds to play, for a 71-70 victory. There was a string of seven more defeats, and not many of them really close.

Williams listed one close game in that stretch that was particularly important to him.

"That is the one game my first year that sticks out and shows that more than anything—we were down to seven scholarship players because Jeff Gueldner was out and Sean Alvarado was out, Lincoln [Minor] and Scooter [Barry], both had knees bothering them. We play Oklahoma here and they were number one in the country. We lost to them in overtime," said Williams.

"At the end of the game, I don't think we had anybody else to put in the game, if one of those guys had fouled out we would have had to put in a JV player. And I think there were a couple guys with four fouls.

"I went down and shook hands with Billy [Tubbs] and their players like I normally do and as I was going off, I realized that the crowd was giving us a standing ovation. I never realize those things are happening. But they were giving us a standing ovation. That was

Mike Maddox, left, Mark Randall, center, and Milt Newton played a meaningful role on the 1988-1989 Jayhawk team.

Above: The 1990-1991 team under coach Roy Williams continued the winning tradition of KU basketball.

Opposite page: Roy Williams did not digress when faced with an NCAA probation during his first year. "I'm always going to put more pressure on myself than they ever could." Within three years, Williams escorted the Jayhawks to the NCAA title game.

just amazing."

KU broke the losing streak with a rousing 111-83 defeat of Colorado and posted two more victories—finishing sixth in the Big Eight at 6-8—before a first-round conference tournament loss to Kansas State.

Williams said he did not think of the NCAA-levied recruiting restrictions during the playing schedule, but sure did after the 1989 season.

"I did not feel like it was any kind of blessing," he said. "The second season, going through the fall recruiting period, I felt so lucky that we had Chris Lindley and Patrick Richey close and we had Steve Woodberry in Wichita, because the most difficult thing I've ever had to do is to recruit kids and not be able to bring them on campus.

"I still think that we are not going to be as good as we could have been next year [1992] if we hadn't had the probation because of the players I think we could have had."

Williams was told of Phog Allen's reputed ability to fall asleep immediately after getting on the bus for a ride home, whether Kansas had won or lost.

He said, "That's a quality I wish I had. I don't lose a moment's sleep over it. I lose nights. The competitiveness, I think sometimes... I even had a goal to try to do better and I didn't."

The Jayhawks opened 1989-1990 practice without even a mention—not one vote—in the preseason rankings. Then a magazine came out and predicted an eighth-place finish.

"When it came out that we were picked last in a magazine, Kevin Pritchard brought it to me and he was so mad," Williams said. "I loved it because I thought we had a chance to be pretty good. Now, it doesn't do any good to be the underdog if you're not any good, but I thought we were going to be pretty good."

Kansas, granted a home-court game for the first round, opened the preseason National Invitation Tournament against Alabama-Birmingham.

"We play Alabama-Birmingham here and they were supposed to have a pretty good team. We've got them [down] 41-11," Williams recalled.

"During the two exhibition games, I was very frustrated because we had jumped out to big leads and put different combinations in and the last four or five

guys in and they would not play well. And then Alabama-Birmingham, we just destroyed them. They couldn't run an offense. They couldn't make a pass.

"That night I told my wife we've got a chance to be pretty dog-gone good."

The NIT still had to be proved, however, and what followed was some of the roughest tournament scheduling ever devised. The Jayhawks' second-round game, which Williams found out about in a 2 a.m. call, was Louisiana State at Baton Rouge, Louisiana.

"The next day, I tell our guys what I want you to do is spend the next 36 hours thinking about how good it would feel to beat LSU. I got some of those crazy looks from some of the players and some of the coaches. Like, 'You've got to be kidding,' said Williams.

"I felt comfortable about that and really pushed our kids to believe that. Finally in the pregame meal, I told our staff, 'Now they believe me. We're going to play our tails off.' And we did."

Kansas came away from Louisiana State an 89-83 winner, with Mark Randall scoring 26 points and outplaying Shaquille O'Neal, but the Jayhawks still weren't getting a lot of respect. That came after the semifinals, in which KU drew Nevada-Las Vegas.

Williams said, "With Vegas, it was a matter of wills. We had to be strong enough to not give in to the pressure, to not get back on our heels, not be tentative. We had to keep attacking. Because I felt that if we did attack, we could be effective against them, too."

The Jayhawks used a balanced attack in which Mike Maddox had 17 points and led six teammates into double figures to put a 91-77 thumping on a UNLV team that would end the season winning the NCAA Tournament. KU completed the stunning run through the NIT by knocking off home-town favorite St. John's, 66-57, behind 25 points from Randall.

"With the St. John's game, it was, now we've gotten this far, let's not feel too good about what you've done. Since you're here let's go ahead and win the dog-gone thing," Williams said.

KU made the unprecedented jump from no votes in one poll to second place in the next. Williams, however, said he didn't consider the team complete yet.

"It's just that we got more attention and more people watched me do the same things that I would be doing anyway."

The NIT set off an amazing 19-game run that included a 150-95 romp over Kentucky and ended with a 132-65 rout of Elizabeth City State. Those games, and eight others, came in a packed Allen Field House. By now, Williams, a part of the Kansas tradition, was also wrapped in it.

"The part that really is emotional to me are game nights in Allen Field House," the coach said. "They are really something special. I've been involved with teams that have played in some pretty good places—Carmichael Auditorium and the Smith Center, for example—and have been everywhere in the country that you can be that is big for college basketball. I've been there. Still, I think, I get a little more of the excitement, the tradition, in the games here."

Kansas rode that excitement to 19-0, and was ranked number one in the country with arch-rivals Missouri and Kansas State up next.

Said Williams, "The border state—the Missouri battles, I can understand the significance, especially because of the town of Kansas City, which is split not just by the state line but by peoples' feelings.

"With Kansas State, it's very similar to North Carolina-North Carolina State—different kinds of schools, one being more agricultural based and one more professional based. So I can understand that and I know the peoples' feelings. And having Mark Turgeon on our staff, it's easy to understand Kansas-Kansas State because he's got some very deep, hard-set feelings."

Those go both ways and Missouri, rated in the Top Five, was very fired up. Four of the Tigers' five starters wound up with at least 20 points. The Tigers set off a domino-style string of upsets of top-rated teams and, by the end of the night, were number one themselves while Kansas slipped one spot to number two.

Said Williams, "We go out to 19 in a row and play Missouri at Missouri and didn't play very well—they had a lot to do with it—then had a week off. Now our next game is going to be at Kansas State. I felt like we had a really big challenge to push the kids to again make them feel

135

Point guard Adonis Jordan emerged as a standout in 1990-1991, directing the Jayhawks to a 27-8 record and the NCAA national championship game.

confident that we could do it. I thought if we lost there that it could really hurt our confidence and there would be problems for us. So the whole week we pushed them pretty hard and very physical, because that's the way K-State plays—instead of sliding through on a screen or something, they'd really bang you. So we'd bang the heck out of all of them.

"We go over there and we're up 12 at halftime and everything we did was like practice. Everything we tried worked. Our execution offensively was unbeliev-able. Our set plays, we're getting layups, we're getting backdoors. It was just an amazing exhibition of basketball.

"I'm pretty big on confidence and I had written something up on the board—'Let's watch them leave early.' Meaning, let's play our game and we'll have the people leaving before the final buzzer. About three minutes left in the game Rick Calloway is shooting a free throw and he yells over, 'Coach.' I said, 'Yeah?' 'They're leeeeavin'.' And sure enough they were and that was a lot of a psychological thing that I was trying to picture."

Kansas ran its winning streak at Kansas State to seven games with an 85-57 rout in which the Jayhawks hit 60 percent of their shots while allowing just 36.5 percent shooting. KU won another four straight games and stood 24-1—and was back at number one since Missouri had lost to Kansas State—going into the rematch with the Tigers.

Williams said he never believed his team was going to lose and "maybe that's the reason I take the losses so hard.

"We lost to Missouri and then turn around and have a great win over K-State. We played pretty well the rest of the time and now we've got Missouri back here and we're back to number one. And we lose again [77-71]. That was a shock. I didn't think there was *any way* they could beat us. And they did.

"It did two things. One, it showed me how good Missouri was, and two, it hurt my confidence, it hurt our team's confidence. It wiped me out. Then we turn around and a couple games later go down and play Oklahoma at Oklahoma and they just destroyed us [100-78]. But that was also their seniors' last home game. The crowd was unbelievable. I don't think anybody could have beaten them that night."

The Jayhawks closed the regular season with a rout of Iowa State, with seniors Kevin Pritchard and Rick Calloway leading the scoring. Williams said, even with a 28-3 record and 12-2 Big Eight record that left them tied for second, he could sense a tightness building.

KU set several records in opening the Big Eight Tournament with a 118-75 victory over Iowa State. In the semifinals, Oklahoma, the new number one team in the country, eliminated the Jayhawks 95-77.

"It was 52-51 with 16 minutes to play in the game. Boy, it's been a great game," Williams recalled of the Oklahoma contest. "Both teams up and down, good plays, people are knocking it in. Then all of a sudden we miss 10 in a row—we miss 10 shots in a row and they're scoring on the other end. And we had good shots. Of those 10, I wanted us to take nine of them when I looked at it on tape. We missed 10 shots in a row and we were the best shooting team in America.

"After that game is when it really hit me that our kids were really feeling the pressure. So when we went to the NCAA tournament, I tried everything I could to give them another speech about, 'This is the icing on the cake. You've already accomplished so much, Let's enjoy this. Let's have fun with this.' But I never did take that pressure off."

The Jayhawks, so long considered the underdog, were the breed of team that played better when it was not rated number one. "The kids were such conscientious kids that they cared about what we thought about them," said Williams. "There is a great amount of pressure that goes with the attention of being number one. There is a great amount of pressure that goes along with being one of the number one seeds that has a chance to go to the Final Four. And our seniors, instead of being the most relaxed ones, they were the ones who felt the most pressure."

Kansas survived a shaky first-round game with Robert Morris, 79-71, for its 30th victory of the year. But KU ran into UCLA in the second round. The Bruins, who have never lost to the Jayhawks, eliminated Kansas 71-70.

Two traits characterize prognosticators: The first is that they never remind anyone about the wrong guesses. The other is that they learn from them and, for good or ill, adjust accordingly. Kansas, picked low in 1989-1990 before winning 30 games, was predicted much higher for 1990-1991. Now Roy Williams was the doubter, admonishing the Big Eight writers for picking Kansas second in the conference.

"I didn't think we'd be that good," the coach said. "I've made the statement about how this was an ugly team. Sometimes in a game it was like, 'How can those guys win a game?' Our practices were like that all the time.

"For every one good practice we'd have where I'd leave practice happy or satisfied that we had accomplished the things that I wanted to accomplish, we had 10 that I left practices wondering. It was really like pulling teeth every single day.

"But it was the most amazing group I've ever been around as far as being competitive and for the most part coming to play every night on game night. Colorado is the only night they didn't

Guard Terry Brown established himself as one of the all-time great long range shooters in Kansas history.

come to play. And they almost pulled that out in the second half."

Williams' style, however, works with interchangeable parts and losses such as those would not be felt as strongly in his system as they might have been in the past. Also, Mark Randall, Terry Brown, and Mike Maddox along with point-guard-elect Adonis Jordan were all back.

"Still, I saw the practices and we were not good," said Williams. "As coaches, we came into the season trying to decide if we could win a game."

Williams said by the time games rolled around, the team was playing better, but a season-opening loss at Arizona State revealed a lack of free-throw shooting "and I knew that would be a problem with us all season long," the coach said.

Kansas did win a game, beating Northern Arizona—"We were bad but they were worse," Williams said—before the Jayhawks played their home opener against Marquette.

Williams said, "Mark [Randall] is not going to play [because of a leg injury] and I talk about how everybody has got to pull together: 'But fellas, remember on October 15 I said that last year everybody talked about how pretty we were, about how we cut people up. This year I want people to talk about our defense.'"

Williams whipped up a defensive frenzy in his team, and Randall decided that, even with staple-like stitches in his leg, he was going to play.

"We go out there and talking about not being able to run an offense. [The Marquette Warriors] couldn't make a dribble or make a pass. We forced 34 turnovers. After the game I told our staff, if we can do something one time we can do it more than once."

Kansas ran past the Warriors 108-71 and followed that up with a victory over Southern Methodist. Then came the payback trip to Kentucky, and the Wildcats were making sure no one forgot the 55-point pasting of a season ago.

"Then we lose to Kentucky," Williams said. "We didn't play well the last seven minutes, but we made a pretty dog-gone good run in a game in an atmosphere that was almost no chance for us to win. For us to come back and make it a one-point game showed me something

about the team."

KU took a trip to Hawaii for one game and a series of practices. Williams said the players determined, by their effort in the first workout of the day, just how much beach they would see. If they didn't work hard in the morning "all they would know of Hawaii would be baseline to baseline," the coach promised. Not once did he have to call more than one practice.

"That really helped us," said Williams. "We came back and played a good Pepperdine team. It's nip and tuck and then we outscore them 21-zip during a run in the second half and win going away [88-62]. That showed me some-

thing. That's the kind of game you have to win if you're going to be an NCAA tournament team.

"We lose at Oklahoma and at Oklahoma State, but had a chance to win both games and should have won both games. Now what my whole thing was, let's make sure the guys don't panic, that 0-2 [in the conference], so what, a lot of people are going to lose at Oklahoma and Oklahoma State.

"That's my thing about the guy asking if it was critical, I said I thought that was a term used for people in the hospital, and that's the way I really felt. But I thought it was more important that our kids felt that way."

Kansas survived that initially rough Big Eight schedule, coming off the 78-73 overtime loss at Oklahoma State and running off 10 consecutive victories.

"After they began to win some," said former head coach Dick Harp, now an Allen Field House season-ticket holder, "the people who sat around where I sat, their expectations immediately jumped from just hoping they were going to be pretty good, to 'Man, maybe we can win the championship,' From that time on the fans were much more dissatisfied when the play wasn't very good."

During the run, Kansas lengthened its winning streak at Kansas State to eight games and defeated Missouri at

Missouri, giving Williams at least one victory in every Big Eight arena except Oklahoma.

The games against the rivals brought out the motivator in Williams.

"It was one of those, throw a chair during halftime thing and go crazy and scream," he said. "It worked at Kansas State. That was one of the screaming halftime talks. It worked at Missouri. That was one of the screamers, the blood rushing to the top of my head and people thinking the veins were going to explode. But it didn't work at Colorado because we'd dug ourselves too big a hole."

Colorado, which shot lights out in the first half, held off a Kansas charge in the second period to end the Jayhawks' winning streak. Still when it came down to the final game of the regular season, KU controlled whether it would win the Big Eight outright or share it with Oklahoma State.

It turned out that Nebraska had even more to say about the outcome and won 85-75, leaving Kansas and Oklahoma State co-champions. As if to show it wasn't a fluke, the Cornhuskers beat Kansas in the Big Eight Tournament semifinals. The Jayhawks, however, were 22-7 and confident of an NCAA Tournament berth.

"My big thing the next couple of days was confidence and that we do have a chance to win it all," Williams said.

"We go over to my house to watch the [announcement] show together. I told my coaches that we've got to act really excited because I don't think our players will. And sure enough it was no big deal. But I was yelling. I was trying to get them to understand what a happy time this could be.

"Then I bring up '83 North Carolina State, '85 Villanova and '88 Kansas. Those were not to the best teams but they won it. If we go game by game, we've got a chance to win it. And I believed that, I really did. Because we were so competitive and because there was only one team that was head and shoulders above everybody else and that was Vegas."

However, Kansas drew every pretender to the UNLV crown—even the eventual usurper. After the nearly traditional sluggish first-round victory, 55-49 over New Orleans, the Jayhawks faced Pittsburgh and won by 11. In regional play there came Indiana, trying to get home to Indianapolis for the Final Four, and KU eliminated the Hoosiers 83-65. Next was second-ranked Arkan-

The fans' expectations were proved true when the 1990-1991 team made it to the NCAA championship game.

sas, and a stunning second-half charge carried Kansas to a 93-81 upset and a ninth trip to the Final Four with regional most outstanding player Alonzo Jamison leading the way.

"I knew that it was going to be unbelievably hard for us to withstand their pressure," Williams said. "At halftime, I made the decision that it was going to be more of a confidence talk instead of throwing chairs and raising Cain.

"It was a pretty heated kind of thing, but it wasn't, 'you haven't done this you haven't done that, you haven't done this.' It was, 'this is all you have to do. You don't have to do any more. If you do what we ask you to do. If you do what we practiced yesterday, if you do what we talked about this morning, you can be there at the end and I'm not so sure they can handle you coming back on them.'"

"But there were times during the Arkansas game," said assistant coach Mark Turgeon, "where you're sitting over there thinking, 'Well, maybe this is as far as this team should go—final eight,' because Arkansas was playing so well the first half and we weren't.

"But that second half, I don't think there was a guy on the bench who didn't think we were going to win when we made that little run at them and got that lead. It's momentum. There was no way it's going to be slowed down."

Kansas headed for Indianapolis in fifth gear, with a date with some old friends coming up.

North Carolina also made a handy run through the NCAA. After beating Duke 96-74 in the ACC Tournament final, the Tar Heels were not even threatened until a three-point game with Temple in the regional championship.

The possibility was first a joke, then it became reality. North Carolina graduate Roy Williams was taking the Jayhawks against Kansas graduate Dean Smith and the Tar Heels. The billing went up immediately: The Coach vs. The Student.

"He down-plays those things," Turgeon said of Williams. "Just like when we played North Carolina State. North Carolina State to him, is just like me playing K-State. He doesn't like North Carolina State. And he tried to down-play it and not act like it was a big game for him. He tried to, but he over-did it.

"I think that's what he tried to do with Coach Smith was down-play it, but knowing that he was going to be fired up more than he had ever been fired up before in his life because it was a Final Four game."

North Carolina entered the game with a 51-percent shooting average, but the Jayhawks' defense limited Williams' old school to 38.4 percent. Rick Fox, Pete Chilcutt, and King Rice—players Williams recruited for North Carolina and who developed into the heart of that team—were a combined eight of 36 shooting. The 79-73 victory had Kansas in the NCAA title game for the sixth time.

All that was left was a partner for the final dance. And Williams wanted the prettiest girl in the place for that final twirl—undefeated and first-ranked Nevada-Las Vegas.

"The pressure with each and every game, I would have given my eye teeth [to play UNLV]," the Kansas coach said. "As a matter of fact, I was mad at our fans during the Duke-Vegas game because they were cheering for Duke, and I was pulling so hard for Vegas it was unbelievable. Because that is who I wanted to play."

Duke, which had been to so many Final Fours only to come away empty, pulled off the upset, however—just as the Blue Devils did in 1986 against Kansas—and went against the Jayhawks for the NCAA title.

"I didn't think there was any way we were going to lose the finals," said Turgeon. "The way we were going, the way we were playing. I thought, man, we are playing so well. I thought, here we go again. It's meant to be."

Duke, however, was destiny's darling in 1991. If any team had suffered for success it had been the Blue Devils, with five trips to the Final Four over six seasons and nothing but a season-ending loss to show for it.

Against Kansas that ended. The Blue Devils went out 7-1 and never looked back. Terry Brown hit a three-pointer that drew the Jayhawks within 26-25 with about seven minutes to play in the half, but Duke pulled away for a 42-34 lead by halftime. Kansas managed to get within 44-40 early in the second period, but Duke stretched it out again, posting a 72-65 victory.

As usual, the losses in a 27-8 season stuck with Williams, a perfectionist who is always trying to figure what he could have done to avoid losing, more than the victories.

"Those eight, I can remember those eight a lot more than I can remember those 27," the coach said.

Williams' first three years at Kansas showed a competitive nature that was worthy of being a part of the Jayhawks' tradition and also gave an indication that he is likely to help it grow.

He's remarkable the way he sees the little things," said Mark Turgeon, Kansas player and assistant coach. "That is what makes him special.

"He can hide things or he sees things that a normal person can't see that he thinks we should take care of. It might not be an 'X' and 'O' thing. It might be a mental thing, which helped prepare the team. That's what makes Coach Williams so good."

Naismith Memorial Hall of Fame

Basketball can be simply described as a contest between two teams in which the side that scores the most points within the time limit wins. But to its fans, basketball could hardly be confined to so simple a definition. And thousands of these fans every years review the game they know and love at the Naismith Memorial Basketball Hall of Fame, which enshrined the memorabilia and history of the game, players, coaches, and supporters.

For basketball fans, 1991 is a landmark year—marking the 100-year anniversary of the invention of the game. James Naismith invented basketball in the winter of 1891 at the Springfield, Massachusetts, YMCA Training School.

Naismith had received a charge from Dr. Luther Gulick, the director of the YMCA Training School in Springfield, Massachusetts, to find a pastime to settle what was a rather unruly physical education class. The men in the class liked the outside the physical activity of football in the fall and track and baseball in the spring, but were bored by the basic calisthenics forced upon them when Massachusetts' winter months kept them indoors.

Naismith fretted over a new game for the men. When he tried to incorporate facets of football, rugby, and his beloved lacrosse, the indoor game became much too rough. Deviations of children's games did not challenge the men enough.

Knowing he must eliminate running with the ball and tackling, Naismith recalled a game from his childhood in Almonte, Ontario, called Duck on a Rock in which he and his friends tried to knock the "duck" off a large rock with smaller rocks.

He replaced the rocks with a ball—a soccer ball seemed the right size—and

Basketball's inventor, James Naismith, examines the equipment he used in the first basketball game in 1891—two peach baskets and a soccer ball.

then, because defense would be too easy with the target on the floor, he raised the goals off the floor.

Naismith asked a janitor for boxes as his targets, but was offered peach baskets instead. Naismith fastened the baskets at either end of the gym to a track 10 feet above the floor.

His unruly class had 18 students, so he split them nine to a side. When he tossed the soccer ball up between two of them, basketball was born.

The game caught on quickly and grew into one of the most popular sports in the world. Naismith's invention was easy to play and did not need much equipment—traits that enhanced its popularity.

In the ensuing 100 years, the game has evolved, with slam dunks, shot clocks, shifting defenses, and the three-point goal changing the face of basketball. But the heart of the sport is still Naismith's. The bottom line is still the same: Get the ball in the basket.

The first major change from Naismith's original set of 13 rules was to limit a team to five players. When the game turned into a battle of stalling in the backcourt, the rules makers of the 1930s decided to put in the 10-second rule and force the offensive team into the front half of the court.

By that time, equipment was standardized, and the ball with the lace was on its way out.

Also by the 1930s, Naismith's onetime exhortation to a former player—"Why, Forrest, you don't coach basketball. You play it."—had been proven wrong, mostly by Forrest C. "Phog" Allen. Coaches put innovations into the game on both ends of the floor, and the game continued to pick up pace and followers.

Basketball acquired an international following. Allen convinced the International Olympic Committee that the game should be included in the 1936 Olympics in Berlin. A nationwide drive collected money to send Naismith to Germany to see his invention played on the world stage. It was, Naismith said, the happiest moment of his life.

In 1939 the National Association of Basketball Coaches established a postseason tournament. After two years, the NCAA took over the administration of that event and the NCAA Division I Men's Basketball Tournament has developed into the premier showcase for basketball.

At that time, the college coaches thought there should be a basketball hall of fame, but it was not until after World War II that action was taken on the idea. NABC officials wanted a place to store and exhibit basketball memorabilia for the public and located the facility in the birthplace of the game and named it after the sport's inventor. The Naismith Memorial Hall of Fame in Springfield, Massachusetts, is a production worthy of basketball.

The Hall has an annual induction ceremony. Candidates are chosen based on moral character, demonstrated abil-ity, and national or international recognition. There are four categories for inductees: player, coach, referee, and contributor. A player or referee must be retired for five years before he is eligible. A coach must be retired for three years or have completed 25 years of coaching to be honored.

The Hall's 24-member Honors Committee receives the nominations and decides on five people each year who deserve a place in the Hall of Fame. At least 18 voting members must approve the person's admission.

The list of electees is long and distinguished. The Naismith Memorial is packed with photos, articles, films, games, and stories about the legendary people in basketball. It honors the great-

est players, coaches, and innovators of the game.

The first five members of the Naismith Memorial Basketball Hall of Fame were elected in March 1959. James Naismith and his first team from the YMCA Training School earned the first spots in the hall.

Six months later, twelve more individuals were inducted, including Angelo "Hank" Luisetti, who electrified the game with his innovative one-handed shot; Forrest "Phog" Allen, head coach of Kansas and "Father of Basketball Coaching;" DePaul legend George Mikan; Dr. Luther H. Gulick; and Amos Alonzo Stagg, whose fame as a football coach did not stop him from promoting Naismith and basketball.

Allen played collegiately at Kansas under Naismith, ironically the only University of Kansas basketball coach with a losing record. Allen never had that stigma and coached for 38 years at Kansas until reaching the mandatory retirement age in 1956. By then, Phog Allen was a record book unto himself.

Allen delivered to Kansas 26 conference championships, three NCAA Regional Championships—in 1940, 1942, and 1943—and three national championships—the Helms Foundation titles in 1922 and 1923, and the NCAA Championship in 1952. Allen's final won-loss record remains one of the best in the history of basketball, 746-264, for a .739 winning percentage. He only had two losing seasons in his 38-year career at Kansas.

Allen was among the coaches who organized the National Association of Basketball Coaches and helped put together that group's postseason tournament, which is now under the auspices of the NCAA. His prompting helped make basketball an Olympic sport.

Phog Allen designed many strategies still in use today, only under different names. Other ideas of his did not fly, but led to various changes. Allen, saying there was nothing sacred about the height of the goal, wanted the basket

Eighteen men played on opposing teams in the basketball games of 1891. Everyone at the YMCA was required to exercise for one hour a day.

The first basketball team was composed of the men in school at the YMCA. They included Amos Alonzo Stagg, who is not pictured here.

raised to 12 feet and would use tall men on his team to prove what he considered the farce of a 10-foot goal.

More important, some of those big men became stars of the game. One of the first was Clyde Lovellette, who was inducted into the Hall of Fame in 1989. Lovellette played at Kansas from 1948 to 1952, led the Big Seven Conference in scoring, and earned All-America honors in each of his three varsity seasons. He led the Jayhawks to the 1952 NCAA title and was voted the Most Valuable Player of that tournament.

Lovellette was known for the accuracy of his two-hand, over-the-head shot, which was the accepted shooting style of the day. But Stanford's Hank Luisetti, Hall class of 1959, made his mark 15 years earlier with his one-handed running shot. With Stanford, under Coach John Bunn, inducted into the Hall in 1964, toying with a rudimentary zone

defense and Luisetti's dazzling shots from behind his ear, the school grabbed the attention of the nation.

The hottest of the hotbeds of college basketball was New York's Madison Square Garden, where promoter Ned Irish established the National Invitation Tournament. Irish, enshrined in the Naismith Memorial Hall in 1964, staged college games in Garden with local teams, including Long Island University, City College of New York, and St. Johns as hosts to the nation's best teams throughout the season.

The games regularly attracted 15,000-16,000 fans, making Madison Square Garden the most visible center of college basketball. It also made money for New York City during the depths of the Great Depression.

Unfortunately, the high visibility attracted gamblers, who enticed some players to participate in point-shaving

schemes. Incidents of point-shaving were uncovered after CCNY won both the NIT and NCAA tournaments in 1950. The following year uncovered extensive gambler involvement in college basketball. Over the period from 1947-1951, games had been fixed in 23 cities and involved some of the top teams in the country. In addition to the 1950 CCNY championship team, the Kentucky team that won the 1951 NCAA title had three players involved.

Recovering from the scandals took time, but by the 1960s, the popularity of the sport was growing again. The NCAA tournament also began to expand. But the largest factor in college basketball in the 1960s was the emergence of John Wooden and the UCLA Bruins.

Under Wooden, the Bruins won the 1964 NCAA championship and collected 10 of the next 12 titles, including seven consecutive national crowns and an 88-game winning streak. Wooden set another record, earning induction into the Hall of Fame twice—as a player from Purdue in 1960 and as an active coach in 1972.

Wooden's first decade at UCLA was not spectacular. He won but not consistently. His style pulled in some of the nation's top talent, and his controlled fast-break offense and six- to seven-man first team rotation turned college basketball into UCLA's game. Players such as Lew Alcindor, Bill Walton, and Henry Bibby played for Wooden's Bruins. And the coach's ability to blend that talent with his innovations made him the most successful coach in recent history. No team dominated college basketball like the UCLA Bruins of the 1960s and 1970s.

Two other legendary coaches, Henry Iba and Adolph Rupp, were esconced in the Hall of Fame in 1968.

Mr. Iba—he is always referred to as

"Mister"—coached at Oklahoma A & M, now Oklahoma State, from 1935-1970 and also coached the United States teams in the 1964, 1968, and 1972 Olympics. He led Oklahoma A & M teams to consecutive NCAA championships in 1945 and 1946.

Those A & M teams were led by 7-0 Bob Kurland, a 1961 Hall of Fame inductee. Kurland was the most valuable player in both the 1945 and 1946 NCAA tournaments and claimed three All-America honors.

Mr. Iba was reknown for his ball-control offense. Careful passing allowed Oklahoma A & M to cut down on the scoring chances of the opposition. Bob Kurland seemed to be an exception to the coach's all-pass attack, as shown by his school record 58-point game against St. Louis in 1946, a season in which he also led the country in scoring.

Adolph Rupp was a different coach in philosophy, but just as successful on the court. Rupp coached the University of Kentucky from 1931 to 1972, and the Wildcats were a terror in conference play nearly every season. Kentucky went to the NCAA's Final Four six times under Rupp, winning four titles.

The 1948 Kentucky Wildcats, known as the Fabulous Five, delivered to Rupp the first of his NCAA titles. Four of those players returned for the 1949 season and the team repeated as NCAA titlist. The 1950 edition went to the NIT quarterfinals—losing to eventual NIT and NCAA champion CCNY—but the 1951 Wildcats won the school's third NCAA championship, a record for both

the coach and school.

Rupp had several other very good teams in the 1950s, but ran into problems with investigations off the court. Violations of NCAA recruiting standards led to the team being barred from the 1953 postseason but Rupp was back in 1954 with what was considered his best team. However, three players from that team were ruled ineligible from the NCAA Tournament because the organization declared that they were eligible to graduate.

Kentucky gave Rupp his fourth championship in 1953, beating Seattle 84-72 in Lexington, Kentucky, in the final game.

The 1960s were a time of great change in the United States and also in college basketball. There were many black players on college teams but opportunities were still decidedly limited. Players the caliber of Bill Russell and K. C. Jones were forced to join their teams as walk-ons rather than being offered scholarships.

In the 1966 NCAA finals, Texas Western, now Texas El-Paso, started a team of five black players against an all-white group of Kentucky Wildcats. Western, rated number-three in the country, knocked off the top-ranked Wildcats, 72-65, an outcome that is considered the game that broke the color barrier in college basketball.

Another dynasty-building coach, inducted into the Hall of Fame in 1982, is Dean Smith of North Carolina. Smith, kiddingly called "Smiles" by his teammates, played for Kansas in 1952 when

John Wooden, shown here with the 1973 UCLA Bruins, was inducted twice—as a player in 1960 and as a coach in 1972.

LA SALLE
Tom Gola

the Jayhawks won the NCAA Tournament. Even before that, however, Smith
planned to become a coach. He worked
with the freshmen team and scouted
opponents with assistant coach Dick
Harp. Smith became the head coach at
North Carolina in 1961, and in 1991
became the sixth coach to amass more
than 700 victories. After that season, his
record was worth the fifth-highest winning percentage of all time.

With Smith's coaching drawing a
great array of talent to North Carolina,
he has been able to match Rupp's record
20 NCAA Tournament appearances.
Smith has had seven teams qualify for
the Final Four and won the 1982 title
with the group that included James
Worthy and Michael Jordan.

Smith is perhaps best known for his
four-corners offense, a delay tactic that
could frustrate Job. The rule makers
dampened the ploy's effectiveness, however, by putting in a shot clock prior to
the 1985-1986 season.

A total of 84 players have been inducted into the Hall of Fame. In 1958,
Elgin Baylor, the keystone of national
runner-up Seattle, earned tournament
MVP honors that season after scoring 25
points in the final game against Kentucky. Baylor is one of the few players to
have scored more than 2,000 points and
collected 1,000 rebounds in his career.

Wilt Chamberlain had the ability to
be a Hall of Famer in several sports, but
basketball seemed to be invented with
him in mind. Chamberlain played for

the University of Kansas in the late 1950s and earned induction in the Naismith Memorial Hall of Fame in 1978 after a long and impressive NBA career. Chamberlain was a factor in the game the second he stepped on the Kansas campus, scoring 42 points in the varsity-freshman game that traditionally graced the Jayhawks' homecoming festivities.

He averaged more than 30 points a game as a sophomore, carrying the Jayhawks into the 1957 NCAA title game where Kansas dropped a 54-53 triple-overtime decision to North Carolina. Chamberlain was the most valuable player of the tournament and was a consensus All-America selection in both 1957 and 1958. He left Kansas before his senior year and played a season with the Harlem Globetrotters before becoming one of the greatest players in NBA history.

"Pistol" Pete Maravich was a fashion statement in his drooping socks and a scorekeeper's nightmare with his shooting ability. Maravich holds the NCAA record with 3,667 points for an average of 44.2 points a game in 83 contests for Louisiana State. He was voted into the Hall of Fame in 1987.

Four years earlier, John Havlicek was given his spot in the Naismith Memorial Hall. Havlicek, another great player as a pro, helped Ohio State to the NCAA championship in 1960. In Havlicek's three varsity seasons, the Buckeyes were 78-6.

Elvin Hayes, a 1990 inductee, and

his Houston team has to be given co-star billing with Lew Alcindor and the UCLA Bruins for making the NCAA Tournament the showcase it is. It was the Houston-UCLA match in the 1968 semifinals that shoved the tournament into the spotlight it has never left. Houston beat UCLA earlier that season, in front of a crowd of 52,693 in the Astrodome, but the Bruins answered in the NCAAs and went on to win the second of its seven consecutive titles.

Hayes piled up 1,214 points that season, a figure second only to the 1,381 amassed by Pete Maravich in 1970.

It is the stars and big names of basketball who have been elected to the Naismith Memorial Hall of Fame But just as important to basketball's popularity and status are the fans and the millions of people who are the daily participants in basketball games across the country, whether those games are contested on playgrounds, gymnasiums, arenas with permanent television lighting, or in backyard courts under a 250-watt spotlight. It is for these people that the Hall of Fame exists and preserves the stories of basketball for generations of people who love the game.

MEMBERS OF THE BASKETBALL HALL OF FAME (178)

PLAYERS (84) May 1991

Archibald, Nate 1990-1991
Arizin, Paul J. 1977
*Barlow, Thomas 1980
Barry, Richard F. D. 1986-1987
Baylor, Elgin 1976
*Beckman, John 1972
Bing, Dave 1989-1990
*Borgmann, Bennie 1961
Bradley, William 1982
*Brennan, Joseph 1974
Cervi, Alfred N. 1984
Chamberlain, Wilt 1978
*Cooper, Charles "Tarzan" 1976
Cousy, Robert J. 1970
Cowens, Dave 1990-1991
Cunningham, William J. 1985-1986
*Davies, Robert E. 1969
*DeBernardi, Forrest S. 1961
DeBusschere, Dave 1982
*Dehnert, Henry G. 1968

The more dominant team in the post-Wooden years was Indiana, coached by Bobby Knight who was inducted into the Hall of Fame in 1991. Knight is pictured above with his 1976 NCAA championship team, the first of three in an 11-year span.

Above: Clarence Gaines, elected to the Hall of Fame in 1981, was head coach at Winston-Salem State, a NCAA Division II power-house with a 70 percent winning record.
Opposite page: Bill Bradley exemplifies the ideals of the Hall of Fame. Bradley was All-America, a Rhodes Scholar, had a sensational pro career with the Knicks, and now serves in the U.S. Senate. He was inducted in 1982.

Endacott, Paul 1971
Foster, Harold "Bud" 1964
Frazier Walter 1986-1987
*Friedman, Max "Marty" 1971
*Fulks, Joseph F. 1977
Gale, Lauren "Laddie" 1976
Gallatin, Harry 1990-1991
Gates, William "Pop" 1988-1989
Gola, Thomas J. 1975
Greer, Harold 1981
*Gruenig, Robert 1963
Hagan, Clifford O. 1977
*Hanson Victor 1960
Havlicek, John J. 1983

Hayes, Elvin 1989-1990
Heinsohn, Thomas W. 1985-1986
Holman, Nat 1964
Houbregs, Robert J. 1986-1987
*Hyatt, Charles "Chuck" 1959
*Johnson, William C. 1976
Johnston, Neil 1989-1990
Jones, K. C. 1988-1989
Jones, Samuel 1983
Krause, Edward W. 1975
Kurland, Robert A. 1961
*Lapchick, Joseph 1966
Lovellette, Clyde 1987-1988
Lucas, Jerry Ray 1979
Luisetti, Angelo "Hank" 1959
*McCracken, Branch 1960
*McCracken, Jack 1962
*McDermott, Bobby 1987-1988
Macauley, Edward C. 1960
*Maravich, Peter P. 1986-1987
Martin, Slater 1981
Mikan, George L. 1959
Monroe, Earl 1989-1990
Murphy, Charles "Stretch" 1960
*Page, Harlan O. 1962
Pettit, Robert L. 1970
Phillip, Andy 1961
Pollard, James C. 1977
Ramsey, Frank 1981
Reed, Willis 1981
Robertson, Oscar 1979
*Roosma, Col. John S. 1961
*Russell, John "Honey" 1964
Russell, William F. 1974
Schayes, Adolph 1972
*Schmidt, Ernest J. 1973
*Schommer, John J. 1959
*Sedran, Barney 1962
Sharman, William W. 1975
*Steinmetz, Christian 1961
Thompson, John A. "Cat" 1962
Thurmond, Nate 1984
Twyman, Jack 1982
Unseld, Wes 1987-1988
*Vandivier, Robert "Fuzzy" 1974
*Wachter, Edward A. 1961
Wanzer, Robert F. 1986-1987
West, Jerry Alan 1979
Wilkens, Lenny 1988-1989
Wooden, John R. 1960

COACHES (43)

*Allen, Dr. Forrest C. 1959
*Anderson, W. Harold 1984
Auerbach, Arnold J. "Red" 1968
*Barry, Justin "Sam" 1978
*Blood, Ernest A. 1960

156

Cann, Howard G.	1967	*Hickey, Edgar S. "Eddie"	1978
*Carlson, Dr. H. Clifford	1959	Hobson, Howard A.	1965
Carnevale, Ben	1969	Holzman, William "Red"	1985-1986
*Case, Everett	1981	Iba, Henry P.	1968
Dean, Everett S.	1966	*Julian, Alvin F. "Doggie"	1967
*Diddle, Edgar A.	1971	*Keaney, Frank W.	1960
*Drake, Bruce	1972	*Keogan, George E.	1961
Gaines, Clarence	1981	Knight, Bob	1990-1991
Gardner, James H. "Jack"	1983	*Lambert, Ward L.	1960
*Gill, Amory T.	1967	Litwack, Harry	1975
Harshman, Marv	1984	*Leoffler, Kenneth D.	1964

Bobby Knight won three NCAA tournaments—in 1976, 1981, and 1987—and was named Coach of the Year three times—in 1975, 1976, and 1987.

*Lonborg, Arthur C. 1972
McCutchan, Arad A. 1980
McGuire, Frank J. 1976
McLendon, John B. 1978
*Meanwell, Dr. Walter E. 1959
Meyer, Raymond J. 1978
Miller, Ralph 1987-1988
Newell, Peter F. 1978
*Rupp, Adolph F. 1968
*Sachs, Leonard D. 1961
*Shelton, Everett F. 1979
Smith, Dean 1982
Taylor, Fred R. 1985-1986
Wade, L. Margaret 1984
Watts, Stanley H. 1985-1986
Wooden, John R. 1972

CONTRIBUTORS (41)

*Abbott, Senda Berenson 1984
*Bee, Clair F. 1967
*Brown, Walter A. 1965
*Bunn, John W. 1964
*Douglas, Robert L. 1971
*Duer, Al O. 1981
Fagan, Clifford 1983
*Fisher, Harry A. 1973
*Fleisher, Larry 1990-1991
*Gottlieb, Edward 1971
*Gulick, Dr. Luther H. 1959
Harrison, Lester 1979
*Hepp, Dr. Ferenc 1980
*Hickox, Edward J. 1959
Hinkle, Paul D. "Tony" 1965

*Irish, Ned 1964
*Jones, R. William 1964
*Kennedy, J. Walter 1980
*Liston, Emil S. 1974
*Mokray, William G. 1965
*Morgan, Ralph 1959
*Morgenweck, Frank 1962
*Naismith, Dr. James 1959
*O'Brien, John J. 1961
*O'Brien, Larry 1990-1991
*Olsen, Harold G. 1959
*Podoloff, Maurice 1973
*Porter, Henry V. 1960
*Reid, William A. 1963
*Ripley, Elmer H. 1972
*St. John, Lynn W. 1962
*Saperstein, Abe 1970
*Schabinger, Arthur A. 1961
*Stagg, Amos Alonzo 1959
*Steitz, Edward S. 1983
*Taylor, Charles H. 1968
Teague, Bertha F. 1984
*Tower, Oswald 1959

*Trester, Arthur L. 1961
*Wells, Clifford 1971
*Wilke, Lou 1982

REFEREES (11)

*Enright, James E. 1978
*Hepbron, George T. 1960
*Hoyt, George T. 1961
*Kennedy, Matthew P. "Pat" 1959
*Leith, Lloyd 1982
Mihalik, Zigmund "Red" 1985-1986
Nucatola, John P. 1977
*Quigley, Ernest C. 1961
Shirley, J. Dallas 1979
*Tobey, David 1961
*Walsh, David H. 1961

TEAMS (4)

First Team 1959
Original Celtics 1959
Buffalo Germans 1961
New York Renaissance 1963

*Deceased
Note: John R. Wooden appears in two separate categories, player and coach.

Kansas All-Time Lettermen

A

Ackerman, Arthur (C)	C,F	1923-1925
Adams, Ira (C)	G,F	1904, 1905
Adams, Irwin (C)	F,G	1903-1904
Alberts, Jerry	F	1953-1954
Alexander, Todd	G	1990
Alford, Donald	F,C	1902, 1903
Alford, Joseph (C)	F,C	1901-1904
Allen, Forrest C.	C,F	1905-1907
Allen, Harry	C	1902-1904
Allen, Milton	F,G	1934-1936
Allen, Robert (C)	C	1939-1941
Allphin, Clyde		1900-1903
Alvarado, Sean	C	1987, 1989
Ames, Loren		1903
Anderson, Ferrel		1937, 1938
Anderson, John (C)	G	1953-1955
Anderson, Robert		1946
Anderson, Scott	F	1977, 1978
Appel, Hilmar	F,G	1915, 1916
Arndt, Howard	F	1967-1969
Arnold, James		1941
Atkinson, Paul	C	1902
Auten, Don		1946, 1947
Avery, Herbert	G	1899

B

Baker, Hoyt		1943, 1946
Baker, Ralph	G	1931
Ballard, John	G	1942, 1943, 1946
Ballard, Eugene		1946, 1948
Banks, Tim	G	1983, 1984
Barlow, Frank	F,G	1904-1906
Barnthouse, Chris	G	1975-1977
Barr, Eugene		1946, 1948
Barrington, Donald	F	1944
Barrow, Wilson (C)	F	1972, 1973
Barry, Richard (Scooter) (C)	G	1986-1989
Bausch, Frank	G	1930, 1932
Bausch, James		1930
Beck, Walter	G	1951
Belgard, Wilferd (C)	G	1924-1926
Benn, Carl		1933
Bennett, Roy	G,F	1919-1921
Bergen, Ralph	C,G	1906-1909
Bernhard, Bernice	Manager	1902
Billings, Robert	G	1957-1959
Bishop, Tom (C)	F	1929-1931
Black, Charles B. (C)	F	1942, 1943,

Black, Charles T. (C)	G,F	1922-1924
Blair, Donald	G	1942, 1943
Bliss, Charles (C)	F	1905
Boagni, Kerry	F	1983
Boehm, Walter	C	1912, 1913
Bohnenstiehl, Roger (C)	F	1966-1968
Bolton, Kerry	G	1963-1965
Born, B. H. (C)	C	1952-1954
Bosilevac, Fred	F	1937
Bosilevac, Fred Jr.	F	1970-1972
Bowman, Waldo	F	1922, 1923
Boyle, Thomas (Tad) (C)	G	1982-1985
Bradshaw, Richard	G	1969
Brainard, William		1954-1956
Branch, Marvin	C	1988
Bridges, Bill	F	1959-1961
Brill, David	F	1963-1965
Brill, William		1943
Brown, Andrew	G	1902-1904
Brown, Loren		1912, 1913
Brown, Roger	C	1969-1971
Brown, Terry	G	1990, 1991
Buescher, John (C)	C	1941-1943
Bukaty, Frank		1939
Bull, Clinton	F,G	1949-1951
Buller, Kenneth	F	1953
Bunn, John	G,F	1918-1920
Burton, Glenn (C)	G	1926-1928

C

Calloway, Rick (C)	F	1990
Campbell, Altonio	G	1985, 1986
Campbell, Clifford	F	1925, 1926
Canfield, Randy	C	1971, 1972
Carlson, Norman	F	1945
Carroll, William	F,G	1979-1980
Chamberlain, Wilton	C	1957, 1958
Chana, Fred	F	1964-1966
Clark, Wendell	G	1946, 1947
Cleland, John	G	1956-1958
Cole, Lawrence (C)	C	1914-1916
Cook, Arthur	C	1904
Cook, Norman (C)	F	1974-1976
Corder, Dean	C	1944-1946
Corlis, Lyman (C)	G,F	1937-1939
Correll, Allen (C)	F	1960, 1961, 1963, 1964
Cox, Forrest (C)	G	1929-1931
Cox, Marvin	C,F	1936
Crawford, John	F	1978-1981

Crosswhite, William	F,G	1926
Curd, Robert	F	1934

D

Daniels, John	F,C	1926
Dater, Edwin	G	1956, 1957
Daum, Gustave	G,C	1945, 1946
Davenport, Lawrence		1952-1955
Davis, Patrick	G	1966, 1967
Deane, Carl	G	1962
Dennis, David	F	1949
Dewell, John	G	1948
Dick, George	G	1942-1944
Diehl, Donald	G	1944
Dishman, Jeffery	F	1982, 1983
Dixon, Armand	G	1943
Dobbs, Dallas (C)	G	1954-1956
Dodd, Leo	C	1928, 1929
Donaghue, Alan	F	1958-1960
Douglas, Greg	F	1968, 1971
Douglas, John (C)	G	1977, 1978
Douglas, Keith	G	1980
Dousman, Donald (C)	F,G	1911, 1912
Dreiling, Greg (C)	C	1984-1986
Dumas, Jimmy (C)	F	1961-1963
Dunmire, Ray (C)	G	1913-1915
Durand, Fenlon	F	1937, 1938
Dye, Everett	F,G	1953

E

Ebling, Donald (C)	F	1938-1940
Ebling, Ray (C)	F	1934-1936
Ediger, Jaye	F	1967
Ellison, Benoyd	F,G	1960, 1961
Ellison, Nolen (C)		1961-1963
Elstun, Donald (C)		1955-1957
Elstun, Doug	G	1991
Emley, Samuel	C	1899
Endacott, Paul (C)	G	1921-1923
Engel, Dale		1949-1951
Engel, Verne	F	1924, 1925
England, Harold	F	1947-1950
Engleman, Howard (C)		1939-1941
Enns, Myron	F,G	1948, 1951
Eskridge, Jack	G	1947, 1948
Evans, Ray	G	1942, 1943, 1946, 1947
Ewing, Mark	C	1982, 1983

F

Fearing, Olin	F	1918-1920
Fees, Charles	G	1901, 1902
Fiddelke, Michael	F	1973
Filkin, Lawrence	F	1933
Fitzpatrick, Wilson		1942, 1943
Flachsbarth, Leland	C	1962
Florell, Loren	F	1938, 1939
Folks, Ray	G	1914, 1915

Forsyth, William		1943
Fowler, Wilmore	G	1978, 1979
Frank, Willard	F	1944
Franklin, Kenneth	G	1972
Franz, Ronald	F	1965-1967
Frederick, Byron	C	1919, 1922, 1923
Frisby, Donald	G	1946

G

Gardner, Jerry	G	1960-1962
Gear, George		1946
Gibbens, Leon		1916-1917
Gibson, Harry (C)	F	1962-1964
Gibson, Milton	G	1975-1978
Giles, Chester	C,F	1979, 1980
Gisel, Richard	G	1960
Goehring, Louis	G,C	1944, 1945
Golay, George	F	1937, 1938
Gordon, Gale	C	1925, 1927
Gough, James	F	1964, 1965
Gray, Gordon	G	1933-1935
Green, Leland	F	1955-1957
Greenlee, Dale (C)	G	1973-1975
Greenlees, Charles (C)	F	1912-1914
Griggs, Adessie	F	1904
Gueldner, Jeff (C)	G	1987-1990
Guiot, Jeffery	G	1983, 1984
Guy, Anthony (C)	G	1979-1982

H

Haase, Dale	F	1972, 1973
Hackett, John	C	1908
Hall, Edward		1941
Hall, Vance	F	1941, 1942
Harmon, Phillip		1967-1969
Harms, Marvin		1919, 1920
Harp, Richard (C)	G	1938-1940
Harrington, Paul (C)	F	1932-1934
Harris, Fred		1934
Harris, Keith	F	1987, 1988
Hauser, Harold	C	1928
Heckert, Henry	C	1924
Heim, Herbert	G,C	1945
Heitholt, Arthur		1952-1954
Heizer, Robert (C)	C	1909-1911
Henderson, Willis	G	1898, 1899
Henry, Carl (C)	G	1983, 1984
Hess, Henry		1899
Hess, William	F,C	1898
Heyward, Ralph	F	1961
Hickman, Robert	G	1958-1960
Hicks, Albert	C,F	1902-1904
Hightower, Wayne	F	1960, 1961
Hill, Everett	G	1945
Hill, James (C)	F	1926-1928
Hill, Lance	G	1982, 1983
Hite, Ora	F	1912, 1913

Hitt, Ward	G,F	1925	Johnson, Jeff	G	1985, 1986	Kline, John (C)	F,G	1939-1941
Hoag, Charlie	G	1951, 1952	Johnson, Jerry		1958	Knight, Danny (C)	C	1973-1975
Hodges, Gregory	G,F	1926	Johnson, Jerry L.	F	1986	Knight, Kelly (C)	F,C	1980, 1982-
Hoffman, James	F	1958-1960	Johnson, Lewis	C	1955-1957			1984
Hogben, William	G	1940	Johnson, Monte	F	1957-1959	Knight, Mark	G,F	1981
Holliday, James		1936, 1937	Johnson, Thomas (C)	F	1909-1911	Knoles, James	F	1918
Hollinger, Blaine	G	1955-1957	Johnson, Wallace		1940-1942	Koenigs, Kenneth (C)		1975-1978
Holmer, Robert		1936	Johnson, William (C)		1931-1933	Konek, Jeffrey	G	1981
Houchin, Claude (C)	G	1947-1950	Johnston, Ronald	G	1955-1957			
Hougland, William	F,G	1950-1952	Jordan, Adonis	F	1990, 1991	L		
Houk, Clarence	F	1921				Larson, Harold	G	1910-1911
House, Jerry	F	1971, 1972	K			Larson, Louis	G	1908
Housey, Arthur	C	1980, 1981	Kaiser, Karl	G,C	1915	Laslett, Howard (C)	G	1917, 1919
Hoyt, Harold		1899	Kampschroeder, Brad	F	1989	Lattin, Clarence	G	1926, 1927
Hull, Rodney	F	1985, 1986	Kappelman, Franics	G	1934-1936	Lawrence, William (C)	G	1968-1970
Hunt, Robert		1938	Kappelman, Lester	G,F	1937-1939	Lewis, Delvin (C)	G	1964-1966
Hunter, Cedric	G	1984-1987	Kauder, Walter	F,G	1916, 1917	Lienhard, William		1950-1952
Hunter, Thomas	G	1940-1942	Keller, John	F,G	1951, 1952	Lindsey, Adrian		1917
			Kelley, Earl (C)	G	1953, 1954	Linquist, William		1944
I			Kelley, Melvin (C)	G	1951-1953	Linville, Aubrey	G	1950
Israel, Warren	F	1942	Kellogg, Ronald	F,G	1983-1986	Lochmann, Riney (C)	F	1964-1966
			Kennedy, Carl	F	1916	Lockley, Robert	F	1956
J			Kenney, Robert		1950-1952	Lonborg, Arthur (C)	G	1918-1920
Jamison, Alonzo	F	1990, 1991	Ketchum, Dee		1959-1961	Lonborg, John		1922-1924
Jeffrey, Balfour	G	1927, 1928	Kindred, Lynn	G	1957-1959	Loneski, Ronald	G	1957-1959
Jennings, Charles		1902	King, Clifford		1974	Long, Verne	F	1909-1911
Jett, Harry	F	1956, 1957	King, Maurice	F	1955-1957	Lopes, Albert	G,F	1965, 1966
Johanning, David	C	1991	Kissell, Max	F,C	1942, 1943	Lovellette, Clyde (C)	C	1950-1952
Johnson, Carl	G	1938	Kivisto, Robert	G	1970, 1971	Loving, Wayne	G	1964
Johnson, Charles		1906	Kivisto, Thomas (C)	G	1972-1974	Lutton, Lyle	G	1937
Johnson, Clinton	G	1975-1978	Klaas, Roy	G	1933	Lytle, Harold	G	1916, 1917

M

Mabry, Guy	F	1948-1950
Maddox, Mike	F	1988-1991
Magley, David (C)	F	1979-1982
Malott, Robert	F	1944
Mandeville, Frank	G	1918
Maney, Robert	G	1927-1929
Manning, Danny (C)	F	1985-1988
Markkanen, Pekka	C	1990
Marshall, Archie (C)	F	1986, 1988
Marshall, Grover	G	1961
Marshall, Mike	G	1984
Martin, Brian (C)	C	1982-1984
Martin, Maurice		1946, 1948, 1949
Martindell, Donald	G	1908-1910
Mask, Neal	F	1970-1972
Mason, Edward	G	1919
Mathews, Kelsey (C)	C	1918, 1919
Mathews, Mark	F	1970-1972
Matt, John	C	1961-1963
Mattox, Marvin	F	1988
McCauley, James	G	1904
McCormick, George	G	1929
McCune, George (C)	F	1907-1909
McDonald, Andrew	F	1921-1923
McElroy, Harold	F	1954
McGuire, Clarence		1928, 1929
McSpadden, Harold (C)	G	1943, 1944
Michaelson, Manley	F	1904
Miller, Howard	F	1918-1920
Miller, Milton (C)	G	1905-1908
Miller, Ralph	F	1939, 1940, 1942
Miller, Richard		1942
Miller, William	C	1905-1908
Minor, Lincoln	G	1988, 1989
Mitchell, Victor	C	1981
Moffett, Charles	F,C	1944, 1945, 1949
Mokeski, Paul (C)	C	1976-1979
Morningstar, Roger	F	1974, 1975
Mosby, James	G	1923

N

Nash, Aubrey	G	1970-1972
Nash, David		1968, 1969
Nash, Macolm	F	1990, 1991
Natsus, Timothy	G	1969
Neal, Douglas	G	1978-1981
Nees, Charles	G	1938, 1939
Nelson, Lawrence (C)	G	1916, 1917
Newland, Carmen	F	1927, 1928
Newton, Milt (C)	F	1985, 1987-1989
Nicholson, Eldon		1953
Noble, Raymond (C)	G,F	1935-1937
Nobles, Herbert	F	1976, 1977
Normore, Clint	G	1988

O

O'Leary, Theodore (C)	F	1930-1932
Olson, Herbert	C	1920, 1921
Owen, Arthur	G	1938
Owens, Eugene	F,C	1898-1901
Owens, Frederick (C)	G,F	1898-1902
Oyler, Robert		1934, 1935

P

Padgett, Gary	F	1954, 1955
Page, Leland (C)	G	1930-1932
Parker, John (C)	G	1955-1957
Patterson, Harold	F	1953, 1954
Pattinson, Darwin	G	1916
Peacock, Charles	G	1982
Peard, Roger	F	1908
Peck, Owen	C,G	1945-1947
Pellock, Mark	F	1985, 1987
Penny, Charles	F	1947-1949
Petersen, Albert	C	1925-1927
Peterson, Arthur		1946, 1949, 1950
Piatt, William		1904
Piper, Chris (C)	F	1985-1988
Plumley, Francis	F	1929

Smith, Dean	F	1952, 1953
Smith, Lester	G	1912, 1913
Smith, Lynwood		1949, 1950
Smith, Tommie	F	1973-1975
Smith, Verni	G	1910
Snow, Mark	C	1980
Snyder, Harry	G	1910-1912
Sollenberger, Marvin	G	1941, 1942
Sorensen, Ephraim	F	1915
Sparks, Loye	F	1962, 1963
Sproull, Ralph (C)	F	1913-1915
Squires, La Vannes		1953, 1954
Stallcup, John (Mac) (C)	F,C	1978-1980
Stallworth, Isaac (Bud) (C)	F	1970-1972
Stramel, Gilbert	F	1946-1948
Stratton, Daniel		1924
Stucker, Charles		1944
Stuckey, George	F	1911, 1912
Sullivan, Nelson	F	1938
Summers, Mark (C)	F	1981-1983
Suttle, Richard	F	1973-1975
Sutton, Walter		1899
Sutton, William (C)		1899

T

Taynor, David (C)	G	1972-1974
Thomas, Richard	G	1967, 1968
Thompson, Calvin	F	1983-1986
Thompson, Gary	F	1957-1959
Thompson, George	F	1981
Thomson, Charles (C)		1928-1930
Toft, James		1956
Tolan, John	G	1902
Tunstall, Sean	G	1991
Turgeon, Mark (C)	G	1984-1987
Turner, Jesse	F	1942, 1943
Turner, Robert		1944

U

Uhrlaub, Ernst (C)	F,G	1917, 1919-1921
Uhrlaub, Rudolf (C)	G,F	1916-1918
Ulrich, Hubert		1942
Unseld, George	C	1963, 1964
Urie, Raymond		1933

V

Vance, Robert	G	1962-1964
Valentine, Darnell (C)	G	1978-1981
Van der Vries, Edward	F	1910, 1914
Vanek, Ernest	G	1932, 1934
Vanoy, Vernon	C	1967, 1968
Von Moore, Donnie	F,C	1975, 1977, 1978
Voran, Bruce	C,G	1939, 1940

Pooler, Arthur		1903, 1904	Royal, Claude		1899, 1900
Pralle, Ferdinand (C)	G	1936-1938	Ruggles, Richard	G	1964
Priest, Richard		1904	Rupp, Adolph	C,G	1923
Pritchard, Kevin (C)	G	1987-1990	Russell, Pierre (C)	F	1969-1971
Proudfit, Herbert	F	1926	Russell, Rusel	G	1899, 1900

Q

Queens, Eugene		1898

R

Ramsey, Floyd	G	1929-1931
Randall, Mark	F	1987, 1989-1991
Reber, John		1916
Reich, Gilbert	G	1953
Reid, Bruce	F,C	1938
Renko, Steve	F	1964
Replogle, Max	G	1939
Reynolds, Albert		1945
Rice, Carl	G	1918
Richey, Patrick	G,F	1991
Roberts, Jay	F	1962, 1963
Robisch, David	F	1969-1971
Rogers, Marshall		1973
Rody, George (C)	F	1929-1922
Rogers, Paul (C)	F	1935-1937
Ross, Ricky	G	1980
Rouse, Carl (Fresh. Coach)		1909

S

Samuel, Nino	F	1973
Sanders, Bradford (C)	G	1976-1979
Sands, Jack	C	1939, 1940
Sanneman, Norman	C	1941
Sapp, Ora (C)	G	1947-1949
Schaake, Elmer	G	1932, 1933
Schaake, William		1951
Schichtle, David (C)	G	1963-1965
Schmidt, George (C)	F	1925-1927
Schmidt, Sylvester (C)	F	1937, 1938
Schnellbacher, Otto (C)	F	1943, 1946-1948
Scott, Closson	G	1945
Scott, Richard	F	1991
Shaffer, Wilmer	F	1934-1936
Sherwood, Homer	C	1944
Short, John	F	1943
Siler, Charles	F,C	1905-1907
Sloan, Bruce (C)	G	1967-1969
Smith, Cecil		1906
Smith, Chester (C)	G	1901, 1902

W

Wagner, Kirk — F — 1990, 1991
Walker, Charles — G,C — 1941, 1942
Watson, Raymond — F — 1910
Waugh, Gerald (C) — C — 1949-1951
Weaver, Arthur — C — 1912-1914
Weidlein, William — G — 1914
Weidner, Carl — G — 1937
Welch, Mark — G — 1981
Wellhausen, Al — C — 1935, 1937
Wells, John (C) — 1934, 1935
Wells, Marion — G,F — 1950, 1951

Wesley, Walter — C — 1964-1966
West, Freeman (C) — F — 1989, 1990
White, Joseph (C) — G — 1966-1969
Whitfield, Claude — F — 1928, 1929
Weinecke, Edwin — 1938
Wilkin, William — F,G — 1923, 1925
Williams, Edgar — F — 1945
Wilson, Robert — G — 1966
Winnagle, Roscoe — G,F — 1905, 1906
Woestemeyer, Armin — F — 1921-1923
Wohler, Paul — 1907, 1908
Wolf, John — G — 1954

Woodberry, Steve — G — 1991
Woodward, Brinton — G — 1962
Woodward, Earl (C) — G — 1907-1910
Woodward, George — 1917
Worrel, Richard — F — 1981
Wulf, John — C — 1921-1923

Y

Yahn, William — 1899, 1900
Yarnevich, George — F — 1967

Z

Zuber, Harold — C,F — 1925-1927

Year-By-Year Scores

1898-1899 Won 7, Lost 4
Coach: Dr. James Naismith
Kansas City YMCA	L	5-16
TOPEKA YMCA	W	31-6
LAWRENCE YMCA	W	14-4
KANSAS CITY YMCA	W	17-14
Topeka YMCA	W	27-15
Topeka YMCA	W	23-12
HASKELL	W	29-8
Kansas City AC	L	5-19
Independence (Missouri)	L	15-21
Independence (Missouri)	L	10-22
William Jewell	W	19-3

1899-1900 Won 3, Lost 4
Coach: Dr. James Naismith
HASKELL	W	14-5
HASKELL	W	13-7
Topeka YMCA	L	14-28
Kansas City YMCA	L	8-18
Nebraska	L	8-48
Omaha YMCA	W	12-10
KANSAS CITY YMCA	L	15-21

1900-1901 Won 4, Lost 8
Coach: Dr. James Naismith
William Jewell	L	6-8
Ajax AC	L	0-2 ++
HASKELL	L	22-40
Independence (Missouri)	L	8-11
Independence (Missouri)	L	13-29
Topeka YMCA	L	7-14
LAWRENCE YMCA	W	28-12
Haskell	L	12-18
TOPEKA YMCA	L	21-23

Ottawa YMCA	W	14-8
LAWRENCE YMCA	W	29-20
HASKELL	W	25-20

++ In dispute over knowledge of the rules, KU walked off the court. Game was forfeited.

1901-1902 Won 5, Lost 7
Coach: Dr. James Naismith
HASKELL	L	19-31
OTTAWA	L	21-25
Haskell	W	27-23
WILLIAM JEWELL	W	12-11
Des Moines YMCA	W	38-23
Muscatine YMCA	L	25-38
Iowa	L	27-40
Fairfield Co. M	L	17-33
Ottumwa	L	10-20
William Jewell	W	19-16
NEBRASKA	L	29-35
Leavenworth YMCA	W	36-7

1902-1903 Won 7, Lost 8
Coach: Dr. James Naismith
HASKELL	L	12-23
William Jewell	L	10-12
Newton AC	W	38-7
Chicago Central YMCA	L	18-43
Monmouth AC	L	21-40
Fond du Lac, AC	L	20-29
Schmelzer AC	L	11-15
Lee's Summit AC	W	31-11
William Jewell	W	23-12
Nebraska	L	19-23
Omaha YMCA	W	26-24
Highland Park	W	21-9

Des Moines YMCA	L	10-16
Ottumwa YMCA	W	29-5
Fairfield AC	W	28-16

1903-1904 Won 5, Lost 8
Coach: Dr. James Naismith
OLATHE YMCA	W	35-10
WILLIAM JEWELL	W	27-10
KANSAS STATE DEAF	W	35-10
TOPEKA YMCA	W	25-22
HASKELL	L	12-28
Topeka YMCA	L	16-18
William Jewell	L	7-27
Kansas City AC	L	10-27
Haskell	L	18-36
OTTAWA	L	21-25
Ottawa	L	16-26
Newton AC	W	18-10
Emporia Teachers	L	13-25

1904-1905 Won 5, Lost 6
Coach: Dr. James Naismith
EMPORIA STATE	W	45-11
Nebraska Wesleyan	L	37-45
Omaha YMCA	L	24-31
Des Moines YMCA	L	19-37
Oskaloosa YMCA	W	37-14
Oskaloosa YMCA	W	56-21
Ottumwa YMCA	L	22-34
Fairfield YMCA	L	20-29
FRATERNAL AID	L	20-37
OSAGE CITY	W	18-8
EMPORIA STATE	W	47-18

1905-1906 Won 12, Lost 7
Coach: Dr. James Naismith
Emporia State	W	33-22
Newton	L	18-23
Chilocco	W	43-17
Baker	L	18-22
CHILOCCO	W	19-11
Washburn	W	22-19
Wyandotte AC	W	40-10
Independence AC	W	43-16
Kansas City YMCA	W	56-6
Nebraska	W	37-17
Des Moines YMCA	W	25-20
Iowa	L	20-28
Armour Institute	W	34-25
Evanston YMCA	L	13-29
Chicago Central YMCA	L	12-35
Muscatine YMCA	L	19-43
Fairfield	L	39-42
WASHBURN	W	39-12
EMPORIA STATE	W	60-13

1906-1907 Won 7, Lost 8
Coach: Dr. James Naismith
LAWRENCE YMCA	W	43-37
KANSAS STATE	W	54-39
OTTAWA	W	37-35
NEBRASKA	L	19-32
Kansas State	L	25-29
Emporia State	W	35-20
Newton YMCA	W	41-27
Baker	L	24-39
Warrensburg	W	34-16
Kansas City AC	L	35-44
William Jewell	L	20-22
Co. F, Independence	L	15-41
KIRKSVILLE	W	65-21
MISSOURI	L	31-34
MISSOURI	L	12-34

1907-1908 Won 18, Lost 6
Coach: Dr. F. C. Allen

+OTTAWA	W	66-22
Ottawa	L	33-39
Newton YMCA	W	37-32
Newton YMCA	W	39-32
William Jewell	L	16-27
NEBRASKA	L	17-20
NEBRASKA	L	21-23
NOME, ALASKA	L	28-34
NEWTON YMCA	W	26-25
KANSAS CITY AC	W	25-16
KANSAS STATE	W	50-12
Washburn	W	19-17
MISSOURI	W	21-20
MISSOURI	W	24-18
WASHBURN	W	39-15
WILLIAM JEWELL	W	19-11
Kansas City AC	W	34-32
Warrensburg	W	34-16
Missouri	W	30-19
Missouri	W	26-22
Des Moines YMCA	L	17-34
Iowa State	W	53-35
Nebraska	W	28-26
Nebraska	W	28-25

1908-1909 Won 25, Lost 3
Coach: Dr. F. C. Allen

Baker	W	21-17
BAKER	W	44-16
Emporia State	W	36-24
Kansas State	W	42-27
Kansas Wesleyan	W	35-18
Bethany	W	36-24
Fairmount	W	65-15
Winfield YMCA	W	47-34
Chilocco	W	39-9
NEBRASKA	W	48-13
NEBRASKA	W	36-17
IOWA STATE	W	65-22
WILLIAM JEWELL	W	63-12
OTTAWA	W	61-22
WASHBURN	W	36-10
Nebraska	W	18-13
MISSOURI	W	24-14
MISSOURI	W	31-23
Warrensburg	W	37-14
Washington (Missouri)	L	26-28
Washington (Missouri)	W	23-18
Missouri	W	25-19
Missouri	L	21-38
WASHINGTON (Missouri)	W	33-28
WASHINGTON (Missouri)	W	27-25
Nebraska	W	28-22
Nebraska	W	24-15
Nebraska	L	29-32

*Indicates overtime
+Dedication game of Robinson Gymnasium

1909-1910 Won 18, Lost 1
Coach: W. O. Hamilton

NEBRASKA	W	33-17
NEBRASKA	W	40-16
WASHINGTON (Missouri)	W	46-7
WASHINGTON (Missouri)	W	34-13
BAKER	W	37-24
Baker	W	27-21
KANSAS STATE	W	44-19
BETHANY	W	47-22
MISSOURI	W	29-15
MISSOURI	W	27-14
Kansas City AC	W	34-31
Washington (Missouri)	W	19-16
Washington (Missouri)	L	15-16

Missouri	W	25-21
Missouri	W	58-22
Drake	W	62-33
Iowa State	W	34-18
Nebraska	W	40-20
Nebraska	W	40-13

1910-1911 Won 12, Lost 6
Coach: W. O. Hamilton

BAKER	W	40-17
IOWA STATE	W	41-21
IOWA STATE	W	54-18
Baker	W	27-21
MISSOURI	W	34-28
MISSOURI	W	27-14
KANSAS CITY AC	W	36-29
NEBRASKA	L	27-36
NEBRASKA	W	37-12
Kansas City AC	L	40-41 *
Missouri	W	32-16
Missouri	W	36-25
Iowa State	W	37-36 *
Iowa State	W	28-17
Grinnell	L	16-17
Cotner	L	26-35
Nebraska	L	26-38
Nebraska	L	24-36

1911-1912 Won 11, Lost 7
Coach: W. O. Hamilton

BAKER	W	45-18
NEBRASKA	L	26-30
NEBRASKA	L	27-30
KANSAS CITY AC	W	43-15
KANSAS STATE	W	37-24
Kansas City AC	W	31-25
Baker	W	34-13
MISSOURI	W	27-16
MISSOURI	W	31-21

WASHINGTON (Missouri)	W	43-16
WASHINGTON (Missouri)	W	30-22
Missouri	W	39-24
Missouri	W	32-26
Washington (Missouri)	L	18-26
Washington (Missouri)	L	28-32
Kansas State	L	28-33
Nebraska	L	21-49
Nebraska	L	28-29

1912-1913 Won 16, Lost 6
Coach: W. O. Hamilton

HASKELL	W	56-27
HASKELL	W	41-25
WASHBURN	W	44-25
KANSAS STATE	L	21-39
KANSAS STATE	L	25-27
Kansas State	W	34-19
Kansas State	W	30-20
Washburn	L	40-41
WASHINGTON (Missouri)	W	44-25
WASHINGTON (Missouri)	W	68-8
MISSOURI	W	22-12
MISSOURI	W	34-20
WILLIAM JEWELL	W	47-19
COLLEGE OF EMPORIA	W	41-29
Missouri	L	20-26
Missouri	W	33-26
Washington (Missouri)	W	29-28
Washington (Missouri)	W	45-29
Warrensburg	W	30-24
Nebraska	L	26-40
NEBRASKA	L	16-18
Nebraska	W	30-24

1913-1914 Won 17, Lost 1
Coach: W. O. Hamilton

IOWA STATE	W	24-18
IOWA STATE	W	38-22

Dean Nesmith, Trainer, 1937-1983

1916-1917 Won 12, Lost 8
Coach: W. O. Hamilton

WASHBURN	W	55-9
EMPORIA STATE	W	36-27
Iowa State	W	30-13
Iowa State	W	25-9
K. C. Poly	W	45-22
KANSAS STATE	W	34-16
KANSAS STATE	W	27-19
Kansas State	L	9-38
Kansas State	L	29-32
MISSOURI	W	24-23
MISSOURI	L	17-26
WASHINGTON (Missouri)	W	34-26
WASHINGTON (Missouri)	W	33-25
NEBRASKA	L	19-21
NEBRASKA	W	30-10
Missouri	L	20-24
Missouri	L	15-38
Washington (Missouri)	L	16-24
Washington (Missouri)	W	29-19
Kansas All Stars	L	20-26

1917-1918 Won 10, Lost 8
Coach: W. O. Hamilton

CAMP FUNSTON	W	37-27
IOWA STATE	W	24-21
IOWA STATE	W	31-20
DRAKE	W	61-24
KANSAS STATE	L	23-36
KANSAS STATE	W	35-32
MISSOURI	L	22-36
MISSOURI	L	21-25
WASHINGTON (Missouri)	W	51-22
WASHINGTON (Missouri)	W	40-25
Nebraska	L	23-24
Nebraska	W	31-25
Missouri	L	21-39
Missouri	W	28-23
Washington (Missouri)	L	23-47
Washington (Missouri)	L	18-32
Kansas State	W	35-33
Kansas State	L	25-32

1918-1919 Won 7, Lost 9
Coach: W. O. Hamilton

Iowa State	W	50-17
Iowa State	L	28-29
BAKER	W	33-30
MISSOURI	L	25-45
MISSOURI	W	15-37
Kansas State	L	30-33
Kansas State	L	27-41
K. C. POLY	W	50-34
Missouri	L	20-34
Missouri	W	36-29
Washington (Missouri)	W	35-31
Washington (Missouri)	W	39-19
KANSAS STATE	L	22-37
KANSAS STATE	L	18-31
NEBRASKA	W	31-17
NEBRASKA	L	24-29

1919-1920 Won 11, Lost 7
Coach: Dr. F. C. Allen

EMPORIA STATE*	W	37-22
WASHBURN	W	50-40
IOWA STATE	W	29-27
IOWA STATE	W	28-18
MISSOURI	L	27-32
MISSOURI	L	16-38
Kansas State	W	33-18
Kansas State	L	12-26
Grinnell	W	42-11

HASKELL	W	49-28	KANSAS STATE	W	39-20
WASHBURN	W	39-28	MISSOURI	W	42-23
Kansas State	W	44-26	MISSOURI	W	44-19
Kansas State	L	25-29	Missouri	W	33-22
KANSAS STATE	W	28-24	Missouri	W	40-26
KANSAS STATE	W	41-16	Washington (Missouri)	W	48-16
WASHINGTON (Missouri)	W	50-19	Washington (Missouri)	W	39-20
WASHINGTON (Missouri)	W	41-11			
Missouri	W	28-25			
Missouri	W	27-21	**1915-1916 Won 6, Lost 12**		
Washington (Missouri)	W	29-18	Coach: W. O. Hamilton		
Washington (Missouri)	W	32-21	IOWA STATE	W	26-25
WARRENSBURG	W	49-22	IOWA STATE	L	21-24
MISSOURI	W	38-22	WASHBURN	W	38-10
MISSOURI	W	31-18	Nebraska	L	33-34
College of Emporia	W	40-25	Nebraska	L	27-40
			KANSAS STATE	L	18-31
1914-1915 Won 16, Lost 1			KANSAS STATE	L	12-26
Coach: W. O. Hamilton			WASHINGTON (Missouri)	W	30-16
Iowa State	W	29-22	WASHINGTON (Missouri)	W	43-13
Iowa State	W	27-23	Missouri	L	24-30
WARRENSBURG	W	46-20	Missouri	L	20-42
WILLIAM JEWELL	W	55-21	Washington (Missouri)	W	30-25
NEBRASKA	W	45-17	Washington (Missouri)	L	24-33
NEBRASKA	W	30-23	Kansas State	L	23-38
Kansas State	W	38-22	Kansas State	L	21-45
Kansas State	W	36-32	EMPORIA STATE	L	25-36
WASHBURN	W	53-28	MISSOURI	L	10-41
KANSAS STATE	L	18-21	MISSOURI	W	31-19

Drake	W	37-18
Missouri	L	21-36
Missouri	L	13-31
Washington (Missouri)	L	27-28
Washington (Missouri)	L	35-37
OKLAHOMA	W	33-28
OKLAHOMA	W	42-26
KANSAS STATE	W	30-24
KANSAS STATE	W	31-23

*Karl Schlademan started season as coach but resigned after first game to concentrate on his duties as head track coach. Dr. Allen replaced him.

1920-1921 Won 10, Lost 8
Coach: Dr. F. C. Allen

DRAKE	W	41-18
DRAKE	W	34-28
Iowa State	W	28-13
Iowa State	W	17-15
GRINNELL	W	35-20
GRINNELL	W	31-17
Missouri	L	22-27
Missouri	L	21-28
KANSAS STATE	L	18-31
KANSAS STATE	L	22-24
WASHINGTON (Missouri)	W	39-28
WASHINGTON (Missouri)	W	46-17
Kansas State	L	30-36
Kansas State	L	18-26
MISSOURI	L	17-33
MISSOURI	L	30-41
Oklahoma	W	33-30
Oklahoma	W	37-32

1921-1922 Won 16, Lost 2
Coach: Dr. F. C. Allen

Minnesota	W	32-11
GRINNELL	W	38-16
DRAKE	W	28-23
WASHINGTON (Missouri)	W	44-17
Nebraska	W	25-15

MISSOURI	L	25-35
Kansas City AC	L	32-34
Oklahoma	W	41-24
IOWA STATE	W	32-21
Kansas State	W	32-23
OKLAHOMA	W	42-28
Iowa State	W	24-18
Grinnell	W	21-14
Drake	W	28-13
Missouri	W	26-16
Washington (Missouri)	W	41-26
KANSAS STATE	W	44-26
NEBRASKA	W	41-18

1922-1923 Won 17, Lost 1
Coach: Dr. F. C. Allen

Creighton	W	29-7
NEBRASKA	W	30-20
IOWA STATE	W	22-12
Iowa State	W	37-17
Grinnell	W	23-8
Drake	W	32-18
Missouri	W	21-19
Washington (Missouri)	W	34-16
WASHINGTON (Missouri)	W	41-14
Kansas City AC	L	23-27
Oklahoma	W	27-21
KANSAS STATE	W	44-23
Nebraska	W	36-15
DRAKE	W	41-11
Kansas State	W	24-17
OKLAHOMA	W	42-18
GRINNELL	W	38-16
MISSOURI	W	23-20

1923-1924 Won 16, Lost 3
Coach: Dr. F. C. Allen

Hillyard Chem. Co.	L	26-28
DRAKE	W	49-16
OKLAHOMA	W	21-19
NEBRASKA	W	19-18
Kansas State	W	36-21

Nebraska	W	13-10
MISSOURI	W	16-14
Kansas City AC	L	23-31
WASHINGTON (Missouri)	W	17-16
Oklahoma	L	20-26
KANSAS STATE	W	23-15
IOWA STATE	W	30-16
Drake	W	28-17
Grinnell	W	37-22
Iowa State	W	20-15
GRINNELL	W	39-19
Washington (Missouri)	W	31-22
Missouri	W	30-17
Missouri	W	15-14

1924-1925 Won 17, Lost 1
Coach: Dr. F. C. Allen

Hillyard Chem. Co.	W	19-15
Grinnell	W	39-26
Iowa State	W	28-8
Drake	W	33-16
KANSAS STATE	L	28-40
Kansas City AC	W	41-17
Nebraska	W	25-20
OKLAHOMA	W	34-20
IOWA STATE	W	33-18
GRINNELL	W	23-20
Washington (Missouri)	W	22-19
Missouri	W	23-22
NEBRASKA	W	28-20
DRAKE	W	27-20
Kansas State	W	27-17
Oklahoma	W	23-22
MISSOURI	W	33-17
WASHINGTON (Missouri)	W	27-21

1925-1926 Won 16, Lost 2
Coach: Dr. F. C. Allen

WASHINGTON (Missouri)	L	18-25
Kansas State	W	25-16
GRINNELL	W	28-20
OKLAHOMA	L	21-29

MISSOURI	W	24-15	IOWA STATE	W	35-23	**1926-1927 Won 15, Lost 2**		
Grinnell	W	36-19	Oklahoma State	W	47-30	Coach: Dr. F. C. Allen		
Iowa State	W	43-21	Oklahoma	W	29-21	Creighton	W	31-29
Drake	W	28-24	Missouri	W	27-22	Drake	W	27-13
Nebraska	W	25-14	Washington (Missouri)	W	29-22	Washington (Missouri)	W	31-15
DRAKE	W	34-18	NEBRASKA	W	30-17	Kansas City AC	W	27-21
OKLAHOMA STATE	W	38-18	KANSAS STATE	W	34-29	IOWA STATE	L	12-15

NEBRASKA	L	24-27
Missouri	W	40-23
Hillyard Chem. Co.	W	30-27
Kansas State	W	35-34
Grinnell	W	41-19
Iowa State	W	27-16
GRINNELL	W	36-16
WASHINGTON (Missouri)	W	27-18
Nebraska	W	34-25
Kansas City AC	W	32-28
MISSOURI	W	36-29
KANSAS STATE	W	29-24

1927-1928 Won 9, Lost 9
Coach: Dr. F. C. Allen

KANSAS STATE	L	13-20
WASHINGTON (Missouri)	W	29-26
MISSOURI	L	22-30
Oklahoma	L	19-45
Oklahoma State	W	34-31
IOWA STATE	W	46-33
Washington (Missouri)	L	28-35
Grinnell	W	36-27
Iowa State	W	21-19
Drake	W	28-27
DRAKE	L	28-40
OKLAHOMA	L	21-30
NEBRASKA	W	33-27
GRINNELL	W	42-21
Missouri	L	29-49
Nebraska	L	28-32
OKLAHOMA STATE	W	46-44
Kansas State	L	30-40

1928-1929 Won 3, Lost 15
Coach: Dr. F. C. Allen

Washburn	L	24-25
Missouri	L	31-38
Notre Dame	L	21-32
Notre Dame	L	17-29
California	L	21-33
California	L	23-30
California	W	24-23
OKLAHOMA	L	25-27
Missouri	L	30-34
Nebraska	L	29-30
IOWA STATE	L	24-27
KANSAS STATE	W	31-24
NEBRASKA	L	31-37
Oklahoma	L	25-40
MISSOURI	L	20-33
Creighton	L	27-44
Iowa State	W	33-32
Kansas State	L	35-36

1929-1930 Won 14, Lost 4
Coach: Dr. F. C. Allen

Washburn	W	42-22
Missouri	W	17-12
California	W	36-25
California	W	31-15
CALIFORNIA	W	38-28
MEXICO (Nationals)	W	39-30
Oklahoma	W	34-22
Oklahoma State	W	44-20
IOWA STATE	W	37-16
Kansas State	W	29-26
NEBRASKA	W	27-20
OKLAHOMA	W	25-23
KANSAS STATE	W	32-30
Missouri	L	18-29
Iowa State	L	27-30
Creighton	L	20-44
Nebraska	W	36-35
MISSOURI	L	18-23

1930-1931 Won 15, Lost 3
Coach: Dr. F. C. Allen

Washburn	W	27-19
Missouri	W	40-26
Kansas Wesleyan	W	47-15
Colorado	W	34-25
Colorado	W	36-28
Colorado	W	25-19
OKLAHOMA	W	44-22
Kansas State	W	37-29
NEBRASKA	L	30-31 *
Iowa State	W	34-27
MISSOURI	W	31-13
OKLAHOMA STATE	W	31-29
Oklahoma	L	30-33
Nebraska	W	34-29
KANSAS STATE	W	40-26
IOWA STATE	W	27-16
Missouri	L	19-26
CREIGHTON	W	38-32

1931-1932 Won 13, Lost 5
Coach: Dr. F. C. Allen

KANSAS STATE	W	32-30
Kansas State	W	27-25
Pittsburgh	W	24-23
Pittsburgh	W	26-20
Pittsburgh	L	22-25
Colorado	L	22-25
Colorado	W	41-22
COLORADO	W	34-25
Oklahoma	L	26-31 *
Nebraska	W	34-21
KANSAS STATE	W	27-26
IOWA STATE	L	29-37
Missouri	L	22-26
Iowa State	W	40-27
Kansas State	W	30-22
NEBRASKA	W	51-19
MISSOURI	W	24-16
OKLAHOMA	W	33-29

1932-1933 Won 13, Lost 4
Coach: Dr. F. C. Allen

| KANSAS STATE | L | 27-31 |
| Kansas State | L | 11-15 |

Ottawa	W	35-27
OTTAWA	W	43-23
STANFORD	W	38-20
STANFORD	W	38-17
STANFORD	W	34-28
NEBRASKA	W	32-29
KANSAS STATE	W	36-24
Oklahoma	L	23-25
MISSOURI	W	35-27
Iowa State	W	35-20
Nebraska	W	34-20
Missouri	L	17-21
IOWA STATE	W	33-19
Kansas State	W	33-25
OKLAHOMA	W	35-26

1933-1934 Won 16, Lost 1
Coach: Dr. F. C. Allen

KANSAS STATE	W	27-13
Kansas State	W	34-20
Warrensburg	W	41-25
Kansas Wesleyan	W	37-22
Nebraska	L	21-24
Missouri	W	27-25
KANSAS STATE	W	32-24
Iowa State	W	31-23
Washburn	W	31-22
OKLAHOMA	W	22-16
OKLAHOMA	W	28-23
IOWA STATE	W	26-23
NEBRASKA	W	25-24
Kansas State	W	39-23
Oklahoma	W	33-26
Oklahoma	W	39-25
MISSOURI	W	23-21

1934-1935 Won 15, Lost 5
Coach: Dr. F. C. Allen

KANSAS STATE	L	35-39 *
Kansas State	W	40-26
EMPORIA STATE	W	32-30
MISSOURI	W	39-29
MISSOURI	W	36-27
KANSAS STATE	W	40-14
OKLAHOMA	W	50-23
OKLAHOMA	L	26-36

KANSAS STATE	W	43-37	Washburn	W	33-30	
Washburn	W	33-27	[Olympic-Missouri Valley District]			
IOWA STATE	W	35-18	Oklahoma State	W	34-28	
NEBRASKA	W	32-21	[Olympic-Missouri Valley District]			
Nebraska	W	32-24	Utah State	W	39-37 *	
Iowa State	L	20-32	[Olympic Playoffs]			
Kansas State	W	39-33	Utah State	L	37-42	
Kansas State	W	36-30	[Olympic Playoffs]			
Missouri	L	21-23	Utah State	L	31-50	
Missouri	L	18-21	[Olympic Playoffs]			
Oklahoma	W	40-31				
Oklahoma	W	47-42				

1935-1936 Won 21, Lost 2
Coach: Dr. F. C. Allen

1936-1937 Won 15, Lost 4
Coach: Dr. F. C. Allen

1937-1938 Won 18, Lost 2
Coach: Dr. F. C. Allen

WASHBURN	W	35-18	WASHBURN	W	30-26	DOANE	W	38-23
OTTAWA	W	53-22	Southwestern	L	22-26	OTTAWA	W	36-17
BAKER	W	34-32	Baker	W	36-35 *	Ottawa	W	41-35
Southern California	W	34-31	SOUTHWESTERN	W	39-27	BAKER	W	41-27
Kansas State	W	38-23	Kansas Wesleyan	W	36-23	SOUTHWESTERN	W	39-29
California	W	32-28	BAKER	L	27-32	MORNINGSIDE	W	26-21
California	W	27-18	Oklahoma	W	28-26	WASHBURN	W	31-15
Kansas State	W	28-17	MEXICO	W	42-22	Southwestern	W	28-24
IOWA STATE	W	38-17	MISSOURI	W	39-27	Drake	L	29-34
Missouri	W	29-25	KANSAS STATE	W	39-28	WASHBURN	W	62-33
NEBRASKA	W	45-23	Washburn	W	42-27	OKLAHOMA	L	46-49
Iowa State	W	42-25	ROCKHURST	W	35-19	Kansas State	W	33-21
Oklahoma	W	43-36	NEBRASKA	W	27-22	IOWA STATE	W	31-17
KANSAS STATE	W	52-34	Iowa State	W	36-26	Missouri	W	37-32
Washburn	W	51-26	Kansas State	L	32-33	NEBRASKA	W	48-33
Nebraska	W	43-36	IOWA STATE	W	41-28	KANSAS STATE	W	35-33
OKLAHOMA	W	51-26	OKLAHOMA	W	39-19	Oklahoma	W	41-38
MISSOURI	W	51-29	Nebraska	L	32-37	Iowa State	W	31-23
			Missouri	W	39-24	Nebraska	W	50-47
						MISSOURI	W	56-36

1938-1939 Won 13, Lost 7
Coach: Dr. F. C. Allen

WARRENSBURG	W	25-20
Oklahoma State	L	15-21
Oklahoma State	L	19-25
Texas	L	34-36
Texas	W	49-35
Southern Methodist	W	46-40
Southern Methodist	W	52-45
CARLETON (Minnesota)	W	39-33
Oklahoma	L	31-43

KANSAS STATE	W	33-29
Nebraska	L	37-48
MISSOURI	W	37-32
Kansas State	W	40-38
Iowa State	L	37-40
OKLAHOMA STATE	W	34-27
Washburn	W	37-34
NEBRASKA	W	49-46
IOWA STATE	W	46-37
OKLAHOMA	W	59-45
Missouri	L	30-55

1939-1940 Won 19, Lost 6
Coach: Dr. F. C. Allen

OKLAHOMA STATE	W	34-30
Warrensburg	L	31-33 *
SOUTHERN METHODIST	W	63-31
SOUTHERN METHODIST	W	37-26
Baker	W	34-18
New Mexico Mines	W	40-24
Washburn	W	52-34
OKLAHOMA	W	46-26
Loyola (Illinois)	W	40-36
KANSAS STATE	W	34-33
Missouri	L	31-42
NEBRASKA	W	40-24
IOWA STATE	W	36-34
Oklahoma State	L	22-24
Kansas State	W	44-33
Nebraska	W	48-41
Iowa State	W	42-29
MISSOURI	W	42-40
Creighton	L	33-35
Oklahoma	L	36-47
Oklahoma	W	45-39
[Big Six Playoff]		
Oklahoma State	W	45-43 *
[Fifth District Playoff]		
Rice	W	50-44
[NCAA Western Playoff]		
Southern California	W	43-42
[NCAA Western Finals]		
Indiana	L	42-60

1940-1941 Won 12, Lost 6
Coach: Dr. F. C. Allen

TEXAS	W	35-27
TEXAS	W	48-45
Fordham	L	42-53
Temple	L	35-40
Loyola (Illinois)	W	41-40
Oklahoma	L	31-42
IOWA STATE	W	44-41
MISSOURI	W	48-41
Kansas State	W	46-41
Wichita	W	54-39
NEBRASKA	W	44-38
Oklahoma State	L	26-30
Missouri	W	35-24
KANSAS STATE	W	50-45 *
Nebraska	W	55-53
Iowa State	L	29-41
OKLAHOMA	L	37-45
OKLAHOMA STATE	W	34-31

1941-1942 Won 17, Lost 5
Coach: Dr. F. C. Allen

DENVER	W	36-35
Bethel	W	61-28
OKLAHOMA	W	54-32
Missouri	W	48-34
Nebraska	W	51-32
Iowa State	L	41-45
KANSAS STATE	W	46-44 *
Iowa	W	53-51

DePaul	W	46-26
Wichita	W	56-37
Great Lakes NTS	L	37-53
CREIGHTON	W	53-49
NEBRASKA	W	58-30
IOWA STATE	W	60-44
OKLAHOMA STATE	W	31-28
Oklahoma State	L	33-40
Oklahoma	L	51-63
Kansas State	W	45-26
MISSOURI	W	67-44
OKLAHOMA STATE	W	32-28
[Fifth District Playoff]		
Colorado	L	44-46
[NCAA Western Playoff]		
Rice	W	55-53
[NCAA Western Cons.]		

1942-1943 Won 22, Lost 6
Coach: Dr. F. C. Allen

| Olathe NAB | L | 29-40 |
| Rockhurst | W | 44-40 |

CREIGHTON	L	33-38
St. Bonaventure	W	53-22
Fordham	W	31-30
St. Joseph's	W	63-38
St. Louis	W	60-25
OLATHE AAB	W	60-32
MISSOURI	W	69-4
Oklahoma	W	48-44
OKLAHOMA STATE	W	36-29
N. Amer. Bombers	W	45-36
Rosecrans A.F.	W	71-22
Camp Crowder	W	57-26
Kansas State	W	40-20
Camp Crowder	L	31-35
Olathe NAB	W	47-36
Great Lakes NTS	L	41-47
Olathe AAB	L	32-42
IOWA STATE	W	44-20
Nebraska	W	56-24
Iowa State	W	37-29
Oklahoma State	W	47-43
NEBRASKA	W	52-33

Engleman finished out season as head coach when Allen was ordered to take a rest after Missouri game of January 7.

1947-1948 Won 9, Lost 15
Coach: Dr. F. C. Allen

Emporia State	L	44-67
Colorado	W	49-39
Kansas State	L	42-56
Nebraska	W	64-60 *
NOTRE DAME	L	49-51
San Francisco	W	57-43
Oregon	L	61-66
Oregon	L	53-61
Nevada	W	52-45
OKLAHOMA	W	39-38 *
COLORADO	W	57-44
DRAKE	W	72-42
Missouri	W	58-46
OKLAHOMA STATE	L	35-47
NEBRASKA	L	57-61
MISSOURI	L	39-42
Iowa State	L	50-52
Kansas State	L	29-48
Oklahoma	L	46-50
KANSAS STATE	L	60-61
Oklahoma State	L	25-37
Nebraska	L	64-70
Colorado	L	60-77
IOWA STATE	W	61-54

1948-1949 Won 12, Lost 12
Coach: Dr. F. C. Allen

Rockhurst	W	67-20
TRINITY	W	63-44
Purdue	L	46-47
Drake	L	44-60
CENTENARY	W	49-41
Missouri	W	62-50
Kansas State	W	60-46
Oklahoma	L	49-52
Oklahoma	L	36-38
Nebraska	L	34-52
MISSOURI	W	42-35
Washington (Missouri)	W	46-41
COLORADO	L	30-42
DRAKE	W	62-37
CREIGHTON	W	79-50
Iowa State	W	62-57
KANSAS STATE	L	48-53
NEBRASKA	L	39-49
Missouri	W	55-37
WASHINGTON (Missouri)	W	43-39
Kansas State	L	36-63
Colorado	L	43-50
OKLAHOMA	L	45-55
IOWA STATE	L	45-49

1949-1950 Won 14, Lost 11
Coach: Dr. F. C. Allen

Rockhurst	W	55-34
Creighton	L	55-59
PURDUE	W	60-52
Cincinnati	L	54-56
Duquesne	L	54-64
Holy Cross	L	53-57
Springfield (Massachusetts)	W	53-43
Kansas State	L	48-58
Iowa State	W	64-43
Michigan	L	47-49
OKLAHOMA	W	56-50
Nebraska	L	56-57
Missouri	W	48-44
IOWA STATE	W	67-42

OKLAHOMA	W	42-35
Missouri	W	47-44 *
Creighton	L	34-56
KANSAS STATE	W	47-30

1943-1944 Won 17, Lost 9
Coach: Dr. F. C. Allen

HERINGTON AAB	W	40-27
HUTCHINSON NAB	L	32-46
FT. LEAVENWORTH	W	31-27
Washburn	W	46-24
Rockhurst	W	45-32
ROCKHURST	W	43-28
OLATHE NAB	L	36-42
FT. RILEY CRTC	W	32-31
Herington AAB	W	22-15
Kansas State	W	62-44
Missouri	W	34-27
PITTSBURG STATE	W	35-21
Missouri	L	28-35
Olathe NAB	L	25-49
NEBRASKA	W	51-27
KANSAS STATE	W	36-30
OKLAHOMA	L	23-24
Iowa State	L	29-40
WASHBURN	W	35-22
Ft. Riley CRTC	L	38-43
Oklahoma	L	35-39
Ft. Leavenworth	W	54-52
Nebraska	W	56-47
Kansas State	W	32-24
MISSOURI	W	40-27
IOWA STATE	L	25-47

1944-1945 Won 12, Lost 5
Coach: Dr. F. C. Allen

Washburn	L	35-40
WASHBURN	W	31-27
Rockhurst	W	47-28
ROCKHURST	W	47-23
Kansas State	W	63-40
Missouri	L	39-48
Missouri	W	45-28
NEBRASKA	W	48-33
Oklahoma	L	43-44 *
IOWA STATE	W	50-35
KANSAS STATE	W	39-36
OLATHE NAB	W	41-26
Nebraska	L	45-59
OKLAHOMA	W	42-27
Kansas State	W	33-31
MISSOURI	W	64-33
Iowa State	L	39-61

1945-1946 Won 19, Lost 2
Coach: Dr. F. C. Allen

WARRENSBURG	W	45-28
OLATHE NAS	W	65-61
Rockhurst	W	59-45
Kansas State	W	71-46
Missouri	W	59-35
ROCKHURST	W	50-21
Olathe NAS	W	52-22
Rice	W	42-34
Oklahoma State	L	28-46
Oklahoma	W	53-46
MISSOURI	W	48-36
Kansas State	W	39-26
Nebraska	W	56-45
OKLAHOMA	W	53-52
Iowa State	W	50-47 *
KANSAS STATE	W	68-43
NEBRASKA	W	72-30
Missouri	W	50-34
IOWA STATE	W	69-41
Oklahoma	W	52-45
Oklahoma State	L	38-49

1946-1947 Won 16, Lost 11
Coach: Dr. F. C. Allen & Howard Engleman

Emporia State	W	48-42
IDAHO	W	42-28
Iowa State	W	55-36
Arkansas	W	53-52
Southern Methodist	L	46-49
St. Louis	W	49-35
Oklahoma State	L	37-47
Tulane	W	65-53
Oklahoma	W	51-45
Oklahoma State	L	39-42
Stanford	W	54-52
Colorado	L	50-52 *
MISSOURI	L	34-39
Oklahoma	L	47-50
Nebraska	L	46-48
Colorado	L	54-59 *
IOWA STATE	W	55-30
KANSAS STATE	W	50-39
Oklahoma State	L	31-33
NEBRASKA	W	69-37
Kansas State	L	45-48
DePaul	W	58-41
OKLAHOMA STATE	W	37-34
Iowa State	L	44-56
OKLAHOMA	W	38-36
Missouri	W	48-38
COLORADO	W	51-39

DRAKE	W	76-50	KANSAS STATE	W	79-68	St. Joseph's (Pennsylvania)	W	60-41
Colorado	L	48-50 *	Oklahoma	L	49-52 *	St. John's	W	52-51
NEBRASKA	W	49-36	Bradley	L	57-59	Kentucky	L	39-68
Kansas State	L	50-55				SPRINGFIELD (Mass.)	W	78-52
MISSOURI	W	59-52	**1950-1951 Won 16, Lost 8**			Iowa State	W	75-51
Drake	W	67-50	Coach: Dr. F. C. Allen			Minnesota	L	51-62
COLORADO	W	76-60	CREIGHTON	W	51-35	Nebraska	W	63-47
Iowa State	W	66-52	UTAH STATE	W	56-38	NEBRASKA	W	66-41

Nebraska	W	69-66
Kansas State	L	64-81
Oklahoma State	L	45-49
IOWA STATE	W	86-68
COLORADO	W	73-68
Iowa State	W	55-50
NEBRASKA	W	90-52
OKLAHOMA STATE	W	66-46
MISSOURI	W	65-54
Oklahoma	W	74-55
KANSAS STATE	W	78-61
Colorado	W	72-55
Texas Christian	W	68-64
[NCAA Regional]		
St. Louis	W	74-55
[NCAA Regional Finals]		
Santa Clara	W	74-55
[NCAA Semifinals]		
St. John's	W	80-63
[NCAA Finals]		
Southwest Missouri	W	92-65
[U.S. Olympic Playoffs]		
LaSalle	W	70-65
[U.S. Olympic Playoffs]		
Peoria	L	60-62
[U.S. Olympic Playoffs]		

1952-1953 Won 19, Lost 6
Coach: Dr. F. C. Allen

Tulane	W	63-50
Rice	L	51-54
SOUTHERN METHODIST	W	83-66
SOUTHERN METHODIST	W	72-55
Nebraska	W	73-66
Missouri	W	66-62
Kansas State	L	87-93
Oklahoma	L	61-76
OKLAHOMA STATE	W	65-53
Iowa State	W	76-57
Nebraska	W	65-59
KANSAS STATE	W	80-66
Colorado	L	68-72
MISSOURI	W	86-62
OKLAHOMA	W	87-59
NEBRASKA	W	77-58
Kansas State	W	80-78
Oklahoma State	L	58-79
COLORADO	W	78-55
IOWA STATE	W	87-62
Missouri	W	69-60
Oklahoma City	W	73-65
[NCAA Regional]		
Oklahoma State	W	61-55
[NCAA Regional Finals]		
Washington	W	79-53
[NCAA Semifinals]		
Indiana	L	68-69

1953-1954 Won 16, Lost 5
Coach: Dr. F. C. Allen

Tulane	L	65-69
Louisiana State	L	63-68
TULSA	W	72-61
Colorado	W	79-62
Missouri	W	69-67
Oklahoma	W	82-73
OKLAHOMA	W	76-72
MISSOURI	W	86-69
Oklahoma State	L	50-54
Kansas State	W	65-62
IOWA STATE	W	76-61
Colorado	L	62-70
Oklahoma	W	93-80
Tulsa	W	71-58
NEBRASKA	W	79-68

MISSOURI	W	61-46
COLORADO	W	54-48
KANSAS STATE	L	43-47
Oklahoma	W	58-52
Northwestern	L	53-54
OKLAHOMA STATE	L	41-46
Nebraska	W	61-52
Missouri	L	38-39
Iowa State	W	56-54
OKLAHOMA	L	59-61
Kansas State	L	51-65
Colorado	W	58-56
IOWA STATE	W	70-64
Oklahoma State	W	37-27

1951-1952 Won 28, Lost 3
Coach: Dr. F. C. Allen

BAYLOR	W	57-46
DENVER	W	84-53
Creighton	W	65-47
Southern Methodist	W	74-51
Southern Methodist	W	58-57
RICE	W	68-48
SOUTHERN CALIFORNIA	W	76-55
Colorado	W	76-56
Kansas State	W	90-88 *
Missouri	W	75-65
OKLAHOMA	W	71-48
Missouri	W	60-59

KANSAS STATE	W	85-74
Iowa State	W	78-70
Nebraska	W	67-62
OKLAHOMA STATE	W	65-55
COLORADO	W	83-62
Missouri	L	67-76

1954-1955 Won 11, Lost 10
Coach: Dr. F. C. Allen

LOUISIANA STATE	W	85-58
TULSA	W	73-66
RICE	W	77-67
RICE	W	100-72
Iowa State	L	81-82
California	L	62-65
Nebraska	W	69-66
MISSOURI	L	65-76
COLORADO	L	54-65
Nebraska	L	62-66
Iowa State	W	73-72
IOWA STATE	L	59-77
Kansas State	W	78-68
OKLAHOMA STATE	W	50-42
Oklahoma	W	87-75
NEBRASKA	L	55-66
Colorado	L	69-80
Oklahoma State	L	49-63
KANSAS STATE +	W	77-67
Missouri	L	71-90
OKLAHOMA	W	71-67

+First game played in Allen Fieldhouse

1955-1956 Won 14, Lost 9
Coach: Dr. F. C. Allen

NORTHWESTERN	W	91-70
Wichita	W	56-55
Wisconsin	W	74-66
Southern Methodist	L	61-81
Rice	L	66-75

SOUTHERN METHODIST	W	62-58
Cornell	W	75-58
Missouri	W	73-56
Iowa State	L	56-67
Oklahoma State	W	65-62
OKLAHOMA	W	77-65
Missouri	L	54-76
Kansas State	W	91-86
IOWA STATE	W	68-63
OKLAHOMA STATE	W	56-55
Iowa State	L	63-79
MISSOURI	L	78-85
NEBRASKA	W	80-56
Oklahoma	L	68-69
Nebraska	W	60-56
COLORADO	W	54-44
KANSAS STATE	L	68-79
Colorado	L	67-75

1956-1957 Won 24, Lost 3
Coach: Dick Harp

NORTHWESTERN	W	87-69
MARQUETTE	W	78-61
Washington	W	77-63
Washington	W	92-78
California	W	66-56
WISCONSIN	W	83-62
Iowa State	W	58-57
Oklahoma	W	74-56
Colorado	W	80-54
MISSOURI	W	92-79
Oklahoma	W	59-51
KANSAS STATE	W	51-45
Iowa State	L	37-39
IOWA STATE	W	75-64
Nebraska	W	69-54
OKLAHOMA STATE	W	62-52
Missouri	W	91-58
OKLAHOMA	W	76-56

Oklahoma State	L	54-56
NEBRASKA	W	87-60
Colorado	W	68-57
Kansas State	W	64-57
COLORADO	W	78-63
Southern Methodist	W	73-65 *
[NCAA Regional]		
Oklahoma City	W	81-61
[NCAA Regional Finals]		
San Francisco	W	80-56
[NCAA Semifinals]		
North Carolina	L	53-54 ***
[NCAA Finals]		

1957-1958 Won 18, Lost 5
Coach: Dick Harp

Oklahoma State	W	63-56
CANISIUS	W	66-46
Northwestern	W	71-65
Marquette	W	82-62
St. Joseph's	W	66-54
WASHINGTON	W	77-59
California	W	58-52
Oklahoma	W	68-50
Iowa State	W	55-48
Kansas State	W	79-65
OKLAHOMA STATE	L	50-52 *
Oklahoma	L	62-64
COLORADO	W	67-46
Missouri	W	68-54
KANSAS STATE	L	75-79 **
NEBRASKA	W	104-46
Colorado	W	60-51
IOWA STATE	W	90-61
MISSOURI	W	84-69
Nebraska	L	41-43
Iowa State	L	42-48
OKLAHOMA	W	60-59 *
Kansas State	W	61-44

1958-1959 Won 11, Lost 14
Coach: Dick Harp

RICE	W	65-49
Canisius	W	75-54
DENVER	L	60-73
U.C.-Los Angeles	L	61-72
Southern California	L	55-68
St. Joseph's	L	65-67 *
NORTH CAROLINA STATE	L	63-66
Colorado	L	52-63
Oklahoma State	L	48-59
Missouri	W	84-73
OKLAHOMA STATE	W	58-49
Missouri	W	69-62
Iowa State	W	69-48
Oklahoma	L	38-45
COLORADO	L	64-66
OKLAHOMA	W	71-44
Louisville	L	74-82
Kansas State	L	72-82
Nebraska	W	63-55
Colorado	L	53-65
NEBRASKA	W	66-50
MISSOURI	W	85-81
KANSAS STATE	L	77-87
IOWA STATE	L	62-67
Oklahoma State	W	63-55

1959-1960 Won 19, Lost 9
Coach: Dick Harp

Northwestern	W	76-67
TEXAS TECH	W	85-71
North Carolina	L	49-60
North Carolina State	W	80-58
KENTUCKY	L	72-77
SAN FRANCISCO	W	73-42
Brigham Young	W	96-64
St. Louis	L	59-66

Oklahoma State	W	67-59
Oklahoma	W	55-54
Iowa State	L	70-83
Nebraska	W	60-47
Colorado	L	61-65
MISSOURI	W	79-63
OKLAHOMA STATE	L	49-62
Iowa State	L	60-72
IOWA STATE	W	70-64
KANSAS STATE	W	64-62
Oklahoma State	W	64-52
Oklahoma	W	54-53
COLORADO	W	75-67
Kansas State	L	57-68
Missouri	W	85-72
OKLAHOMA	W	65-52
NEBRASKA	W	79-74
Kansas State	W	84-82 *
[Big Eight Playoff]		
Texas	W	90-81
[NCAA Regional]		
Cincinnati	L	71-82
[NCAA Regional Finals]		

1960-1961 Won 17, Lost 8
Coach: Dick Harp

NORTHWESTERN	W	86-69
Texas Tech	W	97-75
St. John's	L	54-66
Michigan State	W	93-69
NORTH CAROLINA	L	70-78
Brigham Young	L	70-80
San Francisco	W	60-43
Nebraska	W	78-53
Iowa State	W	76-72
Kansas State	L	66-69 *
Oklahoma	W	58-55
Oklahoma State	W	73-68

IOWA STATE	W	90-59
OKLAHOMA STATE	L	49-54
KANSAS STATE	W	75-66
AIR FORCE	W	78-52
COLORADO	W	88-65
Nebraska	W	38-33
MISSOURI	W	88-73
Colorado	W	90-62
Kansas State	L	63-81
NEBRASKA	L	68-69
OKLAHOMA	W	81-56
Iowa State	W	85-75
Missouri	L	76-79

1961-1962 Won 7, Lost 18
Coach: Dick Harp

ARKANSAS	W	85-74
ST. LOUIS	L	65-79
Southern California	L	70-78
U.C.-Los Angeles	L	61-69
Arizona State	L	58-72
ST. JOHN'S	L	59-64
Marquette	W	76-62
Oklahoma	L	60-61
Colorado	W	75-66
Nebraska	W	69-68
NEBRASKA	L	67-69
Kansas State	L	45-70
Missouri	W	65-54
Air Force	L	72-76
MISSOURI	L	66-79
KANSAS STATE	L	72-91
IOWA STATE	L	72-75
Oklahoma State	L	68-72
COLORADO	L	61-65
OKLAHOMA	L	66-67 *
Nebraska	W	73-70
OKLAHOMA STATE	L	37-56
Oklahoma	L	62-63
Iowa State	W	76-71
Colorado	L	59-63

1962-1963 Won 12, Lost 13
Coach: Dick Harp

MONTANA	W	68-56
Arkansas	L	62-64 *
Michigan State	L	62-81
WYOMING	W	75-57
Arizona State	L	62-71
CINCINNATI	L	49-64
DENVER	W	68-43
Northwestern	W	62-57
Colorado	W	70-64
Iowa State	W	69-51
Kansas State	W	90-88 ****
COLORADO	L	57-73
Iowa State	L	51-55
Missouri	L	56-62
NEBRASKA	W	72-53
IOWA STATE	L	57-69
Oklahoma	W	86-55
Colorado	L	52-62
OKLAHOMA STATE	L	53-54
OKLAHOMA	L	62-64
KANSAS STATE	L	54-67
Nebraska	W	45-39
Kansas State	L	60-74
MISSOURI	W	72-68
Oklahoma State	W	49-48

1963-1964 Won 13, Lost 12
Coach: Dick Harp

ARKANSAS	W	73-60
Cincinnati	W	51-47
TEXAS TECH	W	73-67

SOUTHERN CALIFORNIA	W	60-52
U.C.-Los Angeles	L	54-74
New Mexico	L	54-59
San Francisco	L	58-75
Stanford	L	64-69 *
Colorado	W	74-67
Oklahoma State	L	56-65
Missouri	L	61-63
Oklahoma	L	63-65 *
Oklahoma State	L	48-64
Colorado	W	73-55
NEBRASKA	W	74-48
IOWA STATE	W	74-51
Kansas State	L	55-58
MISSOURI	L	58-59
Iowa State	W	67-65
OKLAHOMA	W	84-72
Missouri	L	60-68
KANSAS STATE	L	46-70
Nebraska	W	64-55
COLORADO	W	73-71 *
OKLAHOMA STATE	W	58-46

1964-1965 Won 17, Lost 8
Coach: Ted Owens

Arkansas	W	65-60
NEW MEXICO	W	59-40
NORTHWESTERN	L	55-58
Penn State	L	48-50
LOYOLA (Illinois)	W	80-60
Cincinnati	L	72-76
Maryland	W	63-61 *
St. John's	W	71-56
Iowa State	W	72-55
Kansas State	W	54-52
Colorado	W	53-51
Nebraska	W	66-56
MISSOURI	W	73-66
Colorado	L	59-61
Iowa State	W	72-60
Kansas State	L	63-71
OKLAHOMA	W	77-68
Missouri	W	71-60
Oklahoma	W	74-57
Oklahoma State	L	64-68
****		
KANSAS STATE	W	86-66
NEBRASKA	W	71-62
COLORADO	W	68-62
OKLAHOMA STATE	L	58-64

1965-1966 Won 23, Lost 4
Coach: Ted Owens

ARKANSAS	W	81-52
Texas Tech	W	74-70
NEW MEXICO STATE	W	102-51
MARYLAND	W	71-62
St. John's	W	61-55
U.C.-Los Angeles	L	71-78
Southern California	L	69-81
Ohio State	W	81-68
Kansas State	W	69-63
Iowa State	W	73-66
Nebraska	W	71-61
Colorado	W	69-55
IOWA STATE	W	82-65
OKLAHOMA	W	89-68
Iowa State	W	49-47
Nebraska	L	75-83
KANSAS STATE	W	69-61
Missouri	W	77-54
OKLAHOMA STATE	W	59-38
MISSOURI	W	98-54
Oklahoma State	W	80-47
Oklahoma	W	86-69

NEBRASKA	W	110-73
Kansas State	W	68-55
COLORADO	W	85-65
Southern Methodist	W	76-70

[NCAA Regional]

Texas-El Paso	L	80-81 **

[NCAA Regional Finals]

1966-1967 Won 23, Lost 4
Coach: Ted Owens

Arkansas	W	73-57
XAVIER	W	100-52
OHIO STATE	W	94-70
Florida State	W	62-48
BAYLOR	W	68-56
PACIFIC	W	70-54
Texas-El Paso	L	67-71 *
St. John's	L	44-68
Colorado	W	72-54
Oklahoma	W	86-73
Iowa State	W	63-57
OKLAHOMA	W	97-73
Missouri	W	70-60
Colorado	L	59-62
IOWA STATE	W	73-65
Iowa State	W	68-50
NEBRASKA	W	84-58
Kansas State	W	60-55
OKLAHOMA STATE	W	52-39
Oklahoma	W	82-74
Oklahoma State	W	60-50
MISSOURI	W	90-55
Nebraska	W	64-57
COLORADO	W	66-59
KANSAS STATE	W	74-56
HOUSTON	L	53-66

[NCAA Regional]

LOUISVILLE	W	70-68

[NCAA Regional Third-Playoffs]

1967-1968 Won 22, Lost 8
Coach: Ted Owens

UTAH STATE	W	84-55
LOUISVILLE	L	51-57
Loyola (Illinois)	L	73-83
CINCINNATI	W	67-61
Texas A&M	W	78-52
STANFORD	W	72-54
Louisville	W	84-76 **
St. Louis	W	68-64
Oklahoma State	L	67-79
Oklahoma	W	73-57
Missouri	W	63-47
COLORADO	W	66-50
Iowa State	W	68-67
PORTLAND	W	80-37
MISSOURI	L	66-67
Kansas State	L	56-71
OKLAHOMA	W	72-70
OKLAHOMA STATE	W	52-50
Colorado	W	75-72
NEBRASKA	W	71-60
Missouri	W	74-65
KANSAS STATE	L	61-64 *
Nebraska	L	69-76
Oklahoma State	W	70-58
Oklahoma	W	85-80 *
IOWA STATE	W	91-58
Temple	W	82-76
Villanova	W	55-49
St. Peter's	W	58-46
Dayton	L	48-61

1968-1969 Won 20, Lost 7
Coach: Ted Owens

ST. LOUIS	W	88-65	MURRAY STATE	W	72-59	Missouri	L	46-47
Wisconsin	L	62-67	Utah State	W	67-61	Iowa State	L	72-78
LOYOLA (Illinois)	W	93-61	Stanford	W	76-67	Kansas State	W	73-67
XAVIER	W	79-56	Nebraska	W	82-56	COLORADO	W	80-70
Creighton	W	78-65	Colorado	W	65-55	OKLAHOMA STATE	W	64-48
SYRACUSE	W	71-41	Oklahoma State	W	56-45	Oklahoma	W	66-59
			Nebraska	W	56-52	Oklahoma State	W	45-41
			IOWA STATE	W	94-61	MISSOURI	L	55-56

182

NEBRASKA	W	79-73
OKLAHOMA	W	83-58
Colorado	L	67-75
KANSAS STATE	L	57-64
Boston College	L	62-78

1969-1970 Won 17, Lost 9
Coach: Ted Owens

MARSHALL	W	96-80
Kentucky	L	85-115
WISCONSIN	W	76-60
Loyola (Illinois)	W	72-71
Notre Dame	W	75-63
SOUTHERN METHODIST	W	89-77
WESTERN KENTUCKY	W	104-81
Oklahoma	L	64-68 *
Oklahoma State	W	72-56
Nebraska	L	73-78
Missouri	L	53-56
IOWA STATE	W	82-62
MURRAY STATE	W	64-62
VALPARAISO	W	74-58
Iowa State	L	89-91 *
COLORADO	W	75-73
OKLAHOMA	W	78-41
Nebraska	L	73-84
OKLAHOMA STATE	W	69-58
Kansas State	L	68-71
NEBRASKA	W	100-87
Colorado	L	73-81
MISSOURI	W	63-45
Oklahoma State	W	78-58
Oklahoma	L	77-82
KANSAS STATE	W	82-79

1970-1971 Won 27, Lost 3
Coach: Ted Owens

LONG BEACH STATE	W	69-52
EASTERN KENTUCKY	W	79-65
SOUTH DAKOTA STATE	W	95-59
LOYOLA (Illinois)	W	94-62
ST. JOSEPH'S	W	80-65
HOUSTON	W	89-73
Louisville	L	75-87
Missouri	W	96-63
Iowa State	W	59-56 *
Nebraska	W	72-52
Georgia Tech	W	84-71
OKLAHOMA CITY	W	101-77
IOWA STATE	W	83-57
OKLAHOMA STATE	W	90-55
Iowa State	W	95-72
KANSAS STATE	W	79-74
Nebraska	W	81-67
COLORADO	W	91-67
Oklahoma State	W	63-50
Oklahoma	W	71-68
MISSOURI	W	85-66
Kansas State	W	61-48
Colorado	W	66-65
OKLAHOMA	W	54-52 *
Missouri	W	71-69 *
NEBRASKA	W	59-54
Houston	W	78-77

[NCAA Regional]

Drake	W	73-71

[NCAA Regional Finals]

U.C.-Los Angeles	L	60-68

[NCAA Semifinals]

Western Kentucky	L	75-77

[NCAA Third-Place]

1971-1972 Won 11, Lost 15
Coach: Ted Owens

XAVIER	W	75-57
KENTUCKY	L	69-79
Indiana	L	56-59
NOTRE DAME	W	88-72
LOUISVILLE	L	65-74
BRIGHAM YOUNG	W	83-67
SOUTHERN CALIFORNIA	L	77-87
Iowa State	L	88-91
Oklahoma	L	69-97
Oklahoma State	L	65-66
Iowa	L	68-81
OKLAHOMA STATE	W	85-58
KANSAS STATE	W	66-63 *
Colorado	L	69-74
IOWA STATE	W	74-71
NEBRASKA	W	57-77 *
Missouri	L	60-64
Iowa State	L	83-84
GEORGIA TECH	W	93-65
OKLAHOMA	W	77-74
Kansas State	L	66-78
Nebraska	L	78-99
COLORADO	W	71-59
MISSOURI	W	93-80
Oklahoma State	L	72-76
Oklahoma	L	82-84 **

1972-1973 Won 8, Lost 18
Coach: Ted Owens

Nebraska	W	63-62
Iowa State	W	76-75
St. Louis	W	79-72
MISSOURI	W	91-86
Iowa State	L	81-96
OKLAHOMA STATE	W	71-60
COLORADO	W	81-59
Kansas State	L	56-66
NEBRASKA	W	72-44
Oklahoma	W	69-54
IOWA STATE	W	76-62
Oklahoma State	W	59-57
Missouri	L	72-87
KANSAS STATE	W	91-53
Colorado	W	78-76
Nebraska	W	79-77 **
OKLAHOMA	W	74-63
Notre Dame	L	71-77
[NCAA Sub-Regional]		

1975-1976 Won 13, Lost 13
Coach: Ted Owens

MURRAY STATE	W	72-56
Southern Methodist	L	66-75
ST. LOUIS	W	70-64
NOTRE DAME	L	64-72
BOISE STATE	W	61-56
KENTUCKY	L	48-54
YALE	W	63-54
LASALLE	W	74-73
Nebraska	W	69-66
Colorado	W	70-50
Missouri	L	69-79
Oral Roberts	L	70-73
Missouri	L	69-99
IOWA STATE	W	68-60
Oklahoma State	L	59-63
Colorado	W	51-50
KANSAS STATE	W	62-57
Nebraska	L	54-57
OKLAHOMA	L	63-64
Iowa State	W	61-53
OKLAHOMA STATE	W	70-60
MISSOURI	L	60-61
Kansas State	L	54-69
COLORADO	L	66-68
NEBRASKA	L	58-62
Oklahoma	W	55-50

1976-1977 Won 18, Lost 10
Coach: Ted Owens

MONTANA STATE	W	104-47
MURRAY STATE	W	81-66
CENTRAL MISSOURI ST.	W	74-52
ORAL ROBERTS	W	79-69
Fordham	W	57-48
Kentucky	L	63-90
MANKATO STATE	W	87-74
ARKANSAS	L	63-67
St. Louis	W	69-68 **
Oklahoma	W	74-70 *
Kansas State	W	81-64
Missouri	L	65-69
MISSOURI	W	77-72
OKLAHOMA STATE	W	62-60
Oklahoma	L	67-71
IOWA STATE	W	73-62
Kansas State	L	65-80
Nebraska	L	57-60
COLORADO	W	79-70
Oklahoma State	W	60-58
OKLAHOMA	W	91-81
Missouri	L	79-87
KANSAS STATE	L	83-86
Iowa State	W	91-89 *

VANDERBILT	L	64-72
INDIANA	L	55-72
MURRAY STATE	W	69-63
IOWA	L	56-69
XAVIER	W	61-54
TEXAS TECH	W	67-51
SAN FRANCISCO	W	60-58
Kentucky	L	71-77
Kansas State	L	70-91
Nebraska	L	72-74
Colorado	L	68-71
Notre Dame	L	64-66 *
COLORADO	W	67-58
Missouri	L	72-75
KANSAS STATE	L	68-77
Iowa State	W	90-78
OKLAHOMA	W	76-69
NEBRASKA	L	45-59
Kansas State	L	66-67
OKLAHOMA STATE	W	75-66
Colorado	L	66-72
Nebraska	L	59-62
MISSOURI	L	63-79
Oklahoma	L	58-60
Oklahoma State	L	87-94
IOWA STATE	L	65-89

1973-1974 Won 23, Lost 7
Coach: Ted Owens

MURRAY STATE	W	103-71
KENTUCKY	W	71-63
Indiana	L	59-72
NORTHERN IOWA	W	94-60
WASHINGTON STATE	W	66-51
OREGON	W	67-49
Vanderbilt	L	72-83
Colorado	L	71-73

Oklahoma	W	82-72
Nebraska	W	75-66
Iowa	W	72-71
NEBRASKA	W	79-64
Iowa State	W	73-69
OKLAHOMA STATE	W	68-66
NOTRE DAME	L	74-76
Oklahoma	W	82-79
Missouri	W	80-67
COLORADO	W	81-66
Oklahoma State	W	80-71
Kansas State	L	71-74
IOWA STATE	W	72-57
OKLAHOMA	W	98-80
Nebraska	W	51-46
Colorado	W	70-68
KANSAS STATE	W	60-55
MISSOURI	W	112-76
Creighton	W	55-54
[Midwest Regional]		
Oral Roberts	W	93-90 *
[Midwest Regional Finals]		
Marquette	L	51-64
[NCAA Semifinals]		
U.C.-Los Angeles	L	61-78
[NCAA Third Place]		

1974-1975 Won 19, Lost 8
Coach: Ted Owens

NE MISSOURI STATE	W	65-50
AUGUSTANA (South Dakota)	W	85-50
INDIANA	L	70-74 *
IOWA	W	89-54
Notre Dame	L	59-75
FORDHAM	W	78-74
WASHINGTON	L	64-74
Kentucky	L	63-100
Oklahoma State	W	88-68

NEBRASKA	W	74-66
Colorado	L	49-58
NEBRASKA	W	61-58
Kansas State	L	67-80

1977-1978 Won 24, Lost 5
Coach: Ted Owens

CENTRAL MISSOURI ST.	W	121-65
FORDHAM	W	99-67
SOUTHERN METHODIST	W	107-71
MURRAY STATE	W	106-71
FAIRLEIGH DICKINSON	W	88-54
KENTUCKY	L	66-73
ST. LOUIS	W	85-65
Oral Roberts	W	91-73
Arkansas	L	72-78
Missouri	W	96-49
Oklahoma	W	79-76
Kansas State	W	67-62
Missouri	W	71-67
Oklahoma State	W	69-57
OKLAHOMA	W	91-61
Iowa State	W	100-82
KANSAS STATE	W	56-52
Nebraska	L	58-62
COLORADO	W	85-56
OKLAHOMA STATE	W	83-65
Oklahoma	W	69-68
MISSOURI	W	72-52
Kansas State	W	75-63
IOWA STATE	W	80-70
NEBRASKA	W	75-70
Colorado	W	70-60
COLORADO	W	82-66
Kansas State	L	76-87
U.C.-Los Angeles	L	76-83
[NCAA Sub-Regional]		

1978-1979 Won 18, Lost 11
Coach: Ted Owens

USSR (Exhibition)	L	84-87
FAIRLEIGH DICKINSON	W	91-68
MURRAY STATE	W	81-66
BOISE STATE	W	82-68
ORAL ROBERTS	W	90-77
Kentucky	L	66-67 *
SOUTHERN METHODIST	W	71-64
Southern California	L	83-89 *
San Diego State	L	69-81
Iowa State	W	75-55
Oklahoma	W	86-75
Colorado	W	72-66
Oklahoma	L	45-68
Oklahoma State	W	82-70
MISSOURI	L	55-58
Kansas State	L	69-96
IOWA STATE	W	80-71
Nebraska	L	64-66 *
COLORADO	W	56-51
OKLAHOMA STATE	W	82-71
Michigan State	L	61-85
Missouri	W	88-85
OKLAHOMA	W	74-62
Iowa State	L	66-68
KANSAS STATE	L	56-58
NEBRASKA	W	66-59
Colorado	W	71-60
IOWA STATE	W	91-70
Missouri	W	76-73
Oklahoma	L	65-80

1979-1980 Won 15, Lost 14
Coach: Ted Owens

YUGOSLAVIA (Exhibition)	L	76-77
NEVADA-RENO	W	93-75
Oral Roberts	L	72-75
Southern Methodist	L	88-89
SAN DIEGO STATE	W	79-66
CALIF-BAKERSFIELD	W	93-53
KENTUCKY	L	56-57
BIRMINGHAM-SOUTHERN	W	90-64
Pepperdine	L	89-96
Arizona State	L	65-73 *
Arizona	W	78-60
WISCONSIN-OSHKOSH	W	109-72
MISSOURI	W	69-66
Iowa State	L	66-67
Nebraska	L	57-64
KANSAS STATE	L	52-61
Oklahoma	W	72-67
COLORADO	W	75-61
Oklahoma State	L	67-71
IOWA STATE	W	72-61
NEBRASKA	L	56-61
Iona	L	77-81
Missouri	L	65-88
OKLAHOMA	W	69-66
Kansas State	W	48-46
Colorado	L	72-81
OKLAHOMA STATE	W	84-74 *
COLORADO	W	75-65
Missouri	W	80-71
Kansas State	L	58-79

1980-1981 Won 24, Lost 8
Coach: Ted Owens

Nevada-Reno	W	91-73
PEPPERDINE	W	81-67
MICHIGAN	L	52-64
ORAL ROBERTS	W	90-66
MOREHEAD STATE	W	90-56
Kentucky	L	73-87
SOUTHERN CALIFORNIA	W	91-68
Southern Methodist	W	73-62
ROLLINS	W	102-47
North Carolina	W	56-55
Memphis State	W	59-49
IONA	W	94-64
IOWA STATE	W	70-58
Oklahoma	W	82-78
MISSOURI	W	63-55
COLORADO	W	66-59
Kansas State	L	43-54
Nebraska	L	54-57
Oklahoma State	L	73-76 ***
OKLAHOMA	W	96-67
Missouri	L	65-79
Iowa State	W	51-49
KANSAS STATE	W	58-50
Colorado	L	50-53
NEBRASKA	W	75-49
OKLAHOMA STATE	W	80-65
OKLAHOMA STATE	W	96-69
Missouri	W	75-70
Kansas State	W	80-68
Mississippi	W	69-66
[NCAA Sub-Regional]		
Arizona State	W	88-71
[NCAA Sub-Regional]		
Wichita State	L	65-66
[NCAA Regional]		

1981-1982 Won 13, Lost 14
Coach: Ted Owens

CHINA (Exhibition)	W	83-63
North Carolina	L	67-74
ARIZONA STATE	W	63-62
TEXAS SOUTHERN	W	67-65
MICHIGAN STATE	W	74-56
ARIZONA	W	86-57
KENTUCKY	L	74-77 *
SOUTHERN METHODIST	W	81-71
St. John's	L	75-76
Indiana	W	71-61
EVANSVILLE	W	72-65 *
ROLLINS COLLEGE	W	82-69
Nebraska	L	55-75
OKLAHOMA STATE	W	77-72
Missouri	L	35-41
Kansas State	L	53-70
ALCORN STATE	W	72-60
COLORADO	W	74-60
OKLAHOMA	W	55-53
Iowa State	L	53-55
Oklahoma State	L	64-79
MISSOURI	L	41-42
NEBRASKA	W	66-63
Colorado	L	80-89
KANSAS STATE	L	53-63
Oklahoma	L	76-79
IOWA STATE	L	61-63
Kansas State	L	62-74

1982-1983 Won 13, Lost 16
Coach: Ted Owens

YUGOSLAVIA (Exhibition)	W	83-74
U.S. INTERNATIONAL	W	91-74
BOWLING GREEN	W	97-68
MISSISSIPPI VALLEY	W	63-51
ST. LOUIS	W	83-69
Michigan	L	74-86
Southern Methodist	W	62-60
MEMPHIS STATE	L	58-64
ALCORN STATE	W	86-74
Kentucky	L	62-83
Ohio State	L	61-64
Oral Roberts	L	71-73 *
Evansville	W	59-54
MAINE	W	79-68
Oklahoma	L	72-95
Oklahoma State	L	74-85
MISSOURI	L	63-76
Kansas State	L	57-58
IOWA STATE	W	75-69
Nebraska	L	61-68
COLORADO	L	74-75
OKLAHOMA STATE	L	69-75
Missouri	L	69-74
OKLAHOMA	W	55-53
Iowa State	W	74-60
KANSAS STATE	L	63-70
NEBRASKA	L	58-60
Colorado	W	74-63
Oklahoma	W	87-77
Oklahoma State	L	83-90

1983-1984 Won 22, Lost 10
Coach: Larry Brown

NETHERLANDS (Exhibition)	W	74-70
Houston	L	91-76
St. Louis	W	67-63
MOREHEAD STATE	W	75-57
JACKSON STATE	W	89-57
KENTUCKY	L	50-72
FLORIDA SOUTHERN	W	85-73
ORAL ROBERTS	W	65-64
Ohio State	L	74-79
Tulane	W	67-64
SW Louisiana	L	45-54
FLORIDA INTERNATIONAL	W	99-47
TEXAS SOUTHERN	W	101-64
COLORADO	W	53-48

Iowa State   L   59-75
Ohio   W   49-38
[NCAA Sub-Regional]
Auburn   L   64-66
[NCAA Sub-Regional]

1985-1986 Won 35, Lost 4
Coach: Larry Brown
CZECHOSLOVAKIA   W   83-69
[Exhibition]
Pepperdine   W   67-61
Washington   W   69-64
Louisville   W   83-78
Duke   L   86-92
SIU-EDWARDSVILLE   W   86-71
WESTERN CAROLINA   W   101-79
North Carolina State   W   71-56
SOUTH ALABAMA   W   72-48
KENTUCKY   W   83-66
ARKANSAS   W   89-78
GEORGE WASHINGTON   W   94-71
Louisiana Tech   W   81-59
Wichita State   W   81-56
Memphis State   L   80-83 *
Detroit   W   60-51
SOUTHERN METHODIST   W   72-56
Nebraska   W   81-70
OKLAHOMA STATE   W   95-72
OKLAHOMA   W   98-92
Missouri   W   81-77
LOUISVILLE   W   71-69
Iowa State   L   77-74
Kansas State   W   64-50
COLORADO   W   100-64
Oklahoma State   W   85-69
MISSOURI   W   100-66
NEBRASKA   W   79-61
Colorado   W   79-74
KANSAS STATE   W   84-69
Oklahoma   W   87-80
IOWA STATE   W   90-70
Kansas State   W   74-51
Oklahoma   W   72-70
Iowa State   W   73-71
North Carolina A&T   W   71-46
[NCAA Sub-Regional]
Temple   W   65-43
[NCAA Sub-Regional]
Michigan State   W   96-86 *
[NCAA Regional]
North Carolina State   W   75-67
[NCAA Regional Final]
Duke   L   67-71
[NCAA Final Four]

1986-1987 Won 25, Lost 11
Coach: Larry Brown
USSR (Exhibition)   W   84-78
TENNESSEE-MARTIN   W   88-69
SOUTHERN   W   87-69
WASHINGTON   W   82-68
Arkansas   L   86-103
COLORADO   W   59-56
TEXAS TECH   W   82-52
THE CITADEL   W   74-71
Pittsburgh   L   76-79
Ohio State   L   78-79 *
Hawaii   W   81-80 *
Wichita State   L   49-54
TEMPLE   W   67-64
Oklahoma State   W   66-63
Oklahoma   L   74-76
MIAMI   W   82-47
MISSOURI   W   71-70
NEBRASKA   W   86-65

MISSOURI   W   73-56
Iowa State   L   56-61
NEBRASKA   W   77-61
KANSAS STATE   W   65-54
Oklahoma   L   84-103
WICHITA STATE   W   79-69
Oklahoma State   L   61-71
IOWA STATE   W   80-72
Nebraska   W   67-66
Missouri   W   72-62
OKLAHOMA   L   82-92
Kansas State   W   63-61
Colorado   L   85-89
OKLAHOMA STATE   W   91-70
OKLAHOMA STATE   W   75-58
Kansas State   W   70-59
Oklahoma   W   79-78
Alcorn State   W   57-56
[NCAA Sub-Regional]
Wake Forest   L   59-69
[NCAA Sub-Regional]

1984-1985 Won 26, Lost 8
Coach: Larry Brown
CHINA (Exhibition) W   91-69
Maryland   W   58-56
Oregon   W   66-49
Alabama-Birmingham L   46-50

DETROIT   W   86-64
SOUTH DAKOTA STATE   W   85-72
ABILENE CHRISTIAN   W   84-72
SOUTH CAROLINA STATE   W   81-54
HOUSTON   W   87-75
George Washington   W   76-70
Kentucky   L   89-92
TEXAS SOUTHERN   W   78-74
Wichita State   W   90-83
WESTERN CAROLINA   W   79-62
South Alabama   W   90-81
IOWA STATE   W   76-72
Oklahoma   L   76-87
MISSOURI   W   70-68
Colorado   W   70-68
Michigan   L   77-96
Kansas State   W   75-57
Nebraska   W   91-80
COLORADO   W   88-69
OKLAHOMA STATE   W   84-72
MEMPHIS STATE   W   75-71
Missouri   L   55-62
Iowa State   L   70-72
KANSAS STATE   W   75-64
OKLAHOMA   W   82-76
NEBRASKA   W   70-65
Oklahoma State   W   88-79
NEBRASKA   W   74-69

North Carolina State W 74-60
IOWA STATE W 72-48
Louisville W 62-58
Kansas State W 80-75 **
OKLAHOMA STATE W 88-63
NOTRE DAME W 70-60
Missouri L 60-63
OKLAHOMA W 86-84
Iowa State L 86-95
KANSAS STATE W 84-67
St. John's W 62-60
Colorado L 56-66
Nebraska L 81-83 *
Oklahoma State W 67-58
Oklahoma W 82-77
Missouri L 65-67
Houston W 66-65
[NCAA Sub-Regional]
SW Missouri State W 67-63
[NCAA Sub-Regional]
Georgetown L 57-70
[NCAA Regional]

1987-1988 Won 27, Lost 11
Coach: Larry Brown
ITALY (Exhibition) W 88-82
Chaminade W 89-62
Iowa L 81-100
Illinois L 75-81
POMONA-PITZER W 94-38
Western Carolina W 68-63
ST. JOHN'S W 63-54
APPALACHIAN STATE W 73-62
RIDER W 110-72
North Carolina State W 74-67
Memphis State W 64-62
St. John's L 56-70
Washington W 67-57
AMERICAN W 90-69
MISSOURI W 78-74
Iowa State L 78-88
HAMPTON W 95-69
Notre Dame L 76-80
Nebraska L 68-70
KANSAS STATE L 61-72
OKLAHOMA L 65-73
COLORADO W 73-62
Oklahoma State W 78-68
IOWA STATE W 82-72
NEBRASKA W 70-48
Kansas State W 64-63
DUKE L 70-74 *
Oklahoma L 87-95
Missouri W 82-77
Colorado W 85-64
OKLAHOMA STATE W 75-57
Oklahoma State W 74-58
Kansas State L 54-69
Xavier W 85-72
[NCAA Sub-Regional]
Murray State W 61-58
[NCAA Sub-Regional]
Vanderbilt W 77-64
[NCAA Midwest Regional]

Kansas State W 71-58
[NCAA Midwest Regional]
Duke W 66-59
[NCAA Semifinals]
Oklahoma W 83-79
[NCAA Finals]

1988-1989 Won 19, Lost 12
Coach: Roy Williams
USSR (Exhibition) L 84-93 *
Alaska-Anchorage W 94-81
California W 86-71
Seton Hall L 81-92
SEATTLE W 98-65
LOYOLA-CHICAGO W 100-80
PACIFIC LUTHERAN W 112-61
Temple W 95-78
NORTHERN ARIZONA W 109-59
Texas Tech W 81-80
Iona W 100-67
SW Missouri State W 82-73
BROWN W 115-45
IOWA STATE W 127-82
SOUTHERN METHODIST W 90-82 *
Miami L 86-87
Kansas State W 75-74 *
Oklahoma L 95-123
Colorado W 89-74
WICHITA STATE W 86-66
KANSAS STATE L 70-71
MISSOURI L 66-91
Nebraska L 70-74
OKLAHOMA STATE L 81-87
Missouri L 80-93
OKLAHOMA L 89-94 *
Duke L 77-102
Iowa State L 89-97
COLORADO W 111-83
NEBRASKA W 80-71
Oklahoma State W 79-78
Kansas State L 65-73

1989-1990 Won 30, Lost 5
Coach: Roy Williams
UA-BIRMINGHAM W 109-83
Louisiana State W 89-83
Nevada-Las Vegas W 91-77
St. John's W 66-57
IDAHO W 87-58
MARYLAND-BALTIMORE CO. W 86-67
TENNESSEE-MARTIN W 103-48
Southern Methodist W 86-53
KENTUCKY W 150-95
PEPPERDINE W 98-73
ARIZONA STATE W 90-67
Texas-Pan American W 103-83
Stanford W 83-61
Wichita State W 93-66
WINTHROP W 94-51
Nebraska W 98-93
Miami (Florida) W 100-73
OKLAHOMA STATE W 91-77
ELIZABETH CITY STATE W 132-65
Missouri L 87-95

Kansas State W 85-57
COLORADO W 90-69
OKLAHOMA W 85-74
Oklahoma State W 83-76
Iowa State W 88-83
MISSOURI L 71-77
NEBRASKA W 94-67
Colorado W 103-71
KANSAS STATE W 70-58
Oklahoma L 78-100
IOWA STATE W 96-63
Iowa State W 118-75
Oklahoma L 77-95
Robert Morris W 79-71
[NCAA Sub-Regional]
U.C.-Los Angeles L 70-71
[NCAA Sub-Regionals]

1990-1991 Won 27, Lost 8
Coach: Roy Williams
Arizona State L 68-70
Northern Arizona W 84-57
MARQUETTE W 108-71
SOUTHERN METHODIST W 80-60
Kentucky L 71-88
RIDER W 103-51
TEXAS-SAN ANTONIO W 101-69
Hawaii Loa W 111-58
Pepperdine W 88-62
N. C. STATE W 105-94
Oklahoma L 82-88
MD.-BALTIMORE COUNTY W 97-46
Oklahoma State L 73-78*
MIAMI (FLORIDA) W 73-60
MISSOURI W 91-64
WICHITA STATE W 84-50
COLORADO W 95-62
Kansas State W 78-69
Iowa State W 85-78
NEBRASKA W 85-77
OKLAHOMA STATE W 79-69
Missouri W 74-70
KANSAS STATE W 69-67
Colorado L 71-79
OKLAHOMA W 109-87
IOWA STATE W 88-57
Nebraska L 75-85
Colorado W 82-76
Nebraska L 83-87
New Orleans W 55-49
[NCAA Sub-Regional]
Pittsburgh W 77-66
[NCAA Sub-Regional]
Indiana W 83-65
[NCAA Regional]
Arkansas W 93-81
[NCAA Regional]
North Carolina W 79-73
[NCAA Final Four]
Duke L 65-72
[NCAA National Championship]

*Indicates overtime contests

Index

KANS
42
KU
UA
3

WALSWORTH PUBLISHING COMPANY
MARCELINE, MISSOURI, U.S.A.